Bill Strobel

# The Scope of Grammar

## of Grammar

### A Study of Modern English

# The Scope
# of Grammar
## A Study of Modern English

Stanley J. Cook
Richard W. Suter

Professors of English
California State Polytechnic University, Pomona

**McGraw-Hill Book Company**
New York   St. Louis   San Francisco   Auckland   Bogotá   Hamburg
Johannesburg   London   Madrid   Mexico   Montreal   New Delhi
Panama   Paris   São Paulo   Singapore   Sydney   Tokyo   Toronto

**The Scope of Grammar: A Study of Modern English**

34567890 HDHD 89876543

Library of Congress Cataloging in Publication Data

Cook, Stanley J        date
    The scope of grammar.

    Bibliography:   p.
    Includes index.
    1.   English language—Grammar—1950–
I.   Suter, Richard W., joint author.   II.   Title.
PE1112.C58        428'.2        79-18123
ISBN 0-07-012460-4

This book was set in Memphis Light by Monotype Composition Company, Inc.
The editors were William A. Talkington and James R. Belser;
the designer was Robin Hessel;
the production supervisor was Donna Piligra.

# Contents

# Preface

What do readers expect to find in a grammar book? This was one of the questions that we asked ourselves when we began planning *The Scope of Grammar*, and it is probably a question that any grammarian/author would ask. We quickly realized, however, that it was not the only question we could or should ask, or even the most important. Other questions soon became paramount, among them the following: What topics should be in a grammar book? Why should certain topics not be in a grammar book? How thoroughly should or could any particular topic be covered? What linguistic theory should be followed? For whom should the book be written? We have tried to answer all of these questions because we strongly believe that all of them are legitimate and important. But we believe that one is of overriding importance.

What is a textbook if it is not written with the best interests of a well-defined audience clearly in mind? A waste of someone's time, more than likely. And who is the audience? For a book such as ours, the audience is primarily college students who are studying English grammar, often at the upper-division level. These students may be enrolled in a grammar course because they plan to become elementary or secondary school teachers, better writers, or linguists, or simply because they desire to know more about the English language. While these students are not likely to deny the value of such a course, they sometimes will approach it with a degree of anxiety. What is most important for such an audience is that the book should be *written with them firmly in mind*. What does this mean? To us, it means that the book should

1 be written in as clear, lively, and interesting a manner as possible;
2 relate grammar to the everyday world and to the people who use the language;

**3** be practical, containing information that students will truly need;

**4** avoid dogmatic adherence to any one linguistic theory, and use the best insights from any and all theories;

**5** recognize the existence of a variety of linguistic systems (grammars), especially those that future teachers can expect to encounter;

**6** present a basic description of standard English; and

**7** provide immediate reinforcement so that students will learn and remember what they learn.

Students, then, are our primary audience and these seven requirements are what we believe a student-oriented grammar must satisfy.

We believe that *The Scope of Grammar* satisfies these requirements. We have tried to come up with a teachable book, one that students will enjoy, one that will educate students rather than puzzle, irritate, or intimidate them. The material, organization, and exercises have proven effective in our classes, but the truth will come from a wider testing—as it must. We will be pleased if this book is well received, but especially if it is well received by students. For in the end, students will be the book's best critics. They are the ones who will have to put their learning to immediate, practical use, and they are the ones who will suffer most if the book fails to present and explain important, practical facts about English grammar in a clear manner. We welcome comments, from students especially, but from teachers and all other users as well, for what we learn from our readers can only help make *The Scope of Grammar* better and its readers more satisfied.

# ACKNOWLEDGMENTS

We would like to express appreciation to those people who have in any way contributed to this manuscript, particularly Don Burden, Carol Napier, Rhona Robbin, Nelson Black, Bill Talkington, and James Belser of McGraw-Hill, who saw the need for a text such as this and helped us develop it. We are also indebted to Harold B. Allen, University of Minnesota; David DeCamp, University of Texas; Dale E. Elliott, California State University; and William G. Stryker, California State University, for their careful appraisals of the manuscript and for their many helpful suggestions. Our colleagues Victor Okada, Larry Robinson, Joseph Farrell, and Ralph Bobb contributed much encouragement and useful feedback, all of it greatly appreciated. Special thanks goes to Walter Roeder and David Winkley, two first-rate reference librarians, who quickly and efficiently fulfilled our often difficult requests for information and sources. Lastly, we thank Janet and Judy, who in many ways made writing the book easier.

Stanley J. Cook

Richard W. Suter

# ONE

# The Scope of Grammar

## ABOUT THE SUBJECT OF OUR STUDY

We do not plan to exhaust the subject of English grammar in the next twenty-two chapters, because this subject is literally inexhaustible. We do, however, intend to give you technical information about grammar and usage that any student of English needs to know. We plan to deal with formal grammatical concepts such as *tense, case,* and *passive voice,* and with how these concepts apply to English as it is actually used in the everyday world. By the time you finish the final chapter, you should have a clearer objective understanding of English. We hope, too, that you will have come to realize that while grammar is described in books, it actually resides in the minds of people, making the study of grammar one of the more human of the sciences.

## WHAT IS GRAMMAR?

Almost every book you go to will vary somewhat in its definition of *grammar,* but most will say that it is a set of rules by which people speak and write. These rules are not always understood consciously, and if you asked people what the rules of English were, they would probably offer one or two or say they did not know. The reason is that the rules we refer to are those that hardly anyone ever thinks about but which allow people to use their language easily and naturally most of the time. One of these rules has us use an article

+ adjective + noun word order in English noun phrases, rather than some other word order, such as one that is permissible in French:

| English | French | | |
|---------|--------|------|------|
| a blue tie | une | cravate | bleue |
| | a | tie | blue |

Another general rule for English says that most declarative sentences should have a subject + verb + object word order. This is not necessary in all languages—Spanish, for example, has object pronouns preceding verbs:

| English | Spanish | |
|---------|---------|---------|
| Paul sees it. | Pablo | lo ve. |
| | Paul | it sees. |

We could cite a great many other rules, but for the present these should suffice. What we want you to be aware of and to remember is that grammar is a set of rules and that every language has such rules.

# WHAT IS A GRAMMAR?

*A grammar* is a written description of the rules of a language. There are many grammars of English, one of the most famous being a seven-volume work by the Danish linguist Otto Jespersen (1860–1943), entitled *A Modern English Grammar on Historical Principles*. Though not a recent grammar, this monumental work is still regarded by many scholars as one of the most thorough and insightful descriptions of the rules of English ever written. Another well-known grammar is the 1120-page *A Grammar of Contemporary English*, written by Randolph Quirk and others, which first appeared in 1972. Most grammars, however, are much shorter, including the one you are now reading. There are grammars of other languages too— grammars of Navajo, grammars of Zulu, grammars of French. The most prestigious grammar of Spanish is the *Gramática de la lengua española*, which is written and periodically updated by the Royal Spanish Academy of the Language in Madrid. Many if not most grammars are written to serve as textbooks in foreign language courses. If you studied a foreign language in high school or college, you almost certainly used one such grammar as your text. Some grammars are longer, some differ in the ways that rules are stated, but they all attempt to do the same thing—to provide a written description of the rules of a language.

# ENGLISH—WHICH ONE?

We come now to a difficult question. Most people, when asked which form (or grammar) of English should be used, would probably say "the best" or "Standard English," the variety used on nationally televised news programs and in newspapers, nonfiction books, and magazines. In your own writing you undoubtedly use Standard written English, so there is no problem. But many people do not write Standard English or do not write it consistently. If you eventually teach, you may find that some, perhaps most, of your students fall into this category. In this situation you may react from your own experience, knowledge, and values and diligently set about "correcting" matters, at which point a problem may emerge because some of your students might balk, not understand, or just plain ignore you.

The United States, unlike France or England, has no one cultural, financial, or political center which can stand as a language model for the rest of the country, especially for speech. In some parts of the country people will tell you they're "sick to" their stomachs, in another part that they're "sick at" their stomachs. Some speakers may say "He here" instead of "He is here," while others may say "He done it" rather than "He did it." You can also hear people say such things as "He might could do that." Yet many of these people will feel as comfortable with their way of talking as you do, and may even mention, to your surprise, that you speak with an accent or that you sound funny. One explanation is that, being a large country, the United States has several centers that serve as models for surrounding areas. Boston was an especially influential center for years, though today its influence wanes as San Francisco, Los Angeles, Denver, and other cities gain people and influence.

The point is that uniformity of speech and writing does not always exist. Diversity is found in literally every city and in many rural areas. Amidst this diversity, however, Standard written English remains useful, important, and, in some situations and places, necessary. We have, therefore, chosen in this grammar to concentrate on Standard written American English.[1] But diversity is important, too, and for this reason we have included discussions of grammatical forms from other dialects. You will find these discussions toward the end of most of the chapters.

# ENGLISH GRAMMAR IN THE SCHOOLS

The writing of English grammars, dictionaries, and other books about the language has a long history, going back at least to the 1500s. Some of these early books were used in the schools as sources of "authority" as to which grammatical forms were considered "correct" and which were not, but the problem was that often the books disagreed and none of the authors possessed enough prestige to be the "final arbiter" in cases of dispute. It was not until 1762 that a grammar which might have been able to claim the status of "final arbiter" appeared: Bishop Robert Lowth's *A Short Introduction to English Grammar with Critical Notes*. Lowth's grammar achieved wide acceptance, and it is upon his grammar that subsequent schoolbook grammars (also called *prescriptive*, *corrective*, or *traditional* school grammars) have been based. Even more successful was the Lowth-based *English Grammar Adapted to Different Classes of Learning* by Lindley Murray, which first appeared in 1795. This grammar proved an immensely successful prescriber of "correct" English in both England and America, went through numerous editions, and achieved sales records which leave modern-day grammarians trembling with envy.

The schoolbook grammars of today are largely inheritors of the Lowth and Murray tradition. These books have been both praised and criticized, but never discarded, despite occasional laments by pupils sullenly conjugating verbs, parsing nouns, or diagraming sentences. The prospect of dropping these books from school curricula would doubtless cause parents, horrified by visions of their sons and daughters *not* being taught Standard English, to raise their voices in loud protest. These grammars continue to exist, then, because both tradition and parent-teacher concern support them. Although not easily provable, it is probably true that students who

---

[1] Standard written American English displays some diversity itself. Major publishing establishments often set up their own guidelines to cover fine points of punctuation, grammar, and word use, and these guidelines frequently vary from one establishment to another. As a result, the English you see in printed material is apt to display some variation. Furthermore, you have probably discovered for yourself that dictionaries and writing handbooks do not always agree as to the fine points of Standard English either, so that the Standard American English you write may be slightly different from that of a friend who consults different dictionaries and handbooks. These variations are very slight, however, and of little or no social consequence.

have been put through their paces in the schoolbook grammars have an easier time adopting standard forms in their speech and writing than students who have not.

# ENGLISH GRAMMAR AND THE NON-NATIVE SPEAKER

Many of us enjoy a circle of friends who are all native speakers of English. Day and night we watch network television shows which use English exclusively. It is easy to believe that the United States is a monolingual country. This, however, is not true.

The United States Bureau of Census reported that in 1970 there were 34 million residents of this country who were not native speakers of English. This figure was more than 16 percent of the population as a whole and did not include substantial numbers of Southeast Asians who entered the country later in the decade, nor many of those non-native speakers who resided in the country illegally, nor those people who for varying motivations reported themselves to be native speakers of English when in fact they were not. This "official" figure of 34 million should be regarded as conservative—other estimates, in fact, have gone as high as 50 million.

Many of the 34 million spoke English perfectly or nearly so; others had problems with the language. Because of their troubles with English (and for other reasons), approximately 4 million Americans in the mid-1970s usually spoke Spanish instead of English in their everyday lives. Nearly 400,000 usually spoke Italian, 300,000 spoke one of the Chinese languages, 300,000 spoke French, 130,000 Vietnamese, and about 100,000 spoke each of the following languages: German, Greek, Japanese, Filipino, Portuguese, and Korean.

These statistics imply a considerable need for learning English among non-native speakers. Meeting this need requires skilled teachers who are, among other things, knowledgeable about English grammar. It is true that a non-native speaker who knows no English whatsoever can be coached in basic expressions by a grammatically naive instructor. However, the student will quickly advance beyond this point. The student will soon raise hundreds of questions that will demand objective answers from the teacher. The teacher who is simply a native speaker will not be able to answer most of these questions; the teacher who has spent time studying the rules of English will.

And where do these non-native speakers learn English grammar? Often non-native speakers end up in a regular public or private school class where they require the special attention of the teacher.

Very often they are enrolled in English classes designed explicitly for the non-native speaker. These classes, called ESL (English as a Second Language) classes, are found in universities and colleges, in night schools, adult schools, and extension schools, in high shools and elementary schools, in churches, factories, and government offices across the country. If you are a native speaker, a visit to one of these classes will cause you to marvel at how much you have taken the grammar of your language for granted. Rules you use without thinking become the subject of careful explanation. The students take notes (often in their native language) and ask questions. Then the students practice each rule carefully—over and over, day after day. Slowly, over the weeks and months, their proficiency in English increases. A great deal of learning, of course, also takes place outside the classroom, especially when the non-native speaker makes an effort to be around native speakers of English. Nevertheless, the student who learns English from a grammatically competent teacher, one who clearly understands and can explain the rules of the language in the classroom, enjoys a tremendous advantage.

## ENGLISH GRAMMAR IN BUSINESS

Finally, we wish to comment briefly upon the role of grammar in the world of business. One of the most insidious and unrelenting forms of prejudice in the United States is the organizational prejudice against nonstandard English. True, you probably have not heard this prejudice discussed on the nightly news telecasts, which frequently report on other cases of prejudice, such as against ethnic minorities, women, or homosexuals. Yet the prejudice against nonstandard grammar is obvious, once you begin to look for it. For example, how often have you heard a high-level corporate executive or government official use such sentences as "Please hand me them earning reports" or "I don't got no information concerning capital gains"? The fact that you seldom hear this kind of grammar used by an executive is no accident. It is an unfortunate fact of life that people who have not mastered standard English grammar are rarely considered for high-level positions in large organizations.

Linguists have verified the existence of this prejudice through experiments that use tape-recorded samples of the speech of both standard and nonstandard speakers. These tapes are heard by various "judges," who then rate the speakers according to the highest occupational level they are capable of attaining. In one of these studies, done in 1971, Roger Shuy used as judges people who actually did the hiring for a wide variety of business organizations. These people were personally responsible for approximately 40,000 jobs in the Washington, D.C., area. In this study and in others similar to it, these judges almost invariably assigned the best jobs to the speakers who used standard English while giving the least desirable jobs to the nonstandard speakers. These studies have also found that nonstandard grammar is more damaging to a speaker's perceived job suitability than are either nonstandard pronunciation or nonstandard vocabulary.[2]

Before we are too hard on employers we should realize that they are only reflecting values transmitted through the schools and reinforced through the media. (By the way, when did you last hear a nonstandard speaker doing the nationally televised nightly news? When did you last see nonstandard grammar used in a newspaper?) Besides, it is common knowledge that many if not most other societies have a standard variety of their language against which all other varieties are measured. There is also evidence that nonstandard-language prejudices have been commonplace throughout history. It is really very unlikely that they will disappear.

What all this means is that knowing how to use Standard English grammar is advantageous. Schools need not apologize for time spent helping students master this skill. If these students eventually become blue-collar workers or owners of their own businesses, they may not need Standard English, though knowing how to use it when they have to will do them no harm. But many students will undoubtedly choose corporate management or similar careers. These students will need to have an excellent control of Standard English grammar. For them, a sound grasp of the Standard variety of English will prove every bit as important as cleverness, competence, or personal charm.

[2] Roger W. Shuy, "Language and Success: Who Are The Judges?" in Richard W. Bailey and Jay L. Robinson, *Varieties of Present-Day English* (New York: Macmillan, 1973), pp. 303–318.

# TWO

# Variety, Variety

## THE GRAMMARS WE HEAR

To many people, a life that lacked variety would be flat and tasteless. The same could be said about language, but more often language variety is thought to be merely needless deviations from a reasonable standard of correctness. Actually language variety means more than the fact that people in California speak differently than those in Minnesota or Georgia or that some people use *ain't* instead of *isn't*. It means those things, certainly, but the word *variety* can also be used to refer to the kinds of speech people use when speaking to different audiences, or to the language differences created by social forces in a community. We can talk of variety within the speech of one individual or use the term to refer to widely used dialects whose grammatical rules differ. Language is full of variety, and this chapter will look at some of the more important kinds. In fact, it can be considered as preparation for the "English in the Everyday World" sections of this book, where bits and pieces of varieties other than the standard are discussed. Our main emphasis will be on grammatical differences, but other matters will also be mentioned.

## STANDARD ENGLISH

*Standard English*, sometimes called *Network* or *Mainstream English*, is that variety found in books, magazines, newspapers, and other printed matter, the speech you hear on radio programs, in most movies, and on most nationwide television programs. It is a dialect that carries few if any indications of the regional, social, or national origins of its users and has distinct advantages. The most important is probably that it is acceptable to a great many people, allowing them to reach and to stand a reasonable chance of being accepted and understood by a wide audience.

In addition to this standard, there are also what some linguists call *regional standards*. This term usually refers to spoken English, to those recognizably different regional varieties that people have always been aware of, commented about, and generally accepted. Practically speaking, it is the English of people from any large metropolitan area, state, or section of the country (New York, Boston, or Charleston, for example) that others may joke about but not label "bad."

# NONSTANDARD ENGLISH

Any variety of American English that differs noticeably from any other variety in pronunciation, vocabulary, and grammar can, by definition, be called a *dialect*. Thus the term *dialect* need carry no other meaning than "different." It is mainly when a dialect becomes associated with certain geographical areas or with social groups characterized by low income and little education that negative judgments arise. Then the dialect is often called *nonstandard* and thought of as "bad," "less worthy," or "linguistically impoverished," although, linguistically speaking, none of these labels is justified. In the last decade speakers of various nonstandard dialects have begun to assert the dignity and value of their own kind of English. By doing so, they have affected the curriculum and the teaching of English in many states and have brought nonstandard English into the classroom to be looked at, listened to, and discussed, hopefully for the good of everyone.

# THE STUDY OF DIALECTS

Many people are intrigued by dialects, though few could define them easily and fewer still could say who study them or how they approach the task. The next several sections will give you a better idea of the people who study dialects. These sections will also describe their methods and distinguish between regional and social dialects.

# Who Studies Dialects?

People who study dialects are usually called *dialectologists*, although the terms *dialect geographer* and *areal linguist* have also been used because most of the early studies were regional in nature. Hans Kurath is a good example of a dialect geographer. Around 1930 he and a group of fellow researchers began work on *The Linguistic Atlas of New England*,[1] which was to be a part of a larger *Linguistic Atlas of the United States and Canada*. The *Linguistic Atlas of New England*, or *LANE*, as it is often called, was published during the years 1939–1943. It took the form of six large volumes containing over 600 maps, with each map recording a feature of grammar, pronunciation, or vocabulary that showed regional or local variation. Today *LANE* stands as probably the most important study of dialects ever undertaken in America.

Over the years after the appearance of *LANE*, many other regional studies of dialects emerged. Gradually, too, interest in the social variation of language grew, partly because the *LANE* project contained information on the social characteristics of the people who had been interviewed. At any rate, linguists studying the relationship between language and society entered the field. William Labov is a good example of one of these scholars, or *sociolinguists*, as they are called. Labov's major work, published in 1966, is *The Social Stratification of English in New York City*.[2] Tremendously influential, it showed, among other things, that social classes could be distinguished by the way their members used certain language features. For example, Labov found that lower-class speakers pronounced a verb like *working* as *workin'* more often than upper-middle-class speakers did and that this contrast was consistent, whether speakers used casual speech or careful speech, read a story, or recited lists of words.

Lately sociolinguists have dominated much dialect work, but regional studies continue and even scholars with interests ranging from theoretical to applied linguistics are adding to our knowledge of dialects, especially to what we know about nonstandard dialects. With dialects the property of everyone and interest at a peak, this trend should continue for some time to come.

---

[1] Hans Kurath et al., *The Linguistic Atlas of New England*, 3 vols. in 6 parts (Providence, R.I.: Brown University, 1939–1943). See also Hans Kurath, *A Word Geography of the Eastern United States* (Ann Arbor, Mich.: University of Michigan Press, 1949), and Hans Kurath et al., *Handbook of the Linguistic Geography of New England* (Washington, D.C.: American Council of Learned Societies, 1939).

[2] William Labov, *The Social Stratification of English in New York City* (Washington, D.C.: Center for Applied Linguistics, 1966).

# Methods

Generally, two basic methods are used in the study of dialects. The first was developed by dialect geographers and is well exemplified in *The Linguistic Atlas of New England*. In any dialect study, and the *LANE* was no exception, the economy, culture, and geography of the area are first studied. This usually results in the area being divided into grids, composed of sets of communities selected because they are important in some way—as being early settlements, centers of culture, on migration routes, or relatively isolated. The communities chosen thus give a broad representation of the linguistic history of the area. Individuals from each community are then selected to take part in the study. For the *LANE* project, the individuals, or *informants*, fell into three categories: (1) old-fashioned speakers of eighth-grade education; (2) younger, more modern speakers of high school education; and (3) speakers of college education. In interviewing them, trained fieldworkers used a pre-tested questionnaire designed to elicit information on a range of topics concerned with everyday life. Among them were terms for food, clothing, and utensils, the names of plants and animals, verb forms—in general, words, pronunciations and expressions known to vary regionally or locally. (For example: Was *lunch* or *dinner* the word for the noonday meal? Was *car* pronounced with an *r*? Was *brought* or *brung* the past-tense form of *bring*?) Once the data were gathered and analyzed, the results were placed on large maps so that the distribution of the various terms, pronunciations, and grammatical expressions, or linguistic *variants*, could be easily seen.

The second method was derived from the first for use in socio-linguistic studies, usually of complex urban centers. Labov's method is a good model, even though researchers in Detroit, Washington, D.C., Los Angeles, and other cities have helped develop, refine, and improve techniques that are now part of the general methodology. Labov used a *survey method*, randomly drawing a set of informants from a well-defined portion of the Lower East Side of Manhattan in New York City and expending considerable effort to interview every person whose name had been drawn. His questionnaire differed from the regional questionnaire in that it sought to isolate contextual styles (casual speech, careful speech, reading style, and word lists) and to measure phonological or grammatical variables (nonstandard pronunciations or verb forms, for example). He was thus able to identify norms shared by a group of people, to compare those norms to others shared by a different group, and to note the speech characteristics of each individual speaker as compared to the group as a whole.

Although these are two basic methods, individual researchers often devise their own after giving careful thought to the nature of their study. Today you can find linguists in bars, restaurants, hospitals, playgrounds, churches—almost anyplace—all studying language. The methods may vary somewhat, but the intent is the same: to discover as much about language and its users as possible.

## What Makes a Dialect?

Kurath's linguistic atlas project disclosed three major dialect areas in the Eastern United States, as shown by the map in Figure 2-1 (the two heavy, unbroken lines separate the three areas). To understand

**Figure 2-1**
(Reprinted from *A Word Geography of the Eastern United States* by Hans Kurath and by permission of the University of Michigan Press.)

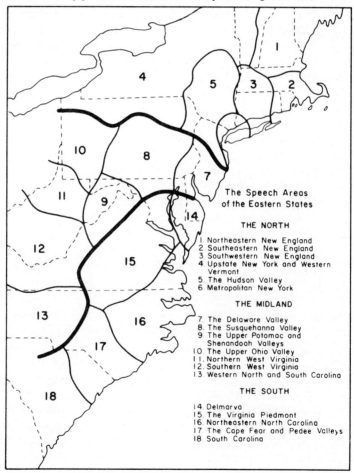

The Speech Areas of the Eastern States

THE NORTH

1. Northeastern New England
2. Southeastern New England
3. Southwestern New England
4. Upstate New York and Western Vermont
5. The Hudson Valley
6. Metropolitan New York

THE MIDLAND

7. The Delaware Valley
8. The Susquehanna Valley
9. The Upper Potomac and Shenandoah Valleys
10. The Upper Ohio Valley
11. Northern West Virginia
12. Southern West Virginia
13. Western North and South Carolina

THE SOUTH

14. Delmarva
15. The Virginia Piedmont
16. Northeastern North Carolina
17. The Cape Fear and Pedee Valleys
18. South Carolina

how these areas became distinct, we must consider their historical development.

The first settlers arriving in this country came from various parts of England and brought with them many different dialects. Contacts with England kept their speech from becoming a different language from British English (compare what happened to the dialects of Latin from which Spanish, French, and other languages sprang), but separation of the settlements and the different mixtures of dialects in each prevented a "common American" speech from forming. In fact, the different mixtures of dialects was so important that most dialectologists say that the obvious dialect differences on the Eastern seacoast (which remain to this day) can be explained by the origin of these first settlers.

But the origin of the first settlers was not the only cause of dialect differentiation. The first settlers were not all English. Their Dutch and German neighbors, the Indians they met, and Ulster-Scots, French, and Spanish speakers arriving later all contributed important elements to the language. The geography of the land had an influence too. Migration routes were partly determined by the lay of mountains and the course of rivers, with some geographical features blocking and others facilitating the spread of speech forms. Features that did not have an English equivalent received French, Spanish, or Indian names, like *mesa*, *prairie*, and *plateau*. As people settled down and developed their own ways of living, cultural centers arose. New York, Philadelphia, Boston, Charleston, and others became influential cities, spreading their linguistic forms to outlying areas, where speakers copied what they felt were prestigious forms. The social structure of the various areas affected dialects, too, with educational and economic differences leading to linguistic differences.

Today no dialect would follow the course it took in the eighteenth or nineteenth century because the country has changed. But similar forces necessary to cause change are still present. New immigrants will arrive, social structures will alter, education will continue to spread, and technology to increase—and the language will reflect whatever happens, as any living language always does.

## Regional Dialects

By *regional dialect* is usually meant a recognizable variety of a language spoken by an identifiable group of people within a specific geographical area. Now just what does this mean? How are the group and the geographical area identified? What does "recognizable variety" mean? To find the answers to these questions, let us do what we would do if we were dialectologists.

First, we would have to decide what part of the country we would like to study—New England, perhaps, as Hans Kurath did. Then we would have to gather as much information about the speech of the inhabitants as possible, using the method of dialect geographers that we discussed previously. Once we had gathered our data, we could sit down over large maps and mark where each variant appeared. Every time we discovered an area where one variant appeared more often than any other, we could enclose that area with a line called an *isogloss*. If we found a great number of isogloss lines coinciding, we would have a *bundle of isoglosses;* the bundle would constitute a dialect boundary. Such a boundary might look like one of the following figures. Remember that each line represents a different item of pronunciation, vocabulary, or grammar and that one form would be used primarily on one side of the line, and a different form on the other (Northern *pail*, Midland *bucket*, for example).

Figure 2-2 shows a bundle of lines like the one separating the Northern dialect area from the Midland dialect area. Figure 2-3 shows a bundle of lines that might be compared to those setting off subdialects within one of the major dialect areas (see the map in Figure 2-1). These lines identify areas containing speech forms recognizably different from those used in other areas outside of or beyond the line. People living within each area so identified could be said to speak the dialect of that area. Everyone's speech would not be the same, of course, for everyone has an *idiolect* (a set of individual speech habits), but there would be many similarities.

**Figure 2-2**

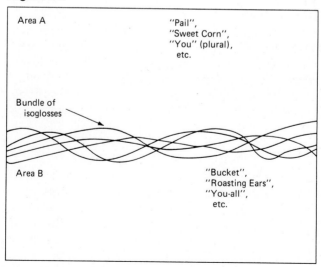

Area A      "Pail",
"Sweet Corn",
"You" (plural),
etc.

Bundle of isoglosses

Area B      "Bucket",
"Roasting Ears",
"You-all",
etc.

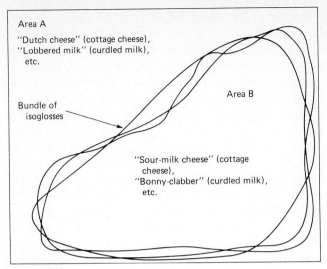

Area A

"Dutch cheese" (cottage cheese),
"Lobbered milk" (curdled milk),
etc.

Area B

Bundle of
isoglosses

"Sour-milk cheese" (cottage
cheese),
"Bonny-clabber" (curdled milk),
etc.

**Figure 2-3**

Drawing isogloss lines on maps to identify dialect areas is useful, but only up to a point and only in certain places. It worked well for Kurath and others when they studied Eastern New England and other older speech areas. In the newer speech areas of the Western part of the United States, however, the isogloss lines "fanned out" instead of forming bundles, making it difficult or impossible to use them with any degree of success. Showing where variants appeared became a matter of marking the dispersion of forms, and a linguistic map of such an area, say, the Pacific Northwest, had to look more like Figure 2-4, where *x*'s and *o*'s stand for variants.

In the end, it should be understood that regional dialects cannot always be clearly distinguished. They are distinguished most clearly in older speech areas, while in newer areas distinctions sometimes become impossible. Time, space, and the history of the speakers work together to shape the speech pattern of any area, and dialectologists describe it as best they can.

**Figure 2-4**

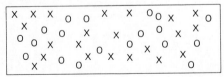

# Social Dialects

Dialects may be classified by social criteria also. Within a large, urban area, each social class will have its own set of speech characteristics. These characteristics, or differences, are attributable mainly to educational and economic factors. For instance, Standard English is typically thought of as the language of most of the upper-middle class. Members of this class, often being college-educated, will consistently use standard forms more often than will members of the lower and lower-middle classes. People from the lower and lower-middle classes will generally use more nonstandard forms, although no class will use one set of forms exclusively. With the lower and lower-middle classes characterized by less money and education, such a stratification of language along class lines seems predictable. The whole matter is complicated, however, and easy generalizations should be avoided. You can always find people with little money or education who use the standard as well as anyone, and people with money and education who can barely handle it. Few can deny, however, the power of education or economic forces, or the fact that education has an important effect on language. In fact, with Standard English being the variety used in and supported by the schools, education will continue to be important.

Age, sex, ethnic affiliation, and professions or occupations also affect the way people talk. Young children use "baby talk," teenagers are noted for their slang, and grandparents often sound a little old-fashioned—at least to the young. Women can use certain lexical items more freely than men, especially adjectives like *precious*, *darling*, *enchanting*, *charming*, and *enthralling*, and nonstandard grammatical forms like *ain't* are more often expected from men than from women. Finally, countless language differences can be traced to one's profession or occupation. There is the "governmentese" of civil service workers, the special vocabularies of engineers, the slang of waiters and waitresses, and, even, the "academese" of academics.

A social dialect differs from a regional dialect, then, primarily in that the people share common speech patterns *and* social status (rather than geographical location). Both are important, but social dialects may be more important today. Clearly, having your language identify you as a member of a particular social class or group can bring both advantages and disadvantages, such as getting a certain job or not getting it. In this matter of jobs, social dialects are definitely more important than regional dialects, which would merely identify a job applicant as coming from a particular place like Georgia or Chicago.

# THAT FINAL TOUCH—STYLE

Just as there is social, historical, and regional variation, so there is stylistic variation. People do not always think about it, but style can be as important as any other aspect of language. It can, in fact, be "that final touch" that means the difference between communicating well or not communicating at all. We will look at three kinds.

## Variation According to Subject Matter

Most people use one variety of language most of the time—the standard, a regional variation, or the speech of their neighborhood—but all have the ability to vary the kind of language they use according to the demands of a particular topic. This variation often involves no more than switching to a different vocabulary. In talking to friends about a recent movie, we would certainly use different words than we would use in talking about a baseball game. Sometimes we know a great deal about a topic, while other times we may know very little. For example, not knowing a Monet from a Rembrandt may very easily leave a person at a loss for words at an art gallery. Most of us know appropriate sets of lexical items for a wide number of topics. We acquire these lexical items as we learn the language, with experience and education helping us broaden our repertoires.

## Variation According to Medium

When we talk about *medium*, we must consider two kinds: speech and writing. Both make their own demands, but they also have things in common. We will look at the differences first.

The most basic difference is that with speech our audience is usually present, offering us immediate feedback. We can be questioned, corrected, argued with, or listened to passively, but the audience is there and we can generally gauge their reaction. The kind of feedback will vary according to the size of our audience, of course, with more feedback coming and expected from a small audience than from a large one. With writing, however, our audience is seldom present, and whether it is large or small, we may have to wait days, weeks, or months for any kind of feedback, if it comes at all. As a result, writing forces us into being more careful and precise than we need to be when speaking. We have to avoid unintentional ambiguity and write for a reader over our shoulder who keeps whispering, "Be clear, be clear." To say what we need to say with clarity, conciseness, and brevity, we must rely on punctuation rather than gestures, intonation, and other devices available to speech.

As for similarities, both forms are used mainly to convey information. Babies may babble meaninglessly and some poets may write for their own eyes, but something more than this usually takes place. Babies learn to talk and most poets publish their poems or read them to others. Both forms also use such closely related symbolic systems that one form can be turned quickly into the other. Speeches are written down and books are read aloud. In fact, the similarities are so obvious that some teachers tell composition students to write the way they talk, forgetful that, although the mediums are alike, each medium has its own personal characteristics, just as twins do.

## Variation According to Attitude

Most people are probably aware that at times their language varies because of their attitudes toward the listener (reader), the topic under discussion, the situation, or the purpose of their communication. This kind of attitude-induced change is often called *stylistic variation* and is usually illustrated by means of a scale going from the most casual to the most careful speech or writing. For the most part, casual speech and writing occur when we feel we can be ourselves, without having to watch our every word. Careful speech and writing, on the other hand, occur when we are more conscious of our language—when we feel, rightly or wrongly, that we are open to the judgment of others for what we say or write. Casual speech and writing often show less regard for what might be considered "proper" English. Careful speech and writing are more likely to have an educated look, with "approved" pronunciations (or spellings), grammatical forms, and vocabulary. The casual "Howdy" could become the careful "How do you do?" A personal letter asserting that "Shrinks don't know everything" might appear in a "Letters to the Editor" column as "Psychologists certainly do not understand every aspect of the human psyche." Such variations according to attitude appear in all dialects of English, standard as well as nonstandard, regional as well as social.

# Exercises

I  In this exercise you will be asked to perform a study, using some of the same techniques that dialectologists employ in gathering and interpreting language data. Your study will not involve pronunciation features, as this would require advanced training in phonetics, nor will it deal with standard and nonstandard features of grammar, since special techniques are needed to overcome the sensitivities of informants about such matters. What your study *will* investigate is variation in vocabulary. The exercise does not pretend to be as thorough as the study a dialectologist would engage in, but it is an interesting and useful way to begin the formal study of dialects.

Try to use at least five people in your study. Your sample should contain as great a variety of people as possible, but it can include friends, neighbors, and relatives. Interview each one separately and keep records of each person you interview. Records should include the person's sex and age (or approximate age, since some people are sensitive about telling how old they are).

Section A asks for background information that should help you make sense of why your informants speak as they do. Section B is a sample questionnaire that will elicit actual words and expressions from your informants. In Section B *you* should read the question *to* the informant. If your informant's response is among the words or expressions listed, circle it. If it is not, add it to the list; then circle it. If you get more than one response to any item, label the responses 1, 2, etc. Suggest a response *only* if your informant cannot think of one. When you have completed the study, discuss the results, pleasures, and problems you had with your instructor and classmates.

A. Background Information.

**1** How long have you lived in this state?

Informant 1 _____

Informant 2 _____

Informant 3 _____

Informant 4 _____

Informant 5 _____

**2** Where were you born, and how long did you live there?

Informant 1 _____

Informant 2 _____

Informant 3 _____

Informant 4 _____

Informant 5 _____

**3** Which other states have you lived in?

Informant 1 _____

Informant 2 _____

Informant 3 _____

Informant 4 _____

Informant 5 _____

**4** Have you traveled extensively in the United States? (if so) Which states have you visited?

Informant 1 _____

Informant 2 _____

Informant 3 _____

Informant 4 _____

Informant 5 _____

**5** Where were your parents born?

Informant 1 _____

Informant 2 _____

Informant 3 _____

Informant 4 _____

Informant 5 _____

**6** Informant's approximate age.

Informant 1 _____

Informant 2 _____

Informant 3 _____

Informant 4 _____

Informant 5 _____

**7** Informant's sex (circle).

Informant 1  M  F

Informant 2  M  F

Informant 3  M  F

Informant 4  M  F

Informant 5  M  F

B.  Questionnaire.

    **1** What do you call a piece of upholstered furniture that seats
at least three people?
Informant 1:  davenport, divan, settee, sofa, (studio) couch
Informant 2:  davenport, divan, settee, sofa, (studio) couch
Informant 3:  davenport, divan, settee, sofa, (studio) couch
Informant 4:  davenport, divan, settee, sofa, (studio) couch
Informant 5:  davenport, divan, settee, sofa, (studio) couch

    **2** What do you call a heavy metal pan that's used to fry foods?
Informant 1:  creeper, fry(ing) pan, skillet, spider
Informant 2:  creeper, fry(ing) pan, skillet, spider
Informant 3:  creeper, fry(ing) pan, skillet, spider
Informant 4:  creeper, fry(ing) pan, skillet, spider
Informant 5:  creeper, fry(ing) pan, skillet, spider

    **3** What do you call the meal that people eat at the end of the
day?
Informant 1:  dinner, supper
Informant 2:  dinner, supper
Informant 3:  dinner, supper
Informant 4:  dinner, supper
Informant 5:  dinner, supper

**4** What do you call the bread made with cornmeal?

Informant 1:   corn bread, corn cakes, corn pone, doughboys, hoecake, johnnycake, spoon bread

Informant 2:   corn bread, corn cakes, corn pone, doughboys, hoecake, johnnycake, spoon bread

Informant 3:   corn bread, corn cakes, corn pone, doughboys, hoecake, johnnycake, spoon bread

Informant 4:   corn bread, corn cakes, corn pone, doughboys hoecake, johnnycake, spoon bread

Informant 5:   corn bread, corn cakes, corn pone, doughboys, hoecake, johnnycake, spoon bread

**5** What do you call the sound that a horse makes?

Informant 1:   bray,   neigh/nigh,   nicker,   whicker/icker, whinny/whinner/whinnow, whinter

Informant 2:   bray,   neigh/nigh,   nicker,   whicker/icker, whinny/whinner/whinnow, whinter

Informant 3:   bray,   neigh/nigh,   nicker,   whicker/icker, whinny/whinner/whinnow, whinter

Informant 4:   bray,   neigh/nigh,   nicker,   whicker/icker, whinny/whinner/whinnow, whinter

Informant 5:   bray,   neigh/nigh,   nicker,   whicker/icker, whinny/whinner/whinnow, whinter

**6** What do you call the bone from the breast of a chicken that people wish on, then pull to break?

Informant 1:   breakbone, lucky bone, pull(y) bone, wishbone

Informant 2:   breakbone, lucky bone, pull(y) bone, wishbone

Informant 3:   breakbone, lucky bone, pull(y) bone, wishbone

Informant 4:   breakbone, lucky bone, pull(y) bone, wishbone

Informant 5:   breakbone, lucky bone, pull(y) bone, wishbone

**7** What do you call a container with a handle used for carrying milk, water, and the like?

Informant 1:   bucket, pail

Informant 2:   bucket, pail

Informant 3:   bucket, pail

Informant 4:   bucket, pail

Informant 5:   bucket, pail

**8** What do you call the strip of grass between the sidewalk and the curb?

Informant 1:   boulevard (strip), curb-line, lawn, parking (strip), parkway, (sidewalk) plot, tree bank/ lawn

Informant 2:   boulevard (strip), curb-line, lawn, parking (strip), parkway, (sidewalk) plot, tree bank/ lawn

Informant 3: boulevard (strip), curb-line, lawn, parking (strip), parkway, (sidewalk) plot, tree bank/ lawn

Informant 4: boulevard (strip), curb-line, lawn, parking (strip), parkway, (sidewalk) plot, tree bank/ lawn

Informant 5: boulevard (strip), curb-line, lawn, parking (strip), parkway, (sidewalk) plot, tree bank/ lawn

**9** What do you call the common worm that is used as fish bait?

Informant 1: angledog, angleworm, bait worm, eace worm, earthworm, eelworm, fish(ing) worm, mud worm, rainworm, redworm

Informant 2: angledog, angleworm, bait worm, eace worm, earthworm, eelworm, fish(ing) worm, mud worm, rainworm, redworm

Informant 3: angledog, angleworm, bait worm, eace worm, earthworm, eelworm, fish(ing) worm, mud worm, rainworm, redworm

Informant 4: angledog, angleworm, bait worm, eace worm, earthworm, eelworm, fish(ing) worm, mud worm, rainworm, redworm

Informant 5: angledog, angleworm, bait worm, eace worm, earthworm, eelworm, fish(ing) worm, mud worm, rainworm, redworm

**10** What names do you have for a small, black animal with a white stripe down its back?

Informant 1: civet/civvy cat, polecat, skunk
Informant 2: civet/civvy cat, polecat, skunk
Informant 3: civet/civvy cat, polecat, skunk
Informant 4: civet/civvy cat, polecat, skunk
Informant 5: civet/civvy cat, polecat, skunk

**11** What do you call the small insect that flies at night and flashes a light at its tail?

Informant 1: firebug/firefly, glowworm, lightning bug
Informant 2: firebug/firefly, glowworm, lightning bug
Informant 3: firebug/firefly, glowworm, lightning bug
Informant 4: firebug/firefly, glowworm, lightning bug
Informant 5: firebug/firefly, glowworm, lightning bug

**12** What other names do you have for a *dragonfly*?

Informant 1: (devil's) darning needle, ear-cutter, eye-stinger, glassmaker, mosquito (skeeter) hawk, snake doctor, snake-feeder, sneeder, water-dipper

Informant 2: (devil's) darning needle, ear-cutter, eye-stinger, glassmaker, mosquito (skeeter) hawk, snake doctor, snake-feeder, sneeder, water-dipper

Informant 3: (devil's) darning needle, ear-cutter, eye-stinger, glassmaker, mosquito (skeeter) hawk, snake doctor, snake-feeder, sneeder, water-dipper

Informant 4: (devil's) darning needle, ear-cutter, eye-stinger, glassmaker, mosquito (skeeter) hawk, snake doctor, snake-feeder, sneeder, water-dipper

Informant 5: (devil's) darning needle, ear-cutter, eye-stinger, glassmaker, mosquito (skeeter) hawk, snake doctor, snake-feeder, sneeder, water-dipper

**13** What do you call the fixture for turning on water in a sink?
Informant 1: faucet, hydrant, spicket, spigot, tap
Informant 2: faucet, hydrant, spicket, spigot, tap
Informant 3: faucet, hydrant, spicket, spigot, tap
Informant 4: faucet, hydrant, spicket, spigot, tap
Informant 5: faucet, hydrant, spicket, spigot, tap

**14** What do you call the soft, lumpy, white cheese that comes in a round container?
Informant 1: (bonny) clabber cheese, cottage cheese, curds, curds cheese, Dutch cheese, pot cheese, smearcase, sourmilk cheese

Informant 2: (bonny) clabber cheese, cottage cheese, curds, curds cheese, Dutch cheese, pot cheese, smearcase, sourmilk cheese

Informant 3: (bonny) clabber cheese, cottage cheese, curds, curds cheese, Dutch cheese, pot cheese, smearcase, sourmilk cheese

Informant 4: (bonny) clabber cheese, cottage cheese, curds, curds cheese, Dutch cheese, pot cheese, smearcase, sourmilk cheese

Informant 5: (bonny) clabber cheese, cottage cheese, curds, curds cheese, Dutch cheese, pot cheese, smearcase, sourmilk cheese

**15** If you are nauseated, you might say, "I'm sick _____ my stomach."
Informant 1: to, at, in, on
Informant 2: to, at, in, on

Informant 3:  to, at, in, on
Informant 4:  to, at, in, on
Informant 5:  to, at, in, on

**16** What do you call what you do when you stay away from school without an excuse?

Informant 1:  bag school, cut school/class, play hooky, skip school/class

Informant 2:  bag school, cut school/class, play hooky, skip school/class

Informant 3:  bag school, cut school/class, play hooky, skip school/class

Informant 4:  bag school, cut school/class, play hooky, skip school/class

Informant 5:  bag school, cut school/class, play hooky, skip school/class

**17** What do you call a sandwich in a long bun that is a meal in itself?

Informant 1:   hero, hoagie, poor boy, submarine, torpedo
Informant 2:   hero, hoagie, poor boy, submarine, torpedo
Informant 3:   hero, hoagie, poor boy, submarine, torpedo
Informant 4:   hero, hoagie, poor boy, submarine, torpedo
Informant 5:   hero, hoagie, poor boy, submarine, torpedo

**18** If you wanted to buy a ticket to a big event, you would probably have to stand _____ line to get it.

Informant 1:   in, on
Informant 2:   in, on
Informant 3:   in, on
Informant 4:   in, on
Informant 5:   in, on

# THREE

# Some Bits and Pieces: Exploring the System

## WAYS OF SIGNALING MEANING

The system that exists in English uses several devices to transmit meaning. Key among these are *word order*, *affixes*, and *words*. We will look at word order first.

### Word Order

Word order is one of the main ways of signaling meaning in English. The following sentences will illustrate:

1 The little boy watched the red ant.
2 The red ant watched the little boy.

In sentence 1 we know that "the little boy" did the watching and that what he watched was "the red ant." In sentence 2 we know with equal certainty that "the red ant" did the watching and that what it watched was "the little boy." Yet exactly the same words appear in both sentences—only the word order is different. Here is another example:

**3** Sally disliked the student opera.
**4** Sally disliked the opera student.

Again, the words in both sentences are identical; the difference in word order has created the difference in meaning.

## Affixes

If we had only word order to rely on for meaning, however, we might find ourselves scratching our heads in puzzlement most of the time. The reason is that a great deal of meaning in English is conveyed through the use of little devices called *affixes*. Affixes are endings (called *suffixes*) and beginnings (called *prefixes*) that we attach onto words in order to communicate certain meanings. Some common prefixes are *un-*, as in *un*necessary and *un*ambiguous; *re-* as in *re*upholster and *re*apply; and *mis-*, as in *mis*understand and *mis*interpret. Some common suffixes are *-ed*, as in want*ed* and award*ed*; *-est* as in bigg*est* and dumb*est*; and *-'s*, as in "Linda*'s* book" and "Paul*'s* car."

That affixes can be as important as word order in communicating meaning is shown by our difficulty in understanding "sentences" such as the following:

\*John watch work long.[1]

This sentence is largely incomprehensible because all the affixes have been deliberately removed. If we replace them, we have the original sentence:

John's watches worked longer.

The *-'s* suffix added to *John* tells us that the watches belonged to John, the *-es* suffix added to *watch* tells us that more than one watch is involved, the *-ed* suffix added to *work* indicates that the action of working took place in the past, and the *-er* suffix added to *long* informs us that John's watches functioned for a greater period of time than some other watches against which they were being compared.

Basically, suffixes are either *derivational* or *inflectional*. We shall discuss derivational suffixes first.

At some time or another you might have heard someone objecting to the use of words like *finalized*, *concretized*, and *plasticized*, as in the sentences "They finalized the agreement," "They concretized the road," and "They plasticized the toy." Asked why, the person objecting might have argued that the words were being used in the

---

[1] An asterisk indicates an unacceptable construction.

wrong way: that *final* is an adjective and *concrete* and *plastic* are nouns, and that they should not be used as verbs. The fact is, of course, that these words sometimes are made into verbs—by a process of derivation. You can derive one word from another by adding a suffix which changes the word's part of speech. Suffixes which do this are called *derivational* suffixes. In the preceding instances, the derivational suffix *-ize* was used, converting an adjective or a noun into a verb. There are many such derivational suffixes in English. For example, *write*, a verb, becomes the noun *writer* when the derivational suffix *-er* is added to it. Add the derivational suffix *-y* to a noun like *speed* and you come up with the adjective *speedy*. One adverb-forming derivational suffix that is fairly common is *-ward*, as in *homeward*. *Home* is a noun meaning "a place or structure where someone lives," while *homeward* is an adverb meaning "toward that place or structure."

The examples in the preceding paragraph allow us to observe the principal defining characteristic of derivational suffixes: when added to a word they change that word from one class ("part of speech") or subclass to another. Add *-ize* to *visual* and you have a verb rather than an adjective. Add *-hood* to *mother* and you have an abstract noun rather than a concrete one (you can touch a mother, but you can only talk about motherhood).

*Inflectional suffixes* differ from derivational suffixes primarily in that the addition of an inflectional suffix to a word does not change the class to which that word belongs.

## Chart 3-1 Inflectional suffixes

|  | Noun | Verb | Adjective |
|---|---|---|---|
| Set 1 | boy | want | red |
| Set 2 | boys | wants | redder |
| Set 3 | boy's | wanted | reddest |

If you scan the first set of words you will note that *boy* is a noun, *want* is a verb, and *red* is an adjective. In the second set the words have a new meaning because each now has a suffix, but they are still nouns, verbs, and adjectives just as they were before. The third set is different from the second because another suffix has been added, but *boy's* is still a noun, *wanted* is still a verb, and *reddest* is still an adjective.

Numbering only eight, the inflectional suffixes in English are easily listed and labeled.

**Chart 3-2   English inflectional suffixes**

---

### With Nouns

---

-*s* plural (cat*s*)
-'*s* possessive (Jane'*s*)

### With Verbs

---

-*s* third person singular
present tense (Carl sing*s*)
-*ed* past tense (she jump*ed*)
-*ing* progressive (is try*ing*)
-*en* irregular perfect (has giv*en*)

### With Adjectives

---

-*er* comparative (bright*er*)
-*est* superlative (bright*est*)

## Words

The actual words of English—*boy, girl, man, woman, work, see, red, good, and, there, the, of, on, in, here, because,* and so forth—carry most of the meaning in any sentence. Without them the language would virtually cease to exist. We could use other devices or signals, of course—gestures, flags (the semaphore system), plastic symbols, or anything else we might be able to assign meaning to—but the fact is that we use words and find them, written or spoken, a highly successful way to communicate.

# GRAMMATICAL CLASSES: IN THE BEGINNING IS THE WORD

Every speaker of English realizes, if sometimes only intuitively, that the words of English constitute various classes. These classes have traditionally been called the *parts of speech.* In all likelihood you studied the parts of speech in elementary school and high school, but as the terminology is important, we shall include a brief review section here.

## Nouns

A *noun* has been traditionally defined as a word that names a person, place, thing, or idea. We can recognize nouns for other reasons, too. For example, most nouns take the possessive and plural affixes (Mary's gloves) and are the usual subjects and objects of verbs in sentences:

*Mozart* composed *operas*.
subject                object

## Verbs

The traditional definition of a *verb* states that it is a word which denotes or implies an action or state of being. Verbs can also be identified by the fact that they take the affixes *-ed*, *-s*, and *-ing* (want*ed*, want*s*, want*ing*) and that together with nouns, they can form complete sentences (Kathy *smokes*).

## Adjectives

Adjectives are said to *modify* (i.e., limit the meaning of) nouns. Thus *old* is an adjective in the phrase "old house" because the meaning of "old house" is more limited or specific than the meaning of *house* by itself. Adjectives also take the "comparative affixes" *-er* and *-est* (or the comparative words *more* and *most*). For this reason, *tall*, *blue*, *expensive*, and *beautiful* can be considered adjectives in the following sentences:

A redwood is tall*er* than an oak.
Monica owns the blu*est* sapphire.
A mansion is *more* expensive than a shack.
The king cobra is the *most* beautiful snake.

## Adverbs

The traditional definition of an *adverb* states that it is a word which modifies a verb, an adjective, another adverb, or a sentence. Adverbs are also said to add the following kinds of information to the words or sentences they modify: "where" (place), "when" (time), "why" (reason), and "how" (manner, degree, or frequency), with "how" adverbs often taking the *-ly* suffix. The following sentences show adverbs performing these various functions:

Mr. and Mrs. Crockett bought the house *yesterday*. (*Yesterday* modifies the verb by telling "when" the buying was done.)

I met her *here*. (*Here* modifies the verb by indicating "where" the meeting occurred.)

Sara drove *carefully*. (*Carefully* modifies the verb by telling "how" or the "manner" in which Sara drove.)

Pascal was *extremely* religious. (*Extremely* modifies the adjective *religious* by indicating the "degree" of Pascal's religiosity.)

Mr. Potter treated his horse *very* cruelly. (*Very* modifies the second adverb, *cruelly*, by expressing the "degree" of cruelty.)

*Certainly*, they were happy. (*Certainly* modifies the sentence "they were happy" by emphasizing the "degree" of truth of the sentence.)

At this point we might note that the terms *adverb* and *adverbial* are sometimes confused. Basically, an adverb is a single word, while an adverbial is one or *more* words which act to modify a verb. All single-word adverbs which modify verbs, therefore, are considered adverbials, but so are multiword constructions such as "last night" in "She saw him *last night*," and "in England" in "He is studying *in England*," since these constructions also modify a verb. Even a longer construction, such as "before the sun rose" in "They finished the tunnel *before the sun rose*" can be called an adverbial as it tells when the act of finishing took place.

## Prepositions

Among the most common prepositions are *at*, *by*, *for*, *from*, *in*, *on*, *over*, *to*, and *with*. Since prepositions carry out many functions in English, they will be discussed in a separate chapter further on in this book.

## Coordinating Conjunctions

The coordinating conjunctions are *and*, *but*, *for*, *nor*, *or*, *so*, and *yet*. These conjunctions serve to connect words, phrases, clauses, and sentences of equal or coordinate value. You can see coordinating conjunctions in the expressions which follow: "Dick *and* Jane"; "the cat *and* the mouse"; "Forrest swims, *but* Jessica plays tennis"; "I am hungry, *so* I'll take your food."

## Other Parts of Speech, and a Word of Caution

There are other parts of speech, most of which you will encounter and study in subsequent chapters. When working with any part of speech, however, keep in mind that used cars and definitions are alike in one way: the closer you look, the more flaws you will find. There is probably no definition that applies only and always to any particular part of speech. For example, adjectives, as you will soon see, are not the only words which can modify nouns, though the traditional definitions seem to imply that they are. For this reason, some grammarians refuse to attempt definitions of the parts of speech and prefer to offer examples of each class and advise the reader to proceed on analogy. We believe that the definitions are helpful starters; they should never, however, be accepted as foolproof and complete. Speakers of English hold much more knowledge about word classes in their minds than linguists have ever been able to capture in their definitions.

# FROM WORD TO PHRASE

*Phrases* are groups of words that are intuitively felt to "belong together." For example, you would probably disagree immediately if someone divided the sentence "The handsome agent threw his briefcase into the river" as follows:

The handsome / agent threw his / briefcase into the / river.

You would be much more likely to divide the sentence in one of these ways:

The handsome agent / threw his briefcase / into the river.
or
The handsome agent / threw / his briefcase / into the river.

These divisions more accurately reflect your intuitions about which words belong together and would thus constitute "natural" phrases. Various kinds of phrases exist in English, three of which will be discussed here.

## The Noun Phrase

A *noun phrase* is a grammatical class consisting of a noun (or pronoun) and any immediate modifiers (the term *modifier* refers to any grammatical element which limits the meaning of some other element). Consider, for a moment, the noun *car*. By itself, *car* could refer to any car in the world—to your car, to the British Prime Minister's car, to any big car, or any little car, to a Toyota or an Aston Martin or a Buick, and so on. If we add the modifier *race* and thus create the construction "race car," we have reduced the list of possible cars referred to; in other words, we have limited the meaning of *car*. By the addition of the word *race*, we have ruled out all the cars in the world which happen not to be race cars. *Race*, therefore, is a modifier of the noun *car*. Now let us add the modifier *yellow* and we rule out all race cars that are not yellow—gone from possible reference are blue race cars and red race cars and orange ones. Finally, we could add the modifier *the* to indicate a particular yellow race car, rather than just any yellow race car, and we have completed our noun phrase, which stands as "the yellow race car."

Remember, though, that a noun phrase is a noun (or pronoun) and *any* immediate modifiers. The word *any* allows the possibility of there being no modifiers present at all. Thus *Joyce* and *it* constitute noun phrases by themselves. A random selection of other noun phrases is shown in the following list. Observe how each of them fits the definition of a noun phrase previously given:

a book
the dull party
the charitable African doctor
Freddy
a most nauseating movie
she
an attractive New England brick house

## The Verb Phrase

In simple sentences such as those that follow, a *verb phrase* consists of a verb, any modifiers of the verb which precede it, and everything following it. A *finite verb phrase* contains a verb that carries full and complete tense, as in the following sentences:

She *left*.
The antelope *easily jumped the fence*.
Marilyn *drives the Porsche daily*.
Blanch *might have left sooner*.
Ms. Stettner *is teaching them Latin*.
The hominy *was purchased at too high a price*.
The rabbi *asked why we had come*.

A *nonfinite verb phrase* contains a verb that lacks full and complete tense, as illustrated in the following examples:

Working late into the night, . . . .
Driven crazy with worry, . . . .
Having gone hungry for a week, . . . .

## The Prepositional Phrase

A *prepositional phrase* consists of a preposition and a noun phrase. Prepositional phrases can modify nouns, verbs, and adjectives, as shown in the following sentences:

People *in the subway* were angry. ("In the subway" consists of the preposition *in* and the noun phrase "the subway." It modifies the noun *people*.)

The car landed *in the river*. ("In the river" modifies the verb *landed*.)

John was the taller *of the two*. ("Of the two" modifies the adjective *taller*.)

# FROM PHRASE TO CLAUSE

We come now to the *clause*, a construction whose basic characteristic is that it contains, minimally, a subject-predicate relationship. The term *predicate* is really just another name for *finite verb phrase*. The predicate serves to make some kind of comment about the subject of the clause, as in the sentence "Michael likes polo," where the subject is "Michael" and the comment is (that he) "likes polo." In the sentence "The gallant knight lost the battle," "The gallant knight" is the subject, and the comment is (that he) "lost the battle."

It is important to remember that any construction containing a subject-predicate relationship is a clause, whether or not the construction constitutes a sentence. Those clauses that can stand as sentences are called *independent* (or *main*) clauses. Those that cannot stand by themselves as sentences are called *dependent* (or *subordinate*) and are typically preceded by an introductory word. Examples of both kinds of clauses are shown in the following charts.

**Chart 3-3  Independent clauses**

| Subject | Predicate |
| --- | --- |
| Monica | visited her uncle. |
| Richard Burton | played Hamlet. |
| A good friend | is hard to find. |
| Most grammarians | drink Scotch. |

**Chart 3-4 Dependent clauses**

| Introductory Word | Subject | Predicate |
|---|---|---|
| because | the hurricane | struck |
| after | the dance | is over |
| whom | her uncle | hired |
| that | he | could lie so |
| until | the Vikings | win |

Sentences formed by adding a dependent clause to an independent clause are called *complex* sentences. An independent clause standing alone is called a *simple* sentence. These constructs are treated fully in later chapters.

# Exercises

I Signaling Meaning.

A. In the spaces provided, list all of the affixes you can find in the following sentences.

*Example:* The wealthy promoters wanted to reconsider.

Inflectional suffixes: ___(for nouns)___ promoters

(for verbs)  want<u>ed</u>  (for adjectives) ___

Derivational suffixes: ___wealth<u>y</u>,  promot<u>ers</u>___

Prefixes: <u>reconsider</u> ___

1 Little Maurice frequently finds the biggest worms.

Inflectional suffixes: ___(for nouns)___

(for verbs) ___ (for adjectives) ___

Derivational suffixes: ___

Prefixes: ___

2 The youthful ship's captain thoughtlessly radioed "Mayday."

Inflectional suffixes: ___(for nouns)___

(for verbs) ___ (for adjectives) ___

Derivational suffixes: ___

Prefixes: ___

**3** Mark liked some of Paul's longer insane stories.

Inflectional suffixes: _(for nouns)_____

(for verbs)_____ (for adjectives)_____

Derivational suffixes: _____

Prefixes: _____

**4** Tom's crew tried to defuse the bomb.

Inflectional suffixes: _(for nouns)_____

(for verbs)_____ (for adjectives)_____

Derivational suffixes: _____

Prefixes: _____

**5** Boorish and pompous, Monroe hated mixing with commoners.

Inflectional suffixes: _(for nouns)_____

(for verbs)_____ (for adjectives)_____

Derivational suffixes: _____

Prefixes: _____

**6** Sensible Tom wants the case closed.

Inflectional suffixes: _(for nouns)_____

(for verbs)_____ (for adjectives)_____

Derivational suffixes: _____

Prefixes: _____

**7** The harmless drudge jumped sideways to safety.

Inflectional suffixes: _(for nouns)_____

(for verbs)_____ (for adjectives)_____

Derivational suffixes: _____

Prefixes: _____

**8** Joan's famous father liked playing silly tricks.

Inflectional suffixes: _(for nouns)_____

(for verbs)_____ (for adjectives)_____

Derivational suffixes: _____

Prefixes: _____

**9** The speediest racer modestly claimed the prize.

Inflectional suffixes: ___(for nouns)___

(for verbs) _____ (for adjectives) _____

Derivational suffixes: _____

Prefixes: _____

**10** The preplanning phase worried the fretful directors.

Inflectional suffixes: ___(for nouns)___

(for verbs) _____ (for adjectives) _____

Derivational suffixes: _____

Prefixes: _____

B.  Change the position of one or two (at the most) words in each sentence so that you get a different meaning.

  *Example:*  Ship the sails.

  *The ship sails.*

  **1** He could do it.

  _____

  **2** Dick arranged to meet Jane secretly.

  _____

  **3** Tom's crew tried to defuse the bomb.

  _____

  **4** Over their objections, he signed the new bill.

  _____

  **5** Always helpful, Benson tried to come to the aid of his uncle.

  _____

  **6** Her playing the activist only made him angry.

  _____

  **7** Rolf got the cheap watch.

  _____

  **8** Jean's friendly banker appeared calm.

  _____

  **9** The harried teacher was constantly returning late papers.

  _____

  **10** My dancing instructor finds sitting still difficult.

  _____

**II.** Parts of Speech.

Identify the part of speech of each word underlined in the following sentences.

*Example:* The paramedics carefully examined the victim.

  noun      adverb   verb

1 Florence Nightingale tended many sick people.

_____

2 Mr. Ibu greeted his guests with a bow.

_____

3 The bulletin warned that heavy rains would follow.

_____

4 They called her Magnanimous Tillie, or "Mag" for short.

_____

5 When in doubt, stamp and shout.

_____

6 The kindly old mayor helped the candidate to his seat.

_____

7 Frantic Jacob hurtled sideways into the crowded elevator.

_____

8 Having been left in the sun too long, the milk turned sour.

_____

9 Racing frantically down the aisle, the tardy groom

upset more than chairs.

_____

10 Creepy crawlers commonly dominate Jane's troublesome

dreams.

_____

**III.** Phrases and Clauses.

    A. In the spaces provided, list all of the *phrases* you can find in the following sentences. Remember that a predicate (verb phrase) may contain noun phrases and prepositional phrases as modifiers.

*Example:* John had a wild trip on the river.

Noun phrases: __John, a wild trip, the river.__

Finite verb phrases: __had a wild trip on the river__

Nonfinite verb phrases: _____

Prepositional phrases: __on the river__

**1** Feeling very ill, the family left the restaurant in a rush.

Noun phrases: _____

Finite verb phrases: _____

Nonfinite verb phrases: _____

Prepositional phrases: _____

**2** The spy satellite had been launched for unknown reasons.

Noun phrases: _____

Finite verb phrases: _____

Nonfinite verb phrases: _____

Prepositional phrases: _____

**3** Having a bad sunburn, Jane avoided the beach.

Noun phrases: _____

Finite verb phrases: _____

Nonfinite verb phrases: _____

Prepositional phrases: _____

**4** Smedley Zapp wore pin-striped trousers on most occasions.

Noun phrases: _____

Finite verb phrases: _____

Nonfinite verb phrases: _____

Prepositional phrases: _____

**5** He can't remember names from one day to the next day.

Noun phrases: _____

Finite verb phrases: _____

Nonfinite verb phrases: _____

Prepositional phrases: _____

**6** The startled gazelles leaped over the fallen log.

Noun phrases: _____

Finite verb phrases: _____

Nonfinite verb phrases: _____

Prepositional phrases: _____

**7** Solar energy is one possible solution to our energy problem.

Noun phrases: _____

Finite verb phrases: _____

Nonfinite verb phrases: _____

Prepositional phrases: _____

**8** The intrepid explorers entered the fearsome forest.

Noun phrases: _____

Finite verb phrases: _____

Nonfinite verb phrases: _____

Prepositional phrases: _____

**9** The fiercest warriors came from Manchuria.

Noun phrases: _____

Finite verb phrases: _____

Nonfinite verb phrases: _____

Prepositional phrases: _____

**10** Intimidated easily, the young child seldom left his mother.

Noun phrases: _____

Finite verb phrases: _____

Nonfinite verb phrases: _____

Prepositional phrases: _____

B. Place parentheses around the *dependent clauses* in the following sentences.

*Example:* Robert Abernathy III is the best designer (that you could find.)

1 Without intending to, Mannie tripped the alarm that Lucy had just installed.
2 Although we laughed at his backhand, we feared his serve.
3 Jan Trovag greeted his American cousins as they stepped from the ship.
4 The news that Paris had surrendered swept Europe.
5 German shepherds, because they are particularly intelligent, are often used as police dogs.
6 Louis became a gatekeeper after the war ended.
7 The song which Jill wrote soon became a sensation.
8 Frank has a tantrum whenever he loses a tennis match.
9 While Susan drove, Benny slept.
10 Since you're involved, you have a right to know.
11 Morgan believes that hard work is its own reward.
12 If the shoe fits, the foot will be happy.
13 The workers who lost their jobs picketed the capitol.
14 Mr. Gurney always arrived when the parking lot was full.
15 Most people appreciate dentists who are painless.

FOUR FOUR FOUR
FOUR FOUR FOUR FOUR
FOUR FOUR FOUR
FOUR FOUR FOUR
FOUR FOUR
FOUR FOUR FOUR
FOUR FOUR
FOUR FOUR
FOUR FOUR FOUR
FOUR FOUR
FOUR FOUR

# Tense

## INTRODUCTION

*Tense,* as we shall define it, refers to the forms that verbs take in order to communicate information. Usually, this information relates to time.[1] For example, the form of the verb *trim* in the sentence "Sandra *trimmed* that tree" indicates that the action of trimming was completed in the past. The verb form *trims* in "Her father *trims* trees," however, shows that the act of trimming occurs repeatedly in time, as it might if her father were a professional tree-trimmer.

Although we are defining tense as verb form, you should know that tense is sometimes defined in other ways. Some grammarians define tense in terms of the meanings communicated, rather than in terms of the verb forms that communicate those meanings. Other grammarians are careful to distinguish between *tense,* which indicates "point in time," and *aspect,* which specifies whether the action or state described by the verb has or has not been completed, does or does not occur repetitively, and so forth. Verb form, point in time, and aspect are actually closely related concepts. They overlap and interact to form a complex network of relationships which has always challenged grammarians. We have chosen to

[1] Verb tense can also communicate other information as well. Sometimes it helps to communicate varying levels of formality or courtesy (Informal: "Who *do* you want to see?" vs. Formal: "Whom *did* you wish to see?"). Tense can also communicate varying levels of probability (Greater Probability: "If I *visit* Bogota, I *will* phone Maria" vs. Lesser Probability: "If I *visited* Bogota, I *would* phone Maria"). Aspects of tense which do not relate to time are discussed later in this book.

define tense as verb form primarily in order to provide an easy to remember framework within which these complex relationships can be discussed.

While you study the tenses described in this chapter, you should also keep in mind the obvious—that tense is just one of several ways available for giving information about time. The following sentences demonstrate a different but commonly used way:

The maestro performs in Boston.
The maestro performs in Boston next month.

The verb forms are identical, yet the action in the first sentence is interpreted as taking place over and over again, whereas the action in the second is clearly assigned to the future, the adverbial "next month," rather than the form of the verb, indicating time.

The adverbial in the next pair causes similar changes:

The President is speaking.
The President is speaking tonight at eight o'clock.

In the first sentence the President is apparently speaking at this very moment. "Tonight at eight o'clock" completely changes things in the second sentence, specifying that the time is the future and being quite precise about it.

Now consider the following pair:

Betty and Sue have lived in Atlanta.
Betty and Sue have lived in Atlanta since 1975.

Here the first sentence implies that Betty and Sue no longer live in Atlanta. In other words, the act of their living in Atlanta was part of their past life. In the second sentence, Betty and Sue are clearly still living in Atlanta at this moment. Although the verb forms are identical, an adverbial, "since 1975," again communicates the essential information about time.

Remember, then, that time in English is communicated by adverbials as well as by verbs. This chapter will focus on verbs, and you will find the most frequent verb tenses described here.

# THE SIMPLE PRESENT TENSE

Daffodils *bloom* in early spring.
Madeline *plays* the harp.
Frank *cheats* at poker.

That old man *is* very tall.
I *hear* a mouse in the attic.
This car *belongs* to Tom.

## Description of Form

The *simple present* tense is formed by using the simple form of the verb. When a third person singular subject (he, she, it, the lady, etc.) is present, an -s ending is added. With *to be*, the form of the verb is changed.

## Meaning

In spite of what you may have been told or may have read, the simple present tense does not ordinarily refer to actions taking place "at this very moment." A quick look at the preceding examples will confirm this point. The daffodils described in the first example were probably not blooming when the sentence was written, nor was Madeline necessarily playing the harp, nor Frank engaged in the act of cheating. Rather than describing events or states existing "right now," the simple present tense is more often used to describe *recurring* actions or states, actions or states that occur repetitively over a period of time. Every time you hear statements such as "Susan dances well," "That river overflows its bank every few years," or "I buy white wines only," you are *not* hearing about things which are being done at the present moment, but about actions that are known to occur over and over again.

Sometimes, however, the present tense *is* used to describe states existing at the present moment. This is particularly true when the verb involved is (1) *be*, (2) a verb of the "senses" such as *hear*, *smell*, *see*, or *taste*, and (3) certain "nonaction" verbs such as *belong*, *know*, *need*, *owe*, or *resemble*. Note that the last three examples at the beginning of this section illustrate the simple present tense being used in this way—to describe states which truly exist "in the present."

The simple present tense, then, has two principal uses. The first describes repetitive actions; the second, limited to certain kinds of verbs, describes states which are in existence right now.

# THE PRESENT PROGRESSIVE

I *am listening* to a Beethoven symphony.
Joyce *is harboring* a fugitive.
The workers *are attending* a seminar in Seattle.
Young Clarence *is being* very attentive.

## Description of Form

The *present progressive* (sometimes called the *present continuous*) tense is formed by using a present tense form of *be* with the progressive form (the *-ing* form) of the verb.

## Meaning

Generally, the present progressive form is used to indicate (or emphasize) that the action or state being described is occurring "right now." The following pairs of sentences illustrate this. The first sentence of each pair contains a verb in the simple present tense, the second a verb in the present progressive. As you go from the first to the second sentence of each pair, notice that the time reference changes from "repetitive action, not necessarily happening right now," to "action happening right now, at this very moment."

1 John *plays* cricket.
  John *is playing* cricket.
2 The twins *listen* to Scott Joplin ragtime.
  The twins *are listening* to Scott Joplin ragtime.
3 Susan *does* her homework.
  Susan *is doing* her homework.

As you see, the present progressive is really more of a "present" tense than the simple present tense is.

The preceding paragraph is a "more or less" accurate statement about the meaning of the present progressive. Unfortunately for grammarians, teachers, and students, not all of the facts of English are accounted for by easy generalizations, especially where tense is concerned. It is not too difficult to think up pairs of sentences in which the "repetitive action" versus "immediate action" distinction is much less apparent. When verbs describing mental or emotional qualities or states are used, the distinction nearly vanishes. Notice, for example, how this happens in the following pairs:

1 I *look* forward to seeing you.
  I *am looking* forward to seeing you.
2 She *feels* fine.
  She *is feeling* fine.

The present progressive can sometimes also be used to refer to future events, as in "Mrs. Lily *is coming* to visit us," and to repetitive actions that are not necessarily happening right now, as in "Betty *is thinking* about going to England," where Betty may not be thinking about the trip at the moment. Lastly, the present progressive cannot be used with some verbs, among them *like* and *know*. Neither of the following sentences is permissible in English:

*I am *liking* cake.
*The students *are knowing* their lessons.

Remember then—the present progressive "usually" refers to the immediate or near-immediate present. As for the exceptions—bless or curse them, whichever suits your fancy.

# THE SIMPLE PAST TENSE

The drought *lasted* for ten years.
Mark *researched* his topic thoroughly.
The Rams *sold* their star quarterback.
Alistair MacLean *wrote* this novel.
Elephants *swam* into view.

## Description of Form

The *simple past* tense is formed by using the simple past form of the verb. For regular verbs, the past form is made by adding *-ed* to the simple form (*kick* + *-ed*, *want* + *-ed*, etc.). For irregular verbs the past forms are more or less idiosyncratic (*wrote*, *swam*, *caught*, *froze*, *went*, etc.).

## Meaning

Actions or states described by the simple past tense usually occurred or were completed in the past. The following sentences are examples:

1 Lincoln *signed* the Emancipation Proclamation.
2 The capital of the United States *was* once New York City.

It is clear from sentence 1 that the act of signing was finished in the past. It is equally clear from sentence 2 that the state described occurred in the past, that, in fact, the state or condition is different today. Sometimes, however, the action or state described by the past tense still exists, but in these cases the *time frame* within which the action or state is being described belongs to the past. For example, a person describing his or her childhood might say, "My father *worked* in Dallas." Possibly the speaker's father still works in Dallas, but the time frame within which the fact is viewed, i.e., the speaker's childhood, has been completed.

In one way or another, all the actions or states described by the simple past tense have associated with them the idea that something was completed in the past. The time of completion may be stated explicitly, as in the sentences "George Washington *died* in 1799," "I *studied* French last summer," and "She *scrawled* her name on the petition yesterday." Or a specific time may be stated early in the discourse and "understood" thereafter. For instance, a writer may establish in the first few pages of a novel that the story will span the years 1910–1930 and not have to mention another date throughout the rest of the book. A third recourse allows time in a story to be stated in relation to other events or actions, as in "Several days after the party, he *saw* her again." In one way or another, simple past tense verbs are usually accompanied by references to specific or relative *times of completion*. It will be important to remember this when we discuss the present perfect tense later in the chapter.

# THE PAST PROGRESSIVE

The townspeople *were sleeping* when the earthquake struck.
The idea came to me as I *was talking* on the phone.
Tony *was hitting* the baseball poorly until his coach helped him.
I met Tony when I *was attending* college.

## Description of Form

The *past progressive* (sometimes called the *past continuous*) is formed by using a past tense form of *be* with the progressive form of the verb.

## Meaning

The past progressive is used to refer to actions or states that were taking place at the time that a second past action or state occurred. A look at the preceding examples will illustrate this. In the first example, the townspeople were sleeping when a second event, the earthquake, took place. In the second sentence, the speaker was talking on the telephone when the idea struck. The third example shows that poor hitting was going on when the second action, help from the coach, arrived. And finally, in the fourth sentence we see that the speaker was attending college when he or she met Tony.

With the past progressive it is common for the second action not to be explicitly referred to in the same sentence, however. For example, in "General Patton *was meeting* with his officers," no second action is mentioned, and may not be until several sentences later, perhaps taking the form, "Suddenly an aide arrived with a message for the general." But the second event could equally well be implied rather than explicitly stated. For example, the sentence "I *was* just *thinking* of you" shows that the speaker was in the act of thinking about a particular person when that person happened to make an appearance or a phone call. Here the appearance or call of this person, though not explicitly mentioned, is understood as the "second event" by both the speaker and the listener.

# THE PRESENT PERFECT: TWO MEANINGS

Set 1:  I *have lived* in New York City since 1975.
We *have played* poker for many years.
Brent *has* always *liked* redheads.
Sally *has been* up all night.

Set 2:  Joan *has seen* that movie.
He *has met* the President.
They *have received* their B.A. degrees.
She *has visited* Copenhagen.

## Description of Form

The *present perfect* tense is formed using a present tense form of the helping verb *have* plus the past participle[2] form of the verb.

## Meaning

The present perfect has *two* principal meanings. The first is illustrated in Set 1 of the preceding examples. Here we see that the actions or states described by the verbs began in the past and continue into the present, right up to the moment of speaking. When this meaning is being used, an adverbial such as "since," "for," "always," or "all night" is almost always present. These adverbials are communicating much of the information about time in these sentences. The present perfect, *together with* these adverbials, signals that a past action is still continuing.

The second meaning of the present perfect is illustrated in Set 2.

---

[2] *Past participle* is the term traditionally used for the verb form that directly follows the helping verb *have* (for example, have *seen*, has *worked*, had *run*).

Here we see that the actions or states described by the verbs were definitely completed in the past. This second meaning is therefore quite similar to that of the simple past tense. There is one important difference in the use of the present perfect and the simple past tense, however. When the time of completion of the past event is stated explicitly, the simple past, *not* the present perfect, is used. For example, "Joan saw that movie last year" is acceptable, but *"Joan has seen that movie last year" is not. You will note that no explicit time of completion is present in any of the sentences in Set 2.

The following pairs of sentences illustrate how natural it is for the simple past tense to occur with time of completion explicitly indicated; they will also show how unnatural it would be to give an explicit time of completion to verbs in the present perfect:

1  I *studied* French last summer.
   *I *have studied* French last summer.
2  They *signed* the agreement yesterday.
   *They *have signed* the agreement yesterday.
3  He *grew* 8 inches when he was 10 years old.
   *He *has grown* 8 inches when he was 10 years old.
4  Jane *received* her diploma in 1972.
   *Jane *has received* her diploma in 1972.

# THE PRESENT PERFECT PROGRESSIVE

William *has been restoring* his antique fire truck.
Susan *has been feeling* better.
The pilots *have been complaining* about that airport.
I *have been wanting* to meet you.

## Description of Form

The present perfect progressive is formed by using a present tense form of *have*, plus the past participle form of *be* (*been*) and the progressive form of the verb.

## Meaning

The meaning of the present perfect progressive is essentially that of the present perfect in its first sense; that is, it indicates that an action or state started in the past and has continued up to the present moment. Observe that the following pairs of sentences are more or less synonymous:

Present Perfect: We *have lived* in Dallas since 1971.
Present Perfect Progressive: We *have been living* in Dallas since 1971.
Present Perfect: We *have fished* in that river for several years.
Present Perfect Progressive: We *have been fishing* in that river for several years.

Many grammarians have argued that there exist slight differences in emphasis between the two tenses. Some argue that the present perfect progressive emphasizes the continuous nature of the activity. Other grammarians have claimed that the present perfect progressive serves to make the action seem more "immediate." A second reading of the preceding two sets of sentences may help you form your own opinion.

Although the present perfect progressive is one of the most complex forms the verb assumes, it nevertheless occurs frequently in our speech and writing. Just think for a moment how familiar such utterances as "I've been studying," "I've been working," "I've been thinking," and so forth sound. With such a long, cumbersome, and esoteric name, it might seem that this form should be reserved only for infrequent, tedious, academic occasions. Prove to yourself that this does not happen by trying one simple experiment—just try *not* to use it.

# THE PAST PERFECT: SEQUENCING IS THE KEY

Michael *had finished* his dinner when Doris arrived.
The villagers returned when the storm *had passed*.
The hunter suddenly stopped. He *had heard* a noise in the bushes.
The Detroit Lions *had won* eight games before they finally lost one.
Oliver felt depressed after he *had quit* his job.

## Description of Form

The past perfect is formed by using the past form of *have* (*had*) plus the past participle form of the verb.

## Meaning

The past perfect is used to indicate that an action or state in the past took place *before* a second past action or state. In the preceding examples, you will notice that the earlier action or state is described by using the past perfect, while the subsequent action or state appears in the simple past. Thus we know that Michael finished his dinner before Doris arrived, that the storm passed before the villagers returned, and that the hunter heard the noise before he stopped, and so on. With the past perfect, you will always find this sort of "x happened first, y happened later" situation.

Often adverbs such as *before* and *after* carry the principal burden of indicating which action or state happened first, and sometimes even common sense makes clear what happened first. In unambiguous cases it is acceptable to describe both the prior and subsequent action by using the simple past tense. Therefore, the fourth and fifth examples could just as easily appear as "The Detroit Lions *won* eight games before they finally *lost* one" and "Oliver *felt* depressed after he *quit* his job."

In sentences like the preceding two, the past perfect might appear primarily as a helpful redundancy. In other sentences, however, the past perfect carries the entire burden of indicating which of two actions or states occurred first. This happens whenever adverbs or common sense are not present to provide the necessary cues. Notice that the first and third examples at the beginning of this section depend entirely on the past perfect to indicate which action happened first. If the past perfect in these sentences were changed to the simple past, we would have:

Michael *finished* his dinner when Doris *arrived*.
The hunter suddenly *stopped*. He *heard* a noise in the bushes.

Notice that the previous information about sequencing has now been drastically altered.

# THE FUTURE: *WILL* IS ONLY ONE WAY

Set 1:  I *will succeed*.
The doctor *will operate*.
Madeline *will graduate* in June.
The New York Yankees *will win* this game.

Set 2:  I *am going to succeed*.
The doctor *is going to operate*.
Madeline *is going to graduate* in June.
The New York Yankees *are going to win* this game.

## Description of Form

The future is ordinarily indicated in English by two forms. The first is *will* plus the simple form of the verb (*shall* plus the simple form of the verb is also acceptable, but uncommon in the United States, especially in spoken English). The second, often called the *going to* future, uses a present tense form of *be* plus the expression *going to* and the simple form of the verb.

## Meaning

Both forms describe events or states taking place in the future. Although both occur frequently in writing, the *going to* future is probably the form most used in conversation. In speech, this form seldom appears in its entirety. Normally the form of *be* is contracted and the *going to* is pronounced *gonna*. It is most often heard as it appears in the sentences "I'm gonna go to college," "I'm gonna do my homework," "He's gonna be sorry," "They're gonna try harder," and so forth.

Finally, as mentioned earlier in this chapter, future time may be indicated without the help of either *will* or *going to*. The job of indicating the future often falls upon adverbials. Examples of this are "They fly to Arizona *tomorrow*" and "She is arriving home *next Tuesday*."

# OTHER TENSES

You are now familiar with the most important, most frequently used tenses. Occasionally, however, you will encounter others. By using your knowledge of the tenses already described in this chapter, you should be able to figure out the names and meanings of these unfamiliar tenses as you encounter them. "They *had been visiting*" illustrates the past perfect progressive, "They *will have been trying*" illustrates the future perfect progressive, and so forth.

# TENSE IN THE EVERYDAY WORLD

In this chapter we have presented a description of verb tense as most people feel it is supposed to be used in Standard English. Even the most casual observer, however, is aware that the actual use of verb tense in English does not always coincide with this prescriptive norm. It is important to be aware of some of the more common variations, for only then is it possible to understand *why* some speakers of English have trouble with standard forms. Understanding is usually the first step toward being able to intelligently help those who wish to learn standard forms and their uses.

One widespread variation is a tendency on the part of some speakers not to use forms of *be*. This practice is especially common in some inner-city areas and with some speakers in the South, although it is found elsewhere, too. When *be* is not present, present progressive forms, for example, appear as "He singin' " (*-ing* is usually pronounced *-in'*) and "You laughin'," rather than the usual "He is singing" and "You are laughing." Here are other examples:

| *Standard Form* | *Without* Be |
|---|---|
| He is coming home. | He comin' home. |
| You are watching television. | You watchin' television. |
| She is getting some food. | She gettin' some food. |

This variation also affects the simple present tense. Sentences that appear in Standard English as "He is lazy" and "You are a genius!" appear as "He lazy" and "You a genius!" Here are other examples:

| *Standard Form* | *Without* Be |
|---|---|
| She is a winner. | She a winner. |
| This is a nuisance. | This a nuisance. |
| They are tough. | They tough. |

*Be* is also often absent in the *going to* future. It is common, in some areas, to hear sentences such as those in the right-hand column of the following list:

| *Standard Form* | *Without* Be |
|---|---|
| He is going to quit. | He gonna quit. |
| They are going to decide it. | They gonna decide it. |
| We are going to win. | We gonna win. |

A second widespread variation is what is commonly called "invariant *be*." This form is also heard in inner-city areas and seems to occur most often in the speech and sometimes the writing of children and adolescents. The invariant *be* is so named because it always has the form *be*, regardless of its grammatical subject. Thus you will hear, "I be . . . ," "You be . . . ," "We be . . . ," and so on. Invariant *be* is apparently used to refer to "repetitive actions" or "general truths," much as the simple present tense is in Standard English. You will find some examples of the invariant *be* displayed in the following list opposite their approximate Standard English equivalents:

| *Standard Form* | *Invariant* Be *Form* |
|---|---|
| Usually we are at the pool. | Usually we be at the pool. |
| Sometimes I am scared. | Sometimes I be scared. |

| | We always be wishin' we |
|---|---|
| We always wish we could find it. | could find it. |
| That man is at meetings most of the time. | That man be at meetin's most of the time. |

In addition to the meaning of "repetitive action" or "general truth," invariant *be* sometimes appears where a "will be" occurs in Standard English and thus indicates future time, as in the sentence "If he finds it soon, he be happy."

A third variation involves the use of nonstandard past-tense and past-participle forms. The variety of these nonstandard forms is truly awesome—just when a grammarian begins to believe that he or she has heard them all, three new ones are apt to pop up in the course of a single week. A small sample of these forms is found in the following list:

| Standard Form | Nonstandard Form |
|---|---|
| He *did* it. | He *done* it. |
| They *knew* it. | They *knowed* it. |
| They have *come*. | They have *came*. |
| I *ran*. | I *runned*. |
| You have *run* away. | You have *ran* away. |
| She had *gone* there. | She had *went* there. |
| We *saw* her. | We *seen* her. |
| He has *written* his name on it. | He has *wrote* his name on it. |

Undoubtedly you can think of many, many more.

# Exercises

I People who are not used to working with tense can sometimes feel a little intimidated by the vocabulary of tense names. When familiarity with tense increases, this intimidation quickly vanishes. This exercise, then, is designed to increase your familiarity with tense names and forms. It is a *practice*, not a test, so refer to the text as frequently as you like for help.

Identify the tense of the underlined verbs in the following sentences:

*Examples:* They <u>buried</u> it.      simple past

           We <u>had abandoned</u> the ship.      past perfect

1 Paolo <u>completed</u> his masterpiece.     _____

2 She <u>has earned</u> the promotion.     _____

3 They <u>are working</u> on the case.     _____

4 She <u>was laughing</u> politely.     _____

5 He <u>had succeeded</u> at roulette.     _____

6 You <u>have been trying.</u>     _____

7 He <u>tried</u> a cigarette.     _____

8 We <u>had lost</u> the jade ring.     _____

**9** I <u>am</u> <u>counting</u>.  _____

**10** It <u>will</u> <u>continue</u>.  _____

**11** She <u>left</u> her briefcase behind.  _____

**12** He <u>has</u> <u>been</u> <u>shaking</u>.  _____

**13** They <u>were</u> <u>swimming</u>.  _____

**14** They <u>take</u> samples.  _____

**15** You <u>have</u> <u>mastered</u> it.  _____

**16** We <u>have</u> <u>owned</u> one since June.  _____

**17** I <u>was</u> <u>digging</u>.  _____

**18** You <u>are</u> <u>joking</u>.  _____

**19** I <u>have</u> <u>been</u> <u>moonlighting</u>.  _____

**20** She <u>interests</u> him.  _____

**21** I <u>have</u> <u>eaten</u> barbecued turtle.  _____

**22** She <u>has</u> <u>tried</u> it.  _____

**23** He <u>had</u> <u>argued</u> with them.  _____

II  Identify the tense of the underlined verbs in the following sentences and summarize the information about time that they are conveying.

*Examples:*

John will marry her.

Tense: *will* future

Time: The event will take place in the future.

Secretariat won the race. Joe had bet wisely.

Tense: past perfect

Time: Joe's bet occurred prior to the winning of the race.

1 My life flashed before my eyes as the airplane was falling.

Tense: _____

Time: _____

2 Bill and Margaret have been taking tightrope walking lessons.

Tense: _____

Time: _____

3 Ancient man invented the wheel.

Tense: _____

Time: _____

**4** Alex <u>is</u> <u>making</u> too much noise.

Tense: _____

Time: _____

**5** The evidence <u>had</u> <u>vanished</u>. Mark was furious.

Tense: _____

Time: _____

**6** Mr. Platt <u>designs</u> submarines.

Tense: _____

Time: _____

**7** Sam <u>has</u> <u>been</u> a devil since childhood.

Tense: _____

Time: _____

**8** Marie <u>has</u> <u>read</u> all of Shakespeare's works.

Tense: _____

Time: _____

# Be–The Busy One

## TWO *BE*S

This chapter title is an appropriate one, for once you look for *be*, it appears everywhere. It occurs so often not because it is a verb laden with intrinsic meaning, but because it plays two roles—that of a verb and that of an auxiliary.

The verb *be* is often called a *copulative* or *linking* verb. As a linking verb it carries little meaning, serving mainly to "link" a noun, adjective, or adverb to a subject, as in the following sentences. Notice that it would be difficult to say what *be* means in any of them, other than that some vague notion of "existence" is perhaps involved.

1 They *are* doctors.
2 The tree *was* tall.
3 The boy *is* here.

Such linkages are characteristic of the verb *be*. In fact, it is seldom that the verb *be* is not followed by one of these three constructions. You can find such sentences as "God is," "I am," or "Let them be," but they appear infrequently. Moreover, in each sentence *be* could easily be replaced by words that would specify the meaning more exactly, like *exist* ("God exists") or *alone* ("Let them alone" or "Leave them alone").

When *be* is used as an auxiliary, it no longer links two constructions; instead it helps a verb express some meaning, mainly by carrying the tense (present or past) or by helping to form the progressive[1] or the passive.[2] This is why *be* as an auxiliary is also called a *helping* verb. In the following sentences *be* is used as an auxiliary:

[1] See Chapter 4.
[2] The passive form is explained fully in Chapter 6.

**4** He *is* helping them. (present progressive form)
**5** It *was* raining. (past progressive form)
**6** She *was* seen by them. (past passive form)
**7** The problem has *been* solved. (present perfect passive form)

Note that in each of these sentences a verb (*help, rain, see,* and *solve*) follows *be*.

Since *be* can be both a verb and an auxiliary, you might even find it playing two roles in the same sentence:

**8** They *are being* silly.

In "They are being silly" the first *be* ("are") is an auxiliary and the second *be* ("being") is a verb. The order of occurrence will help you distinguish them, for the auxiliary is always first.

## THE FORMS OF *BE*

In the previous section *be* appeared in several different forms in our few examples. The following list is the complete set: *am, is, are, was, were, be, been,* and *being*. When and where each form is used in standard English is explained in Chart 5-1, which you will find further on in this chapter.

## PERSON AND NUMBER WITH *BE*

The terms *person* and *number* can be used to describe the pronoun or noun that occurs with a particular form of *be*.

In English *number* refers to singular and plural forms. *Boy* is singular and *boys* is plural. *Person* is used in talking about both nouns and personal pronouns,[3] but it is mainly used in referring to the forms that pronouns take and to the meanings they have. First person singular means the person speaking: "*I* am the one." With first person plural, however, the speaker and various other persons may be included. For example, in the sentence "*We* just arrived," *we* includes the speaker and the entourage, but not the person spoken to who might be meeting them. In the sentence "*We*'re going to have a good class," *we* includes the speaker and the audience. The first person plural could also mean the person speaking, the person or persons spoken to, and one or more "others" spoken about, as in "*We*'re all responsible for the crime," where the accused

---

[3] Nouns are all third person, whether singular or plural.

implicitly referred to by the speaker may not even be present. Finally, two other meanings of we are worth mentioning. One, commonly referred to as the "editorial we," may be found in editorials and magazines or newspaper columns where the writer refers to himself or herself as "we": "We would like to think that Congress could act more responsibly." Another, where we refers to the person spoken to, is regularly used to soften orders, especially by adults speaking to children, as in "We're going to be a good boy, now, aren't we?" Second person means the person or persons spoken to, while third person means the person, persons, thing, or things spoken about.

The various forms that pronouns take are presented in Chart 5-1, along with the appropriate present-tense forms of be. Such a chart provides a convenient set of labels for the pronouns and allows you to quickly state which form of be each pronoun takes. For example, the first person singular takes am. The chart represents Standard English, but in the everyday world you will find frequent variations.

**Chart 5-1**

| Person | Number | Pronoun | Form of Be[4] |
|--------|--------|---------|---------------|
| first | singular | I | am |
| first | plural | we | are |
| second | singular | you | are |
| second | plural | you | are |
| third | singular | he, she, it | is |
| third | plural | they | are |

## BE IN THE EVERYDAY WORLD

Be is not only busy; it also has the distinction of showing more variety than any other verb and the honor of arousing comments and criticism out of all proportion to its size and shape.

You have probably heard such expressions as these used repeatedly:

---

[4] In the past tense was is used with I, he, she, and it, while were is used at all other times. Other forms of be are be (simple form), being (progressive form), and been (past participle form).

1 If I *was* you, I wouldn't do that.
2 That *ain't* right.
3 You (They) *was* there.

You have probably also heard these expressions denounced soundly, for across the country many speakers immediately notice these forms in the speech of others and call them incorrect or nonstandard. People continue to do so even though the forms appear regularly in the speech of many and sporadically in the speech of others, including some highly educated people who use them in casual conversation among friends and intimates.

The first example is considered nonstandard because the sentence should contain the so-called "subjunctive *were*." Standard English requires the use of this form in sentences expressing wish, doubt, and possibility, regardless of the number or person of the subject noun or pronoun. Thus, the following sentences are said to take *were* rather than *was*, at least in more formal speech and writing:

4 I wish that Jane *were* here.
5 If he *were* reliable, I'd loan him the money.
6 *Were* I to be invited, I might attend.

Despite injunctions against it, *was* occurs frequently, especially in speech, and has since the seventeenth century. Probably only the grammar-book teaching of *were* as the correct form has kept *was* from becoming completely respectable.

*Ain't* in sentence 2 might be considered the most recognizable nonstandard form of *be* in the United States. This construction is widely used as a substitute for the negatives "am not," "are not," and "is not." One hundred years ago *ain't* was acceptable; today it is not. One can even find students who have been told that *ain't* is not a word, or that it does not exist, despite the fact that they need only listen to hear it on playgrounds, campuses, city streets, and almost any other place where casual speech is used. Speakers who object to *ain't* generally follow the usage shown in Chart 5-1, except in negative questions where *I* is the subject and *be* is in the present tense. Then some favor "aren't I" ("*Aren't I* dressed properly?"), while others use "am I not" ("*Am I not* right?"). With *ain't* in such disfavor, chances are that it will not be acceptable in any but the most informal situations for a long time to come.

Our last example ("You *was* there") contains what is sometimes called "invariant *was*." Some speakers use the past-tense form *was* with all subjects, even though Standard English requires the use of *were* with plural nouns like *cows* and with the pronouns we, *you*, and *they*. Sentences with these words as subjects would take the following form with users of "invariant *was*":

**8** The cows *was* grazin'.
**9** We *was* really scared.
**10** You *was* late yesterday.
**11** They *was* jabberin' away.

Like the other forms, "invariant *was*" once had a better reputation. In fact, in the eighteenth and nineteenth centuries, "you *was*" as a singular form was common in the speech of British aristocrats. This usage also appeared in plays and novels of the time, a good indication that it received a better reception in those days than it does now.

The preceding examples are three common nonstandard forms of *be*. If you do not use them, it might be instructive to raise the matter in class to see whether other students do. An open discussion could reveal a multitude of attitudes and lead to a better understanding of where and when such forms are and are not used.

# Exercises

I  Identify the *be* as linking verb and the *be* as auxiliary by underlining the linking verb once and the auxiliary twice.

*Example:* You <u>are</u> <u><u>being</u></u> childish.

1 If you wish, you can be whatever you like.
2 That is Reuben's responsibility.
3 They are working at the same place.
4 She was aware of their feelings.
5 He is the only one Julie trusts.
6 He is going over her head.
7 We were there for part of the performance.
8 You aren't being very consistent.
9 They were criticized for their actions.

II Supply the appropriate forms of *be* as linking verb or *be* as auxiliary in each of the following sentences (use the tense form requested, if one is asked for). In the blank to the left of each sentence, put "L" for linking verb or "A" for auxiliary.

*Example:* \_\_\_\_\_ John can't \_\_\_\_\_ serious.

\_\_L\_ John can't \_be\_ serious.

\_\_\_\_\_ 1 George and Hilda \_\_\_\_\_ coming to the party. (present tense)

\_\_\_\_\_ 2 That copying machine \_\_\_\_\_ working now. (present tense)

\_\_\_\_\_ 3 Both the boy and the girl \_\_\_\_\_ expecting surprises. (present tense)

\_\_\_\_\_ 4 The students \_\_\_\_\_ aware of the outcome. (past tense)

_____ **5** Gloria's main passion _____ horses. (present tense)

_____ **6** The top scholar _____ chosen for an award. (past tense)

_____ **7** Julio is _____ silly.

_____ **8** The youngest boy _____ guilty of hiding the chalk. (past tense)

_____ **9** Norman _____ not feeling very well. (past tense)

_____ **10** This exercise could have _____ easier.

**III** "Correct" the following nonstandard sentences by substituting the appropriate standard form of *be*.

**1** Ain't I more important than that?

_____

**2** They was just strolling through the park.

_____

**3** If he was to leave, I'd be glad.

_____

**4** Morris talks like he ain't coming back.

_____

**5** Admit it—you was wrong!

_____

**6** If only Maria was here now.

_____

# SIX

# Passives

Passive sentences have been helping you out of tight situations ever since you were a youngster. Although you might not realize it, they have been helping you escape conflict, avoid embarrassment, protect sources of confidential information, and conceal your ignorance of certain things. Before we discuss in detail the merits of these helpful grammatical devices, let us first see just what a passive sentence is.

## THE PASSIVE DEFINED

Many English sentences may appear in either of two forms—the *active* form (i.e., the normal subject + verb + object form) or the *passive* form. In either form the sentence communicates the same meaning.

In the following list you see how five sentences look in both their active and passive forms. You will notice too that the meaning remains the same regardless of the form used.

| *Active Form* | *Passive Form* |
|---|---|
| The Dodgers beat the Yankees. | The Yankees were beaten by the Dodgers. |
| Shakespeare wrote this poem. | This poem was written by Shakespeare. |
| Warblers eat spiders. | Spiders are eaten by warblers. |
| Millions of people play baseball. | Baseball is played by millions of people. |
| Joseph planted that tree. | That tree was planted by Joseph. |

Let us now consider the steps that must be taken in order for a sentence to be converted from its active form into its passive form. (For various reasons the active form is considered the "basic" form and the passive a conversion of this basic form, rather than vice versa). In the demonstration to follow, each step has been isolated to show step by step how the passive form is built. In reality, of course, all the steps take place simultaneously.

*Active Form:* <u>Shakespeare</u>   <u>wrote</u>   <u>this poem.</u>
            subject     verb     direct object

*Step 1:*   Switch the subject and direct object.

*Result:*   | This poem |   wrote   | Shakespeare |
       direct object            subject

*Step 2:*   Insert the appropriate form of *be* immediately in front of the verb.

*Result:*   This poem   | was |   wrote     Shakespeare.
                             verb

*Step 3:*   Change the verb to its past participle form.

*Result:*   This poem was   | written |   Shakespeare.
                          verb

*Step 4:*   Insert the word *by* immediately in front of the subject.

*Result:*   This poem was written   | by |   <u>Shakespeare.</u>
                                            subject

And there you have it. The active sentence has been successfully converted into its passive form, "This poem was written by Shakespeare."

Now compare the active and passive forms in the following set of sentences. You will see that each passive is simply the result of all four steps being applied to the active.

| *Active Form* | *Passive Form* |
|---|---|
| The farmer saw the missing elephant. | The missing elephant was seen by the farmer. |
| The new doctor treated Susan. | Susan was treated by the new doctor. |
| All six senators signed the bill. | The bill was signed by all six senators. |

# SUBJECT DELETION: THAT USEFUL OPTION

You are now familiar with Step 1 of the conversion procedure—the step in which you switch the subject and direct object. There is one more thing you should know about this switch—you have the option of deleting the subject. In the illustrative sentences that follow, each active form has been converted into two passives—one with the subject retained and one with the subject deleted. Both types of passives are perfectly grammatical. The only difference is that in one the subject that performed the action is clearly expressed, while in the other the subject is not mentioned. As we shall see in the final section of this chapter, there are times when the option not to mention the subject is quite appealing.

| *Active Form* | **1** *Passive Form with Subject Stated* <br> **2** *Passive Form with Subject Deleted* |
| --- | --- |
| Paul cheated Susan. | **1** Susan was cheated by Paul. <br> **2** Susan was cheated. |
| A tipster alerted the police. | **1** The police were alerted by a tipster. <br> **2** The police were alerted. |
| Pam fed the horse. | **1** The horse was fed by Pam. <br> **2** The horse was fed. |
| Chrysler Corporation built that car in 1958. | **1** That car was built by Chrysler Corporation in 1958. <br> **2** That car was built in 1958. |

When the subject is deleted, we can no longer say that the meaning of the passive form is exactly the same as the meaning of the active. The difference, of course, is that the subject is no longer clearly defined.

# LIMITATIONS ON ACTIVE-PASSIVE CONVERSIONS

You should be aware that not all actives with direct objects can be converted into passives. Actives in which the direct object is a reflexive do not convert successfully. "He hated himself" converts into the unacceptable *"Himself was hated by him." Certain verbs, such as *resemble*, block successful conversion also. "She resembles her aunt" becomes the unacceptable *"Her aunt is resembled by her." There are many other things which prevent successful conversion, so be forewarned. You can never be absolutely sure that a conversion will work until you have tried it.

# THE *GET* PASSIVE

If you are under the impression that passives are not very common in everyday conversation, you should realize that a great many children and many adults (especially in informal situations) insert a form of *get* instead of a form of *be* in front of the verb in a passive. This results in passives such as "I got cheated," "I got hit," "He got paid," "She got hired," "We got beaten," "She gets asked out," and "The accounts get audited." Passives are certainly not uncommon grammatical constructions.

# LOOK-ALIKES

After you have learned what the passive is, you will soon come across constructions that look like passives but that do not act the way passives are supposed to act. There are not many verbs that this happens with, but they do occur fairly often and it is only for this reason that we mention them.

Three of the most common look-alikes are shown in the following sentences:

1 He is gone.
2 The moon is risen now.
3 They are finished.

Notice that none of these sentences seems to have gone through the process of subject deletion (dropping the *by* + noun phrase). *"He is gone by John" is not possible, and "They are finished by the people" changes the meaning of the sentence as you probably first understood it.

These sentences look like passives, of course, because they have the passive form. The explanation goes back to a time in the history of English when it was possible to use *be* instead of *have* to form a perfect. This construction survives in only a few verbs today, and these verbs have their own characteristics and meanings, which are different from either the perfect or the passive. As a result you can say such things as "The moon is risen now" as a statement of fact. Just remember that such constructions are not passives.

# A NOTE ON TERMINOLOGY

The direct object that has been moved to the front of a passivized sentence is sometimes called the *grammatical subject* of the sentence, since it determines the form that *be* takes. The original subject, the one moved to the end of the sentence, is called the *logical subject* because it names the performer of the action and remains the true subject as far as the meaning of the sentence is concerned. The "subject" we refer to throughout this chapter is always the logical subject.

# PASSIVES IN THE EVERYDAY WORLD

Passives are used for a variety of reasons in the everyday world. One important reason is that people frequently feel the need to use a sentence form that does not require them to identify (or to misrepresent) the subject. For example, how many times have you heard the active "I made an error" discarded in favor of the passive equivalent so that the subject could be deleted? The resultant "An error was made" (or "An error has been made") allows the perpetrator of the mistake to be hidden behind a grammatical smoke screen—temporarily, at least. Next time you are faced with this kind of passive smoke screen, you might try insisting on a translation to the active. You might be surprised at how many times the "unknown" subject turns out to be the speaker.

Sometimes people wish to avoid mention of the subject in order to keep the source of their information secret. For example, a person might hesitate to use the active "Ralph informed me that George gambles heavily" for fear of compromising Ralph. The passive form of the sentence, "I was informed that George gambles heavily," protects Ralph while still spreading the gossip successfully. Consider now the active sentence "Your assistant told me that sometimes you overlook this violation." This active form clearly jeopardizes the assistant. He or she is easily protected by the passive "I was told that sometimes you overlook this violation." In other contexts, you have undoubtedly taken the "I was told . . ." tack yourself.

Sometimes people use passives because they do not know the identity of the subject. Rather than struggling with vague subjects such as "somebody," "they," or even "I don't know who it was," these people switch to the passive form in order to get rid of the subject altogether. This is one reason for using sentences such as "This highway was built in 1939," "The contract was signed," or "The car was stolen." Such sentences are also used when the identity of the subject *is* known but is not considered worth mentioning.

So far in this section we have discussed only those passives in which the subject has been deleted. Why do people use passives in which the subject has *not* been deleted? For one thing, to break up a long chain of actives and thus introduce welcome variety into speech and writing. A string of sentences such as "A Ferrari won the first race. A Maserati won the second race. A Porsche won the third race," etc., can quickly become irritating or boring. The introduction of an occasional passive helps to make such strings of sentences a little more tolerable. Compare the preceding string with "A Ferrari won the first race. A Maserati won the second race. The third race was won by a Porsche."

Another reason why people use these passives is that sometimes they wish to place emphasis upon the direct object of a sentence. If a writer wished to emphasize the direct object "Greenland" in the sentence "Eric the Red discovered Greenland," he or she might decide to switch to the passive form, which would move the direct object to the front of the sentence. This would result in "Greenland was discovered by Eric the Red." It is interesting that some readers apparently do not sense any gain in emphasis when this stylistic device is used. Most readers, however, apparently do; hence the use of passives in emphasizing direct objects continues to be a valuable rhetorical device.

# Exercises

I  Convert the following active sentences into their passive equivalents. Give the full passive version (i.e., include the *by* phrase).

*Example:* Active:  The late rain helped the crops.

Passive:  The crops were helped by the late rain.

1 Active:  A licensed mechanic fixed the brakes.

Passive:  _____

2 Active:  A former actor directed the school play.

Passive:  _____

3 Active:  Felipe solved the supply problem.

Passive:  _____

4 Active:  Christopher Wren designed this church.

Passive:  _____

5 Active:  Henry Aaron set a new home-run record.

Passive:  _____

6 Active:  Jonathan deceived almost everyone.

Passive:  _____

7 Active:  Many people prefer older homes.

Passive:  _____

**8** Active: Many science majors take this course.

Passive: _____

**9** Active: The authorities arrested the tax evader.

Passive: _____

**10** Active: The Franciscan missionary Junipero Serra founded many California missions.

Passive: _____

_____

**11** Active: A neatly dressed middle-aged man with a cheerful smile robbed the bank in Denver.

Passive: _____

_____

**II** Convert the following active sentences into passives with subjects deleted.

*Example:* Active: Someone fixed the back gate.

Passive: The back gate was fixed.

**1** Active: People abandoned the idea.

Passive: _____

**2** Active: They nominated Senator Humphrey.

Passive: _____

**3** Active: Sally sold the vintage Cadillac.

Passive: _____

**4** Active: Carmen detected several flaws.

Passive: _____

**5** Active: The company manufactured twelve thousand pumps.

Passive: _____

**6** Active: Ludwig approved the initial design.

Passive: _____

**7** Active: Richard lost your application form.

Passive: _____

**III** Convert the following active sentences into *get* passives with subjects deleted.

> *Example:* Active: Someone lost your paycheck.
>
> Passive: Your paycheck got lost.

1 Active: The plumber fixed the faucet.

Passive: _____

2 Active: The newspaper published Marilyn's letter.

Passive: _____

3 Active: The company hired both Marvin and Sam.

Passive: _____

4 Active: The Chicago Cubs beat the San Francisco Giants.

Passive: _____

5 Active: Meredith finished the job.

Passive: _____

6 Active: I wrecked your car.

Passive: _____

**IV** From your own reading in textbooks, magazines, and newspapers, collect five full passives and eight passives without subjects. For each passive without a subject, suggest why the subject may have been omitted.

Full passives:

1 _____ .

2 _____ .

3 _____ .

4 _____ .

5 _____ .

Passives without subjects:

1 _____ .

Possible reason for subject not being stated:

_____

_____ .

**2** _____ .

Possible reason for subject not being stated:

_____

_____

_____ .

**3** _____ .

Possible reason for subject not being stated:

_____

_____

_____ .

**4** _____ .

Possible reason for subject not being stated:

_____

_____

_____ .

**5** _____ .

Possible reason for subject not being stated:

_____

_____

_____ .

**6** _____ .

Possible reason for subject not being stated:

_____

_____

_____ .

**7** _____ .

Possible reason for subject not being stated:

_____

_____

_____ .

**8** _____ .

Possible reason for subject not being stated:

_____

_____

_____ .

# SEVEN

# The Third Person Singular -S

## INTRODUCTION

In an earlier chapter, it was mentioned that every present-tense verb must carry the suffix -s when it has a third person singular subject, as in the following sentences:

*Shirley asks* too many questions.
*She wants* to go to Bermuda.
*It takes* years to master chess.
*He knows* enough.

Whenever the present-tense verb has a subject other than the third person singular, no suffix is added:

*I speak* French well.
*You like* Mexican food.
*We work* in a brickyard.
The *workers receive* a raise every year.
*They allow* reservations.

The grammatical fact that any present-tense verb with a third person singular subject must have an -s ending is referred to as *third person singular agreement*. Earlier in the history of the English language, present-tense verb endings were required not only for the third person singular but for all other subjects as well. For example, in several dialects of Middle English (c. A.D. 1100–1400), present-tense verbs were required to have the ending -s with *I*, -est with *thou*, -es with *he*, *she*, *it*, and singular nouns, and -en with plural nouns and pronouns. All endings except -es (later shortened to -s) have since been lost.

Some people feel that English would be simpler today if the -s had gotten lost also, for then *all* present-tense verbs would lack endings. There would be one less "exception" to complicate the grammar. But most see the -s as present tense rather than agreement and insist that it be used properly. Without this pressure to preserve it, -s might be lost, for there is often a leveling tendency operating in language which eliminates exceptions to rules, as you will see in the next section of this chapter.

# THIRD PERSON SINGULAR -*S* IN THE EVERYDAY WORLD

Although the third person singular -s is required in standard written and spoken English, it is often missing from the speech and writing of speakers of at least one widespread nonstandard dialect. In inner-city areas throughout the United States and in many areas of the South, verb forms such as those shown in the right-hand column of the following list occur with considerable frequency:

| *Standard Form* | *Without Third Person -s* |
|---|---|
| That baby *cries* all the time. | That baby *cry* all the time. |
| He *works* in a hospital. | He *work* in a hospital. |
| She *doesn't* like excuses. | She *don't* like excuses.[1] |
| He *buys* lemonade every time he *goes* shopping. | He *buy* lemonade every time he *go* shoppin'. |
| Robert *wants* a racing pigeon. | Robert *want* a racin' pigeon. |

This nonstandard dialect demonstrates the results of leveling that we mentioned earlier. You might even say that its speakers have (unconsciously) taken the logical step of removing one exception, a suffix, that held little semantic or grammatical meaning, thereby simplifying the system.

The third person -s suffix is also accidentally omitted at times by people learning English as a second language. These people must often struggle to remember the third person -s suffix because it doesn't fit the suffixless pattern found with other present-tense verbs. The -s contitutes just one more "exception" for these non-native speakers to master. In addition, the third person -s is not really essential to communication since the meaning of a sentence can usually be understood without it. The result? Many non-native speakers inadvertently get into the habit of not using the -s ending.

---

[1] This particular form is used by many speakers throughout the United States and is not limited to inner-city areas or the South.

This habit may sometimes prove troublesome, but can be overcome if the people are asked to work at tasks which force them to focus on and practice using the third person -s.

Once in a while native speakers of standard English will also omit the -s, though this usually happens through carelessness or the limitations of short-term memory. You have surely found yourself using a third person singular subject and then becoming so involved in what you were saying that you neglected to add the -s to your verb. An example of such a sentence might be "The roller coaster at Bimbo Pier has a 300-foot drop and *attain* a maximum speed of 60 miles an hour." Sometimes a nearby plural will trip up hasty writers, as in "One of the cars *sell* for eight thousand dollars." Careful proofreading is usually sufficient to protect against this kind of error.

# Exercises

I Substitute the third person singular subject in parentheses for the original subject in the following sentences. Then change the form of the verb as called for by the agreement rule.

*Example:* These horses eat both alfalfa and oats.
(This horse)

This horse eats both alfalfa and oats.

1 I detest the color blue.
(She)

2 They grow prize-winning beets.
(He)

3 Cowards die many deaths.
(A coward)

4 They love children.
(He)

5 Those students excel at mathematics.
(That student)

6 Coffee plants require a lot of moisture.
(The coffee plant)

**7** You always cheer for the underdog.
(She)

_____

**II** Rewrite the following sentences as they would appear in a dialect which does not contain the third person singular -s agreement rule.

**1** Marjorie loves to watch baseball on television.
*
_____

**2** The teacher knows the answer.
*
_____

**3** Harvey swims with Randal.
*
_____

# EIGHT

# The Modals

## THE MODALS AND THEIR MEANINGS

The modals constitute a very small but very important class of words in English. There are nine modals: *can*, *could*, *may*, *might*, *must*, *shall*, *should*, *will*, and *would*. They are often listed according to the meanings they convey, as illustrated in the following categories.

### Ability

The modal *can* expresses a present ability to do something. The past form *could* indicates that the ability existed at some time in the past.

> Wilbur *can* hypnotize a chicken.
> Wilbur *could* hypnotize a lizard when he was 6.

### Advisability and/or Obligation

The modal *should* is often used to express advisability or a sense of moral obligation.

> Advisability: You *should* get your reservation in early if you want a good seat.
> Moral Obligation: People *should* show respect toward their elders.

### Necessity

*Must* is the modal of present necessity. As there is no past-tense form for *must*, past necessity is usually indicated by the nonmodal expression *had to*.

Present Necessity: I *must* work full time in order to pay for books and tuition.

Past Necessity: I *had to* work full time in order to pay for books and tuition.

## Possibility

Possibility is indicated through use of the modals *may* and *might*.

It *may* snow before nightfall.
It *might* snow before nightfall.

## Probability

*Must* and *should* indicate probability. *Must* is used primarily to express strong probability in the present, while *should* frequently expresses the probability of a future event.

Brenda grew up in Naples. She *must* know how to speak Italian.
Our team is clearly superior. We *should* win Saturday's game easily.

## Requests for Permission

The modals *can*, *could*, *may*, and *might* are used for requesting permission.

*Can* I speak with you?
*Could* I speak with you?
*May* I speak with you?
*Might* I speak with you?

## Other Requests

For requesting something other than permission, the following modals are used: *can*, *could*, *may*, *might*, *will*, and *would*.

*Can* you lend me a dollar?
*Could* you lend me a dollar?
*Might* you lend me a dollar?
*Will* you lend me a dollar?
*Would* you lend me a dollar?
*May* I have a dollar?

## Repetitive Past Actions

Repetitive past actions are described by using the modal *would* or the "pseudo-modal" expression *used to*. *Used to* is a construction with no present tense and no other meaning. It should be distinguished from other constructions closely resembling it, such as "to be *used to*," which means "to be accustomed to" ("I am *used to* getting up early") and the verb *use*, meaning "to make use of" ("An ax is *used* to chop wood"). Note that the letter *d* in the pseudo-modal *used to* is not pronounced, which may explain its common misspelling of *use to*, as in *"I use to collect stamps."

*Would* and *used to* indicate that a past action occurred repeatedly, often habitually. The two terms are essentially synonymous.

When we were young, we *would* keep spiders as pets.
When we were young, we *used to* keep spiders as pets.

## Hypothetical Conditional Events

Conditional statements are of the "If this happens, then that will happen" variety. In other words, one event is conditional upon the occurrence of another. When the situation described in the clause beginning with *if* is of a hypothetical nature, the clause which describes the conditional event must contain *would*, *could*, or *might*, as shown below:

| If *Clause Expressing a Hypothetical Situation* | *Conditional Event* |
|---|---|
| If I visited the South Pole, | I *would* bring a warm coat. |
| If she became a movie star, | she *could* afford a new home. |
| If he built better houses, | people *might* buy them. |

Note that the verbs in the *if* clauses are in the *simple-past-tense* form. Hypothetical conditionals constitute one of the few instances where past-tense verb forms are used to indicate something other than past time.[1] What the past-tense forms indicate in this case is that the situation being described is hypothetical in nature. In other words, the situation does not exist now, and it is quite probable that it never will. Whenever a *present-tense* verb appears in the *if* clause, however, the meaning changes. The situation is then much more likely to occur, and can no longer be viewed as hypothetical. Observe this change in the following sentences:

[1] For another instance, see Chapter 4, footnote 1.

**1a** Verb in Past-Tense Form: If I *became* President, I would lower taxes. (Becoming President is viewed as a hypothetical occurrence.)

**1b** Verb in Present-Tense Form: If I *become* President, I will lower taxes. (Becoming President is viewed as a genuine possibility. A legitimate candidate for President might make such a statement.)

**2a** Verb in Past-Tense Form: If I *bought* a castle, I would install air conditioning in it. (The purchase is being viewed in a hypothetical sense.)

**2b** Verb in Present-Tense Form: If I *buy* a castle, I will install air conditioning in it. (This speaker is apparently considering such a purchase seriously and not speaking in hypothetical terms.)

When the situation is no longer being viewed hypothetically, the modal *would* is changed to *will*, as in the preceding examples.

## Other Hypotheticals

Hypothetical future events can be described without the use of *if* clauses. When this happens, the modals *could* and *would* are most often used:

Student A  (daydreaming) I wish I *could* buy my own jet airplane.

Student B:  What *would* you do with it?

Student A:  I *would* fly to Jamaica every Saturday.

Student B:  Then on Sundays you *could* fly me to Bimini.

The modals *can* and *will* are not used in such hypothetical statements. Observe how substituting *can* and *will* for *could* and *would* in the previous examples alters the hypothetical nature of the discussion. The events being described now appear far more probable.

Student A  (daydreaming) *I wish I *can* buy my own jet airplane. (This sentence is ungrammatical. The verb *wish* is normally used with respect to presently unattainable situations, while *can* denotes present ability. The resultant logical contradiction contributes to the unacceptability of the sentence.)

Student B:  What *will* you do with it? (*Will* makes the purchase seem almost certain.)

Student A:  I *will* fly to Jamaica every Saturday. (Again, future certainty is implied.)

Student B: Then on Sundays you *can* fly me to Bimini. (*Can* makes the Bimini trips appear probable.)

## Future Actions or States

*Shall* and *will* are the modals used to indicate future time, with *will* being by far the more common. When *shall* is used, it is used mainly with a first-person subject (e.g., "I *shall* retire soon," "We *shall* continue to negotiate") and much more often and extensively in Great Britain than in the United States.[2] In fact, many Americans seldom or never use *shall* in this way. However, choosing between these two modals is seldom an issue, partly because the contractions *I'll*, *we'll*, *he'll*, etc., appear so frequently, in both spoken and written English.

It *will* rain tomorrow.
You *will* be hearing from me.
The show *will* open on Friday.
I *shall* miss you.
*I'll* take care of it.
*We'll* have a great time.

## Generalizations

The modal *will* is frequently used for generalizations, particularly in scientific or technical discourse. In the following examples, it is clear that *will* is referring not to a specific future occurrence but to a general truth, something that is true not only of the future, but of the present and past as well.

Water *will* boil at 212°F.
Stainless steel *will* resist corrosion.
Hereford cattle *will* gain weight fastest on a diet of corn, hay, and molasses.
Even smart bass *will* strike at a rubber worm.

# MODALS AND SUFFIXES

Modals will not take suffixes, even in situations where it seems that the rules of English would require them to do so. For example, a present-tense modal with a third person singular subject will *not*

---

[2] In addition to being used to indicate the future, *shall* is also used by some Americans in questions which invite choice, e.g., "Shall we go?"

take the -s suffix required for verbs. Thus, "It closes," "She swims," and "He works" are correct; *"It mights," *"She musts," and *"He cans" are not. Modals will not take the -ed suffix either, even when past time is indicated. *Can* in its past-tense form is *could*, not *canned*. The past tense of *must* is expressed by *had to* rather than by *musted*, and so on. Nor do verbs immediately following a modal bear suffixes. Note that the following verbs lack suffixes that would be required were it not for the presence of the modal:

She must *visit* (not *visits*) her sick aunt each morning.
He can *play* (not *plays*) the piano even though he is blind.
Our neighbor would plow (not *plow*ed) his fields in late October.

# MODALS IN THE EVERYDAY WORLD

Like other elements of English grammar, the modals display some variation in the everyday world. One noteworthy example is the *double modal*, a term that refers to the occurrence of two modals in succession, something that is not possible in Standard English. The construction is commonly heard in the South, but rarely elsewhere, except from some "transplanted Southerners" or others influenced by Southern speech. Those of you who have lived in or visited the South may remember using or hearing sentences like the following:

I *may can* fix it.
You *might could* help them do it.
You *might should* keep that.
She *might would* let them have it.
He *must could* not have done it.

Perhaps someone in your class familiar with Southern speech can supply you with other possible modal combinations.

A second interesting use of modals is found among immigrants and others learning English as a second language who are unaware that suffixes cannot exist in modal constructions. These people will occasionally write sentences such as *"The plane can flies very fast" or *"My father could lifted heavy things." Unless you teach English to the foreign-born, you may never see or hear such sentences. If you do, though, a brief explanation about modals and suffixes, plus some practice, will usually set things right.

Finally, concern sometimes arises in the everyday world over the levels of formality, or "politeness," shown by the various modals of request. Requests with *can* ("Can I ask you something?") seem a little less formal than requests with the other modals ("*May* I ask you something?" "*Could* I ask you something?" "*Might* I ask you something?"). Some people commonly use *can* around the house ("*Can* I have some peace and quiet around here?") but shift to *could* or *may* during formal interviews with the boss or some other social "superior" ("*May* I make a suggestion?"). Some consider *might* the most formal modal of all ("*Might* I keep this?"), but *might* does not seem to be used in requests as often as other modals, for reasons that are not entirely clear.

# Exercises

I Into each of the following sentences, insert a modal which expresses the meaning given in parentheses.

*Example:* Mr. James _can_ (present ability) play rugby well.

1 Jeff _____ (possibility) fail his algebra class.

2 Admiral Nelson _____ (repetitive past action) plan all his attacks carefully.

3 You _____ (advisability) change the oil in your car's engine frequently.

4 Sally just bought another large diamond. She _____ (present probability) be wealthy.

5 Margaret _____ (past ability) waltz beautifully in her youth.

6 _____ (request for permission) I open a window?

7 People _____ (moral obligation) do what they can to help others in distress.

8 I _____ (necessity) pay the rent each month.

9 Kathy _____ (future time) sell her ranch in September.

10 _____ (request) I borrow your expensive new car?

II Change the following statements of possibility into hypothetical conditionals. Underline the changes you are required to make in the wording of each sentence.

*Example:* If I resign from my job, I will face poverty.

If I resigned from my job, I would face poverty.

**1** If Bill moves to Switzerland, his health will probably improve.

**2** If all crime suddenly ceases, everyone will be overjoyed.

**3** If I try to quit smoking, I will be doing myself a favor.

**III** Rewrite the following sentences, inserting the designated modal in front of the verb.

*Example:* Felix climbed mountains when he lived in Nepal. (could)

Felix could climb mountains when he lived in Nepal.

**1** Peter works hard for a living. (must)

**2** Sylvia programs computers. (can)

**3** Benjamin thinks I am a liar. (may)

**4** We fished for salmon when we lived in Iceland. (would)

**5** The young duke charmed even his enemies. (could)

What additional change in the original form of each sentence were you required to make because of your insertion of the modal?

**IV** You will find several modals after each of the following sentences. Discuss how each modal, inserted in the blank, would change the meaning of the sentence. Be prepared to point out situations where (1) no change in meaning results, (2) ambiguity results, or (3) the change is in the tone rather than in the meaning.

**1** Paul _____ be there with the rhinoceros by Friday. (should) (can) (might) (may) (must) (would)

_____

_____

_____

_____

_____

**2** _____ you help me tow my car? (Can) (Could) (Might) (Will)
(Would)

_____

_____

_____

_____

_____

_____

_____

**3** Pine trees _____ grow in rather poor soil. (will) (can) (must)
(might)

_____

_____

_____

_____

_____

**4** Sheila _____ juggle six plates at once. (can) (would) (must) (may)
(will)

_____

_____

_____

_____

_____

**5** The climbers _____ camp on the summit. (could) (should) (must) (will) (may) (might)

_____

_____

_____

_____

_____

_____

**6** Daisy _____ get home after dark. (used to) (would) (must) (had to) (should)

_____

_____

_____

_____

_____

_____

_____

_____

_____

_____

_____

_____

_____

_____

_____

_____

NINE

# Asking about Things: The Interrogative

Like all other languages, English possesses a means by which its speakers can ask questions. The system used for asking questions in English is quite simple, requiring only a knowledge of a grammatical element known as the *auxiliary*. The auxiliary (often abbreviated AUX) is a grammatical class containing (1) the modals, (2) the various forms of *be*,[1] (3) *have* (or *has* or *had*) when used as a helping verb in one of the perfect tenses, and (4) the auxiliary *do*. The auxiliary class is shown schematically in the following box. The important thing to remember is that each of the grammatical elements within the box is considered an auxiliary—a modal is an auxiliary, a form of *be* is an auxiliary, *have* in one of the perfect tenses is an auxiliary, and so on.

AUXILIARY =

> **1** the modals
> We *can* read.
> You *may* go.
> etc.
> **2** *be* in its various forms[1]
> She *is* here.
> I *was* working.
> etc.
> **3** *have*, *has*, or *had* in the perfect tenses
> He *has* gone.
> You *have* studied.
> etc.
> **4** the auxiliary *do*

[1] Technically, in regard to *be*, only the forms which serve as helping verbs are true auxiliaries. To facilitate the description of interrogatives and negatives, however, we will consider all forms of *be*, even those functioning as copulative or linking verbs, as auxiliaries.

Many textbooks refer to auxiliaries as *helping verbs*. The two terms are synonymous.

Now that you are familiar with the auxiliary system, let us look at the kinds of questions in English and observe the role the auxiliary plays in each.


# YES-NO QUESTIONS

*Yes-no questions* are those which are capable of being given a simple "yes" or "no" answer. Some sample yes-no questions are "Can you swim?", "Is John married?", "Has the bus left yet?", and "Do you smoke?" Notice that each of these questions might be answered with a short "Yes" or "No."

To understand how yes-no questions are formed, one must first be aware of the usual word order found with declarative (i.e., statement) sentences. The word order is subject first, then auxiliary, then verb or adjective. This order is illustrated in the following chart:


**Word order in a declarative sentence**

| Subject | Auxiliary | Verb or Adjective |
| --- | --- | --- |
| Sam | will | recover. |
| Susan | is | tall. |
| The taxpayers | were | complaining. |
| That person | has | paid. |

To convert any statement into a yes-no question, it is necessary only to reverse the order of the subject and the auxiliary. This procedure is diagramed as follows:

| *Auxiliary* | *Subject* | *Verb or Adjective* |
| --- | --- | --- |
| Will | Sam | recover? |
| Is | Susan | tall? |
| Were | the taxpayers | complaining? |
| Has | that person | paid? |

That is all there is to it. Any statement can be converted into a yes-no question by switching the positions of the subject and the auxiliary. If a statement contains two auxiliaries, then the *first* auxiliary switches places with the subject. Thus, "Babe Ruth's

number *has been* retired" would appear in question form as "*Has*
  1   2

Babe Ruth's number *been* retired?" and "Claudius *is being* perse-
  2               1   2

cuted" would change to "*Is* Claudius *being* persecuted?"

It so happens, however, that not all statements will contain auxiliaries. Observe how this is true of the following statements:

> Bulldogs snore.
> Sally likes Nova Scotia.
> Rome conquered Carthage.

How can these statements without auxiliaries be converted into yes-no questions? Basically, in just the same way that statements *with* auxiliaries are converted, that is, by moving an auxiliary in front of the subject. The only difference is that since no auxiliary is present, one must be "created." The auxiliary which is created in such cases is the auxiliary *do*, which seems to have little if any inherent meaning by itself. It is not the same as the verb *do*, which means "perform," as in "He *does* the housework quickly." The auxiliary *do* exists, in this instance, solely for the purpose of switching position with the subject in order to make a question possible. The rule is as follows:

When no auxiliary is present in a statement . . .

| Subject | Auxiliary | Verb, Adjective, Object, etc. |
|---|---|---|
| Bulldogs | _____ | snore. |
| Sally | _____ | likes Nova Scotia. |
| Rome | _____ | conquered Carthage. |

. . . form a yes-no question by creating the auxiliary *do* and placing it in front of the subject.

| Auxiliary | Subject | Verb, Adjective, Object, etc. |
|---|---|---|
| Do | bulldogs | snore? |
| Does | Sally | like Nova Scotia? |
| Did | Rome | conquer Carthage? |

Note that two of the verbs in the preceding statements (*likes* and *conquer*ed) contain suffixes indicating tense. When the auxiliary *do* is created, these tense markers have to be moved from the verbs and jumped to the auxiliary. Doing so creates *does* and *did*, and leaves behind the tenseless forms *like* and *conquer*. This phenomenon, called *tense jumping*, is a characteristic of questions that are formed by using the auxiliary *do*.

Finally, we should point out that in some dialects (especially in British English), the verb *have* sometimes behaves like an auxiliary and switches positions with the subject. For this reason, we can sometimes hear yes-no questions such as "Have you a match?", "Have you a dime?", or "Have you the time?"

# *Wh-* QUESTIONS

Many questions in English cannot be given a simple "yes" or "no" answer. You can prove this for yourself by trying to answer "yes" or "no" to the following questions:

Who is Dina?
Where is Bangladesh?
How does a clock work?

Questions which cannot be answered by "yes" or "no" are called *wh-questions* because they begin with one of the interrogative words, all but one of which start with the letters *wh-*. The interrogative words are *who, whom, whose, what, which, why, where, when,* and *how.*

In some *wh-* questions, the interrogative word itself functions as the subject of the sentence, as shown in the following chart:

| Interrogative Word as Subject | Auxiliary | Verb or Adjective |
| --- | --- | --- |
| Who | is | ill? |
| What | has | happened? |
| Who | can | help? |

When this happens, the subject precedes the auxiliary, resulting in the same word order found in statements.

Frequently, however, the interrogative word is not the subject of the sentence. Then the auxiliary must precede the subject, as it does with the yes-no questions:

| Interrogative Word | Auxiliary | Subject | Verb |
|---|---|---|---|
| What | can | Betty | buy? |
| When | is | Labor Day? | |
| Why | has | the noise | stopped? |
| Why | does | Henry | gamble? |

In the last example the auxiliary *do* is used because no other auxiliary is available. This is the same principle that we saw operating with the yes-no questions.

# TAG QUESTIONS

*Tag questions* are statements which become questions by having a yes-no question element "tagged" on at the very end. Examples are as follows:

The wine is in the refrigerator, isn't it?
Bill can pick you up after work, can't he?
Maria has finished that assignment, hasn't she?
It seems stuffy in here, doesn't it?

Observe that when the statement is positive, the tag ordinarily appears in negative form. Conversely, when the statement appears in the negative, the tag is positive:

The wine isn't in the refrigerator, is it?
Bill can't pick you up after work, can he?
Maria hasn't finished that assignment, has she?
It doesn't seem stuffy in here, does it?

The word order in the tags is auxiliary before subject, just as it is for all yes-no questions and for many of the *wh*-questions.

Some tag questions are intended to be questions in the rhetorical sense only. At such times they are mainly one more way of expressing an opinion, as in "Becky doesn't seem herself tonight, does she?" The speaker here might well be expressing the opinion that Becky in fact does not seem herself. Doubt, irony, and even sarcasm may be expressed by using a positive statement followed by a *positive* tag, as when the skeptical boss says, "Oh, he's worth twice his salary, is he?" or the poorly advised bettor complains, "So that racehorse could outrun all the others, could it?" or the bitter scapegoat protests, "So I'm to blame, am I?"

# ECHO QUESTIONS

One exception to the auxiliary-before-subject word order is the *echo question*. The echo question is either a partial or complete repetition of someone else's statement, and is usually accompanied by a rise in the intonation (or pitch) of the voice. Echo questions frequently indicate surprise, and are often requests for further information rather than true questions. Examples are as follows:

First Speaker:   Joseph was arrested last night.
Second Speaker:   (echo question) Joseph was arrested last night?

First Speaker:   George has willed his belongings to his pet cat.
Second Speaker:   (echo question) To his pet cat?

First Speaker:   The boss wants your report by four o'clock.
Second Speaker:   (echo question) By four o'clock?

# EMBEDDED *Wh-* QUESTIONS

The last kind of "question" we will take up is really not a question at all. *Embedded* wh- *questions* contain the words found in *wh*-questions, but the word order and meaning are those of a statement. Embedded *wh-* questions are embedded (i.e., "inserted") into a larger statement, as illustrated in the following list, where the embedded *wh-* questions are underlined:

I don't know where Pasadena is.
He's not sure when he might leave.
We don't care why she has stopped.
People wonder how it began.

As you can see, the auxiliary does not precede the subject in these constructions, as it would in true questions. Note also that the meaning being conveyed is not that of a true question, since nothing is really being asked. More likely than not, a statement containing an embedded *wh-* question is either a response to a question, or a comment, reaction, or response to a previous statement. For example, someone might say "The Rose Bowl is in Pasadena" and another might respond with "I don't know where Pasadena is," or someone might ask, "When might he leave?" and someone else might answer with "He's not sure when he might leave."

# QUESTIONS IN THE EVERYDAY WORLD

Questions seem to show less variation in the everyday world than one might expect. One of the few notable variations concerns embedded *wh-* questions, which are sometimes constructed with the nonstandard word order of auxiliary before subject. Consequently, embedded *wh-* questions may appear as shown in the right-hand column of the following list:

| *Standard Form* | *Auxiliary-before-Subject Form* |
|---|---|
| I don't know *why he might do it*. | I don't know *why might he do it*. |
| I'm not sure *how I won it*. | I'm not sure *how did I win it*. |
| I don't care *when the party is*. | I don't care *when is the party*. |
| Dennis asked *if he could do it*. | Dennis asked *could he do it*. |

Another variation in question formation involves the deletion of auxiliaries. When this happens, the standard question form "Why do they try it?" becomes "Why they try it?", "Are we going?" becomes "We goin'?", and so on.

Finally, it is important to remember that questions are really only one means we employ to elicit information from other people in the everyday world. Just observe sometime the techniques of interrogation used by someone you feel is an especially skilled questioner—perhaps a counselor, attorney, teacher, police officer, reporter, salesperson, physician, or job interviewer—and you will find a great amount of grammatical variety apparent. Questions are used, it is true, but so are various kinds of statements as well as several types of commands. For example, consider the teacher quizzing a class on a subject such as state capitals. The teacher might use a direct question for one student: "Molly, what is the capital of Texas?" With the next pupil, the teacher might employ a direct command: "Lucas, tell me the capital of Missouri." Perhaps a more formal, polite command would follow: "Aimee, I wish you'd name the capital of Nevada for me." Then a statement might be employed: "Trevor, I bet you can't identify the capital of New Hampshire," followed by another kind of statement, one which requires completion: "Christina, the capital of Indiana is _____," and so on. Skillful questioners, whether they are concerned with education, business, law enforcement, medicine, journalism, or jurisprudence, or are simply eliciting the latest gossip, employ grammatical variety of this sort.

# Exercises

I  Convert the following statements into yes-no questions.

*Example:* Carson City is the capital of Nevada.

   <u>Is Carson City the capital of Nevada?</u>

   1  Sylvester will refuse the offer.

   2  The bakers were on strike.

   3  The senators had tried to investigate.

   4  He could send a substitute.

   5  I am too old to join the FBI.

   6  A winner has been chosen.

Describe the operation you performed in order to convert statements 1–6 into questions.

**7** Orchid plants require frequent watering.

_____

**8** Ann prefers Indian cuisine.

_____

**9** Love conquers all.

_____

**10** The doctor saved her life.

_____

**11** The judge asked for more evidence.

_____

Describe the operation you performed in order to convert statements 7–11 into questions.

_____

_____

_____

**II** Write down the _wh-_ question which presumably triggered the embedded _wh-_ question response.

_Example:_ Response: I don't know where Iron Mountain is.

Question: _Where is Iron Mountain?_____

**1** Response: I don't know when our next holiday is.

Question: _____

**2** Response: I'm not sure how old Billy is.

Question: _____

**3** Response: I don't know what the Prince will think.

Question: _____

**4** Response: I don't give a darn what Spencer thinks.

Question: _____

**5** Response: I'm not sure where the maid has gone.

Question: _____

**6** Response: I'm not sure why she insisted.

Question: _____

**7** Response: I don't know when they can pay.

Question: _____

**8** Response: I'm not sure what they have gotten themselves into.

Question: _____

Explain how the word order of the embedded *wh-* questions in the preceding questions differs from the word order of the *wh-* questions you have written.

_____

_____

**III** Change the following statements into tag questions.

*Example:* Yoruba is an African language.

Yoruba is an African language, isn't it?

1 I can park here overnight.

_____

2 It is supposed to rain tomorrow.

_____

3 The McGregors have checked out of their room.

_____

4 The Green Bay Packers won the game.

_____

5 My aunt hasn't telephoned yet.

_____

6 Sonny isn't a real secret agent.

_____

7 Elaine can't speak Lithuanian.

_____

# The Negative: Ways of Saying "No"

We have said that all languages possess means of asking questions. It is also true that all languages possess means for forming negative statements. In English, the auxiliary plays a crucial role in the formation of the negative, just as it does in the formation of questions.

## FORMING THE NEGATIVE WITH AUXILIARY + *NOT*

The most common way of making a negative statement in English is to place the negative word *not*, often in contracted form, immediately after the auxiliary. This process is illustrated as follows:

Affirmative:    I <u>could</u> pass that course without studying.
                     AUX

Negative:      I <u>could</u> [not] pass that course without studying.
                     AUX  ↑

Affirmative:    George <u>is</u> interested in modern dance.
                        AUX

Negative:      George <u>is</u> [not] interested in modern dance.
                       AUX ↑

Affirmative:    We <u>were</u> sleeping.
                     AUX

Negative:      We <u>were</u> [not] sleeping.
                     AUX  ↑

Affirmative:    The doctor <u>has</u> seen her today.
                        AUX

Negative:      The doctor <u>has</u> [not] seen her today.
                       AUX ↑

When more than one auxiliary is present in an affirmative statement, the word *not* is placed immediately after the *first* auxiliary, as shown in the following sentences:

The swimmer <u>could</u> not <u>have</u> lasted much longer.
$$\text{AUX} \quad \uparrow \quad \text{AUX}$$
$$\quad 1 \qquad\qquad 2$$

I <u>am</u> not <u>being</u> praised enough.
$$\text{AUX} \ \uparrow \ \text{AUX}$$
$$\ 1 \qquad\quad 2$$

Many affirmative statements, however, lack an auxiliary, a fact discussed in the chapter on interrogatives. The following sentences are of this kind:

Pine trees grow quickly.
Betsy liked snow cones.
The pharmacist works long hours.

How can negatives be made from sentences which lack auxiliaries? They can be made the same way that questions were made, that is, by "creating" the auxiliary *do*. As in questions, *do* is nonemphatic and essentially meaningless here, serving principally to enable us to follow the AUX + *not* rule. The formation of negatives with the auxiliary *do* is illustrated as follows:

*Affirmative:* Pine trees grow quickly.
*First Step in Negative
Formation* (creation
of the auxiliary *do*):        Pine trees <u>do</u> grow quickly.
$$\qquad\qquad\qquad\qquad\qquad\qquad\quad \text{AUX}$$

*Final Step in Negative
Formation* (placing *not*
after the auxiliary):        Pine trees <u>do</u> not grow quickly.
$$\qquad\qquad\qquad\qquad\qquad\qquad\quad \text{AUX} \ \uparrow$$

*Affirmative:* Betsy liked snow cones.
*First Step in Negative
Formation* (creation
of the auxiliary *do*):        Betsy <u>did</u> like snow cones.
$$\qquad\qquad\qquad\qquad\qquad\qquad \text{AUX}$$

*Final Step in Negative
Formation* (placing *not*
after the auxiliary):        Betsy <u>did</u> not like snow cones.
$$\qquad\qquad\qquad\qquad\qquad\qquad \text{AUX} \ \uparrow$$

*Affirmative:* The pharmacist works long hours.

*First Step in Negative Formation* (creation of the auxiliary *do*):

The pharmacist <u>does</u> work long hours.     AUX

*Final Step in Negative Formation* (placing *not* after the auxiliary):

The pharmacist <u>does</u> [not] work long hours.     AUX ↑

You will notice in the preceding examples that tense "jumps" from the verbs onto the auxiliary *do* when *do* is created, leaving the verb forms tenseless. This is the same "tense jumping" phenomenon that we observed taking place in the formation of questions.

Very often, particularly in conversation, the auxiliary and the word *not* are contracted; that is, the two words are joined and one or more letters are deleted. Doing this produces a shorter, more quickly pronounced combination of words. Some of the most common negative contractions are *can't, couldn't, won't* (*will* + *not*), *isn't, aren't, wasn't, hasn't, haven't, doesn't, didn't,* and *don't*.

# FORMING THE NEGATIVE WITH ADVERBS OF NEGATION

Placing the word *not* after an auxiliary is only one way of forming a negative sentence. A second way is to use the *adverbs of negation*, which are *barely, hardly ever, never, rarely, scarcely,* and *seldom*. Of these words, only *never* shares *not*'s ability to completely negate an affirmative statement. The approximate synonymity of *not* and *never* can be observed in the sentences "I did *not* play jacks as a child" and "I *never* played jacks as a child," where both *not* and *never* render the statements more or less equally negative. The other adverbs of negation convey the idea that the action or state being described "usually" does not or did not happen or exist, but could have occasionally. For example, most people feel that sentences such as "I *seldom* played jacks as a child" and "I *rarely* played jacks as a child" are negative, though not in the "absolute" sense that sentences with *not* and *never* are.

Adverbs of negation typically appear immediately before the verb in a sentence; less commonly they follow the verb. When an auxiliary is present, they may either precede or follow the auxiliary. The adverbs of negation, then, enjoy considerably more freedom of distribution in sentences than does the negative word *not*, which is usually obliged to occur immediately after the auxiliary. Some of the possible positions of adverbs of negation are illustrated as follows:

I <u>never</u> <u>said</u> you were pompous.
   ADV VERB

Dorothy <u>could</u> <u>never</u> <u>bait</u> the hook right.
       AUX  ADV  VERB

He <u>never</u> <u>could</u> <u>think</u> for himself.
   ADV  AUX  VERB

We <u>see</u> them <u>rarely</u>.
  VERB      ADV

They are rarely at home.
     AUX ADV

We <u>rarely</u> <u>are</u> ill.
  ADV AUX

# NEGATIVES WITH *NO*

A third method of forming a negative statement in English is to use the word *no*, which precedes the noun it negates, as shown below:

Erasmus owns *no* property.
That minister has *no* faults.
*No* tourists are allowed beyond this point.

That statements such as these are true negatives can be proved by the fact that they may be cast in a form using *not* with no resulting change in meaning. In other words, the three previous examples could just as well appear as follows:

Erasmus does *not* own property.
That minister does *not* have any faults.
Tourists are *not* allowed beyond this point.

# THE NEGATIVE PREFIXES

Also capable of rendering statements negative are the negative prefixes, particularly *il-*, *im-*, *in-*, *ir-*, and *un-*. Thus statements such as the following:

She has been *un*able to improve her reading scores.
This action is *il*legal.
It is *im*possible to find a store open at this hour.

are actually just as negative as synonymous forms with *not*:

She has *not* been able to improve her reading scores.
This action is *not* legal.
It is *not* possible to find a store open at this hour.

## NEITHER/NOR

The negative conjunctions *neither/nor* can be used where two discrete elements are part of a negative statement, as in the following sentences:

*Neither* the Coast Guard *nor* the Navy was able to locate the missing freighter.
That third baseman can *neither* hit well *nor* throw accurately.

The discrete elements present in the first sentence are (1) "the Coast Guard," and (2) "the Navy," while in the second example they are (1) "hit well," and (2) "throw accurately."

## NEGATIVES IN THE EVERYDAY WORLD

The negative is a particularly rich source of variation in English. We described in an earlier chapter the frequent nonstandard use of *don't* in negative statements with third person singular subjects. This feature is so widespread that sentences such as "She don't believe me," "He don't care," and "It don't matter" are actually more natural for some speakers than the standard "She doesn't believe me," "He doesn't care," and "It doesn't matter." In another earlier chapter we touched on the negative contraction *ain't*, which is a variant of *'m not* (am + *not*), *isn't*, and *aren't*. Both the standard and nonstandard variants are illustrated as follows:

Standard: I'm *not* going to let him.
Nonstandard: I *ain't* gonna let him.
Standard: That *isn't* his helmet.
Nonstandard: That *ain't* his helmet.
Standard: They *aren't* here.
Nonstandard: They *ain't* here.

*Ain't* is also substituted for *hasn't* and *haven't*, as in the following examples:

Standard: He *hasn't* got an uncle.
Nonstandard: He *ain't* got no uncle.
Standard: They *haven't* tried it.
Nonstandard: They *ain't* tried it.

The so-called "double negative" is another widespread nonstandard negative construction. The term *double negative* is actually a misnomer, because as we shall see, this construction also occurs in triple and quadruple form. For this reason, we refer to the double negative as the *multiple negative*. But before we see just what this construction entails, we need to introduce a class of words known as the *indefinites*. Some of these are defined and discussed in Chapter 12, so we will just name a few which concern us at this time: *any*, *anybody*, *anything*, *anywhere*, *ever*, and *either*. These indefinites occur frequently in standard negative sentences, such as the following:

I don't have *any*.
He wasn't trying to see *anybody*.
They don't want *anything*.
He couldn't work *anywhere*.
I don't *ever* want to see her.

Observe in these sentences that the negative word *not*, in contracted form, appears immediately after the auxiliary, exactly as it is supposed to in the Standard English negative. Speakers who employ the multiple negative also place *not* immediately after the auxiliary, but go one step further—they also convert any subsequent indefinite into its negative form. The preceding standard sentences are repeated in the following list, this time with their nonstandard multiple-negative equivalents. In each case of multiple negation, note how the indefinite has been changed into its negative form:

Standard Form: I don't have *any*.
Multiple-Negation Form: I don't have *none*.
Standard Form: He wasn't trying to see *anybody*.
Multiple-Negation Form: He wasn't tryin' to see *nobody*.
Standard Form: They don't want *anything*.
Multiple-Negation Form: They don't want *nothin'*.
Standard Form: He couldn't work *anywhere*.
Multiple-Negation Form: He couldn't work *nowhere*.
Standard Form: I don't *ever* want to see her.
Multiple-Negation Form: I don't *never* want to see her.

Perhaps now you see how the term *multiple negation* came about.

It refers to the multiple occurrence of negative forms within a single simple sentence. Sometimes a sentence can have four, five, or even six negative forms. A sentence with four negative forms is the following:

Standard Form:     I *won't* *ever* have *any* fun *any-where* except here.

Multiple-Negation Form:     I *won't* *never* have *no* fun *no-where* 'cept here.
1     2     3     4

Notice, however, that whether one negative form (as in the standard negative) is used or whether two, three, four, or more are used, the sentences are still negative sentences. The oft-quoted statement "Two negatives make a positive" applies in algebra, but it is untrue when applied to English grammar.

Placing *not* after the auxiliary and converting subsequent indefinites into their negative forms, then, is the basis for the multiple negative. It should be noted that there are several slightly different versions of the multiple negative, each characteristic of a particular nonstandard dialect; all, however, operate on the basic principle previously outlined.

Another variation of the negative encountered in the everyday world is called *negative inversion*. This is one of the few nonstandard grammatical constructions which is capable of legitimate misinterpretation by speakers of standard English who are unfamiliar with it. The form of negative inversion discussed here is most often found in the speech and occasionally in the writing of many speakers living in poor inner-city areas, and is illustrated as follows:

*Didn't nobody* tell her that.
*Wasn't nobody* in there.
*Can't nobody* do it like that.
*Don't no house* rent for that much 'round here.
*Ain't nothin'* left.

Notice that the auxiliary in these examples precedes the subject—the word order found in the standard yes-no question. For this reason, some standard speakers might interpret the five preceding sentences as questions, when in fact they are all intended as *negative statements*.[1] These auxiliary-before-subject negatives apparently connote a higher degree of emotionalism or excitability

[1] The likelihood of such misunderstanding is greatly reduced, however, by the fact that these sentences are pronounced in the same way as statements; that is, they terminate with a lowering in the intonation (or pitch) of the voice.

than the usual negative—at any rate, they seem to be found more frequently during excited, animated speech. The five examples of the inverted negative are repeated in the following list, along with the standard sentences which probably most closely approximate their meaning:

Inverted Negative: *Didn't nobody* tell her that.
Equivalent Standard Negative: *Nobody told* her that(!)
Inverted Negative: *Wasn't nobody* in there.
Equivalent Standard Negative: *Nobody was* in there(!)
Inverted Negative: *Can't nobody* do it like that.
Equivalent Standard Negative: *Nobody can* do it like that(!)
Inverted Negative: *Don't no house* rent for that much 'round here.
Equivalent Standard Negative: *No house* rents for that much around here(!)
Inverted Negative: *Ain't nothin'* left.
Equivalent Standard Negative: *Nothing is* left(!)

Although the inverted negative carries emphasis, it need not always be strong emphasis, hence the use of parentheses around the exclamation marks in the preceding examples. A slightly different variety of negative inversion uses inversion but not multiple negation. It is heard in many parts of the South. An example is the sentence "Didn't anybody rough the kicker!", which an irate Texas football fan screamed during a game attended by one of the authors.

Linguists at this time have really only a partial knowledge of the denotations, connotations, forms, and varieties of negatives found in the everyday world. Anyone undertaking research in this area is almost certain to increase our understanding of this important part of English grammar.

# Exercises

I Convert the following affirmative statements into negative statements which contain the word *not*.

*Example:* You should give up.

You should not give up.

1 I will go to college next year.

2 Mrs. Bens is eager to visit her aunt.

3 Alice has owned poodles before.

4 The three soldiers would steal from civilians.

5 Clark is traveling in Madagascar this summer.

6 The young lowland gorilla had learned its lesson.

7 Millicent can throw a football 160 feet.

8 The Emperor was considering torture.

9 I have known many exciting people.

Where (grammatically speaking) did you place the word *not* in all the sentences you have created?

_____

_____

II Convert the following affirmative statements into negative statements containing the word *not*. Be prepared to explain how these sentences differ from those in Exercise I.

*Example:* Those banjo players practice every day.

Those banjo players do not practice every day.

1 Pam and Ed own a home in Mexico.

_____

2 Frank drives carefully.

_____

3 Winston lost his jade ring.

_____

4 Making new friends came easily for Dorothy.

_____

5 My father enjoys soap operas.

_____

6 Tea plants grow well in Wisconsin.

_____

7 Mr. Baynes envies his rich acquaintances.

_____

8 Thomas Jefferson invented the rocking chair.

_____

How are the original sentences in this exercise different from those in Exercise I?

_____

_____

This difference required you to take one extra step before using the word *not* in your negative statements. Describe this extra step.

_____

_____

**III** Contract the auxiliary + *not* constructions in the following sentences.

    *Example:* That rumor is not true.

                That rumor isn't true.

1 Clarissa should not invest so heavily in tungsten mines.

2 The judge was not impressed.

3 These orchids have not been watered for days.

4 Don's car does not fit his personality.

5 The California condor will not survive the century.

6 Canadians are not fond of lazy hockey players.

7 This student has not paid his fees.

8 I do not know where Laufenburg is.


**IV** Change the following affirmative statements into negative statements by using the words in parentheses. These parenthetical words are either negative adverbs or the negative word *no*.

    *Examples:* I enjoyed life on the ship.   (seldom)

               I seldom enjoyed life on the ship.

               Rattlesnakes are found in Hawaii.   (no)

               No rattlesnakes are found in Hawaii.

1 Miss Ormsby goes to church on Sunday.   (never)

2 Hector made large profits on his real-estate investments.   (rarely)

3 That tennis player outsmarts the opposition.   (hardly ever)

**4** My brother does well in the sciences.   (seldom)

_____

**5** Rain is predicted for this evening.   (no)

_____

**6** Walter has mechanical ability.   (no)

_____

**7** There is hope.   (no)

_____

**V** Change the following affirmative statements into negative statements by using the negative prefixes discussed in this chapter (*il-*, *im-*, *in-*, *ir-*, and *un-*).

*Example:* The young duke was a faithful husband.

The young duke was an unfaithful husband.
_____

**1** This physician's signature is legible.

_____

**2** The students were very attentive.

_____

**3** Most of the people were inspired by the speech.

_____

**4** Farley is one of the most polite ushers I know.

_____

**5** Doris is happy with her new contract.

_____

**6** The regiment's new executive officer proved to be a responsible administrator.

_____

_____

**7** The race driver turned in a consistent performance in 1977.

_____

**8** The informer's story is true.

_____

**VI** Translate the following standard negatives into nonstandard multiple negatives.

*Example:* They didn't find any evidence.

      \*They didn't find no evidence.

1 We didn't catch anything that day.

   \*

2 Thomas didn't go anywhere yesterday.

   \*

3 I don't need any help.

   \*

4 The old dog didn't bother anybody.

   \*

**VII** Translate the following standard negatives into nonstandard inverted negatives.

*Example:* Nobody would tell me.

      \*Wouldn't nobody tell me.

1 Nothing can be done.

   \*

2 Nobody should do that.

   \*

3 Nobody saw it.

   \*

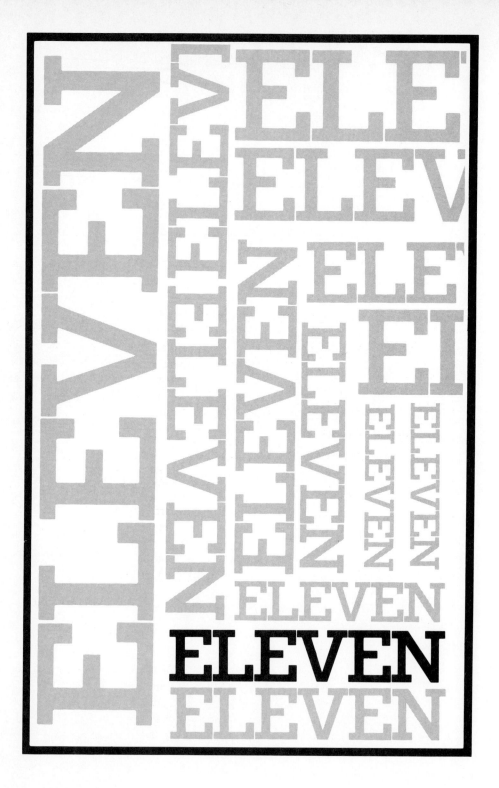

# Giving Orders

## THE IMPERATIVE DEFINED

A teacher who walks into a classroom and says, "All right, students, *open your books*, please" has just used the imperative. A parent who says, *"Come to dinner*, now" has just used it. So has a Marine Corps drill instructor who shouts, *"MOVE it!"* The term *imperative*, as defined here, refers to any predicate which expresses an order or command. Two kinds of sentences are traditionally and most commonly called imperatives. These will be discussed in the next two sections.

## IMPERATIVES WITH AN IMPLIED SUBJECT

If you will examine the following imperative sentences, you will notice that all of them lack something—a visible subject:

Send the invoice to the following address.
Ask Tillie to do it.
Let sleeping dogs lie.
Tell me a story.
Finish your milk.
Be quiet.

If asked to supply a subject for each of the preceding sentences, you would be able to comply quickly—and find yourself in agreement with the vast majority of people given this task. You would say that the subject was implied and most likely to be the pronoun *you*. How did you know? You might say that the context made the answer obvious, or that you knew it intuitively. Traditional grammarians would agree with you, since they have long referred to this *you* as the "understood" subject of imperatives. Linguists today agree that the subject *you* is implied in these kinds of commands and believe that leaving the subject *you* out of a sentence is one important signal that a command is intended. A second important signal is lack of verb tense. None of the verbs in the preceding examples, you will notice, carries tense.

# IMPERATIVES WITH A STATED SUBJECT

In each of the following imperative sentences, the subject *you* is stated explicitly (although tense, again, is lacking):

Ramona, *you* be quiet now.
Jay, *you* be a good boy.
Junior, *you* leave that cookie jar alone.
*You* lead the procession, Morris.

Often the subject *you* is included in an imperative as a signal of extreme forcefulness, especially when normal imperatives fail to achieve a desired result. Any parent will be familiar with the following situation:

Parent: Brian, close the door.
Brian: (no movement toward the door)
Parent: Brian, close the door.
Brian: (no movement toward the door)
Parent: Brian! *You* close that door!!!

It is worth pointing out that the modal *will* could be added to the last command and that doing so would make the sentence even more forceful:

Brian! You *will* close that door!!!

Imperatives with stated subjects can take other forms, too. For example, they can appear with full verb tense as complete declarative sentences:

I wish you'd open the window.
The colonel wants these barracks cleaned now.
The senator needs you in his office, immediately.
I hope you are going to take your muddy shoes off before you go
  inside.

Imperatives with stated subjects can also take the form of questions:

Would you close the door, please?
Could you turn the music down a little?
Could I see you for a moment? (boss to subordinate)

All of these sentences convey unmistakably the idea that a command is intended, though in some cases this command is extremely gentle. All of them, therefore, can be considered imperatives.

# IMPERATIVES IN THE EVERYDAY WORLD

The various forms of the imperative can have interesting effects on people in the everyday world. The way commands are phrased can literally mean the difference between a poke in the mouth and friendly compliance. Imperatives with the subject not stated are generally considered most direct. In the military and in parent-child relationships, direct commands are an accepted part of life and are usually effective. Military orders such as "Hold your fire," "Speed it up," "Reload," and "Stand at attention" are not apt to cause any problems, nor are Mom or Dad's imperatives such as "Clean up your room," "Turn down the television," "Get that thing out of here," or "Go to sleep now." Direct commands can cause a great many problems if delivered in inappropriate settings, however. Imagine what could happen if a man walked onto a hot, crowded bus and abruptly told one of the passengers, "Move over" so that he could sit down, or consider the new boss whose first order to a secretary is a blunt "Change that typewriter ribbon." A police officer who says, "Give me your driver's license" to a motorist stopped for a routine traffic violation is also using a form of the imperative which is inappropriate for the situation. Insensitivity in handling the imperative has led to more than one fight or brawl, and to countless hurt feelings.

When it becomes necessary, as in the preceding situations, for one stranger to deliver an imperative to another, most people employ the so-called "gentle imperatives," which ordinarily take the form of questions. These imperatives are frequently softened further by various apologetic introductions, deferential terms of address such as *ma'am* or *sir*, and similar devices. The man who commands "Move over" on a hot, crowded bus is apt to get noncompliance or even a fight, while the one who says, "Excuse me, sir, could you move over just a little?" will probably get a seat.

The new boss who says, "Change that typewriter ribbon" invites a hostile, bitter attitude on the part of a secretary. This could be avoided by using a more gentle imperative, such as "When you have a minute, would you change that typewriter ribbon?" The police officer who elicits hostility and citizen complaints with the brusque "Give me your driver's license" could do his or her job more effectively by simply switching to "Could I see your driver's license, sir (or ma'am)?"

From your own personal experience you could probably supply many more examples of imperatives, as well as anecdotes about the effect they have had on you or on the people to whom you have given orders. So could everyone. Since the way in which imperatives are given and received is important, they will always be a touchy but integral part of our language.

A final and much less critical aspect of the imperative concerns its use with the exclamation point in writing. The convention today is to not use the exclamation point unless the imperative clearly conveys a sense of urgency, as in the following sentences:

Look out!
Grab the rope!
Help me!

# Exercises

I Various circumstances which call for the imperative are described in the following list. In each case give the required imperative, using the simplest form possible.

*Example:* Circumstance: You want someone to turn down the music.

Imperative: <u>Turn down the music.</u>

1 Circumstance: You want someone to drop the gun.

Imperative: _____

2 Circumstance: You want someone to stop lying to you.

Imperative: _____

3 Circumstance: You want someone to give you a chance.

Imperative: _____

4 Circumstance: You want someone to quit fooling around.

Imperative: _____

5 Circumstance: You want someone to kiss you.

Imperative: _____

6 Circumstance: You want someone to listen carefully.

Imperative: _____

**II** Repeat the procedure required for the previous exercise, but this time give the imperative in two forms—one near the top of the politeness scale and one near the bottom.

*Example:* Circumstance:  You want someone to hand you the newspaper.

Imperatives:
Top of Politeness Scale:  Would (or Could) you hand me the newspaper, please?

Bottom of Politeness Scale:  Hand me the newspaper.

1 Circumstance:  You want someone to check the air pressure in your tires.

Imperatives:
Top of Politeness Scale: _____

_____

Bottom of Politeness Scale: _____

**2** Circumstance:   You want someone to sign the receipt.
Imperatives:
Top of Politeness Scale: _____

Bottom of Politeness Scale: _____

**3** Circumstance:   You want someone to close the door.
Imperatives:
Top of Politeness Scale: _____

Bottom of Politeness Scale: _____

**4** Circumstance:   You want someone to do you a favor.
Imperatives:
Top of Politeness Scale: _____

Bottom of Politeness Scale: _____

# TWELVE

136

# Pronouns: There Is No Substitute for Them

## THE ADVANTAGES OF USING PRONOUNS

*Pronouns* are words that are often substituted for nouns and noun phrases. In the sentence "Sam has an old green sports car, and *he* drives *it* to work," the pronoun *he* substitutes for (i.e., "stands for") the noun *Sam*, while the pronoun *it* substitutes for the noun phrase "an old green sports car." The noun or noun phrase that a pronoun substitutes for is called the *antecedent* of that pronoun. In the above sentence, *Sam* is the antecedent of the pronoun *he*, and "an old green sports car" is the antecedent of the pronoun *it*.

At first glance, the advantages of using pronouns may not be obvious, but their advantages, indeed their utter indispensability, can easily be proved. The following passage will illustrate:

> John and Mary drove to John's father's house, parked John and Mary's car, and got out. As John and Mary began unloading John and Mary's luggage, John's father rushed out of the house and down the sidewalk to greet John and Mary.

This constant repetition of the nouns *John* and *Mary* is intolerable, and if people spoke or wrote in such a manner, they would be neither listened to nor read, at least not for long. By substituting pronouns for those longer noun phrases, we are able to overcome the monotony problem, and we are also able to communicate more quickly, for pronouns are almost always shorter than their antecedents.

# PRONOUNS IN REVIEW

Because there are so many pronouns, we will break them into subclasses. Doing so will permit us to cite important characteristics that each subclass possesses.

## Personal Pronouns

In Chapter 5 we demonstrated how personal pronouns have person and number. They also have *case*, a way of showing their function in a sentence. If a pronoun is functioning as the subject of a clause, it is said to be in the *subjective* (or *nominative*) case; if it is functioning as an object, it is in the *objective* (or *accusative*) case; and if it shows possession, it is said to be in the *possessive* (or *genitive*) case. The case forms of the personal pronouns are shown in the following chart:

**Chart 12-1**

| Case | 1st person sing. | 1st person plural | 2d person sing. | 2d person plural | 3d person sing. | 3d person plural |
|---|---|---|---|---|---|---|
| Subjective (subject) | I | we | you | you | he, she, it | they |
| Objective (object) | me | us | you | you | him, her, it | them |
| Possessive | my/ mine | our/ ours | your/ yours | your/ yours | his, her/ hers, its | their/ theirs |

Because of distinctions in case, a given antecedent may be replaced by any one of several different pronoun forms, depending on its function in the sentence. For example, notice how all the following pronouns have exactly the same antecedent—"the twins."

The twins were bored. *They* (subjective case) found nothing which interested *them* (objective case). *Their* (possessive case) vacation was fast becoming a disaster.

Personal pronouns serve mainly to replace nouns that appear in the first part of a sentence:

*Jason* asked the people to listen to *him*.
*Miranda's* book was in *her* suitcase.
When *Tim* called to *Rosalyn*, *she* ignored *him*.

Sometimes, however, the pronoun can occur before the noun:

Although *he* died young, *Mozart* accomplished miracles.
When *he* changed the rules, *Myron* spoiled the game.

One final note about possessive pronouns. One form is used before a noun and one is used when the noun is not stated:

Estella laid *her* book on the table.  (noun stated)
Estella laid *hers* on the table.  (noun not stated)
Give me *my* yellow credenza.
Give me *mine*.
Do you have *your* wits about you?
Do you have *yours*?
Cornelius envied *their* wealth.
Cornelius envied *theirs*.

## Reflexive Pronouns

Reflexive pronouns consist of the objective or possessive form of a personal pronoun and *-self* (or *-selves*, plural): *himself*, *herself*, *myself*, *itself*, *themselves*, *ourselves*, and *yourself* (*-selves*). They replace a noun or pronoun that is identical semantically to another noun or pronoun *in the same clause*:[1]

*Raymond* loved *himself*. (*Raymond* loved *Raymond*.)
The *dog* scratched *itself*. (The *dog* scratched the *dog*.)
*We* laughed at *ourselves*. (*We* laughed at *us*.)

When more than one person is involved or when the noun or pronoun is plural, the reflexive takes the plural form:

John and Mary considered *themselves* a perfect couple.
The troops fed *themselves* quickly.
We have *ourselves* to thank for that.
You must educate *yourselves*.

[1] This limitation does not always apply to clauses containing infinitive and gerundive phrases. These types of phrases are taken up in Chapter 16.

Reflexive pronouns used for emphasis are called *intensive pronouns*. Intensives usually occur immediately after the subject, although they can be found elsewhere, too:

I *myself* will do that.
Clayton *himself* had never failed before.
Mary developed the plan *herself*.

## Reciprocal Pronouns

The reciprocal pronouns are *each other* and *one another*. In Standard English, *each other* is preferred when there are two antecedents, while *one another* is preferred when there are more than two. The following sentences illustrate typical usages:

Philip and Rosemary admired *each other*.   (two antecedents)

The five gorillas looked at *one another*.   (more than two antecedents)

## Relative Pronouns

Because relative pronouns will be discussed in detail in Chapter 19, we will do no more than present them here. They include *who*, *whom*, *whose*, *which*, and *that*. *Who* (subject), *whom* (object), and *whose* (genitive) are used with human antecedents, although *whose* may also be used with nonhuman antecedents:

Where's the clown *who* started the riot? (human)
The person of *whom* you speak is my husband. (human)
She's the actress *whose* name slipped me. (human)
The old regime, *whose* time had finally come, quietly faded from the political scene. (nonhuman)

*Which* is used with nonhuman antecedents, while *that* is used with both human and nonhuman antecedents:

The lamp *which* George purchased was a Tiffany. (nonhuman)
She picked a corsage *that* smelled fragrant. (nonhuman)
He fired the worker *that* insulted his wife. (human)

## Interrogative Pronouns

The interrogative pronouns help us ask questions. They are the same as the relative pronouns except for two differences: *that* does not occur as an interrogative, and *what* is used with nonhuman subjects. Since these pronouns were explained along with other interrogative words in Chapter 9, only a few illustrative examples will be given here:

*Who* is rapping at my front door?
To *whom* were you speaking?
*Whose* Mercedes is parked in front of our house?
*What* happened while I was gone?

## Demonstrative Pronouns

Demonstrative pronouns come in pairs that semantically distinguish differences in distance: *this*, singular, and *these*, plural, showing "nearness"; and *that*, singular, and *those*, plural, indicating "farness." Here are some examples:

*This* (thing here) is larger than *that* (thing over there).
*These* (apples on the scale) weigh more than *those* (pears on the table).

The distance can be in time as well as space:

*This* is an atrocious hour to get out of bed.
*That* was a horrible week for all of us.

## Universal Pronouns

The universal pronouns are *each* (one), *everyone*, *everybody*, and *all*. *Everyone* and *everybody* have collective reference (to three or more), while *each* refers to a person or thing that is part of a group of two or more. *All* may have either a singular or a plural meaning, depending on the context in which it is used. The following sentences are illustrative:

Michael and Jason think alike, but *each* (one) has his own way of doing things.
Thirty beggars came and she gave a gift to *each* (one).
There's enough here for *everyone*.
They're watching *everybody* these days.
*All* is confusion. (The situation is chaotic.)
*All* are eager for the play to begin. (A number of people are eager.)

At times *each* and *all* are used *after* noun phrases or pronouns:

John and Helene *each* won an award.
You *each* deserve a share of the blame.
The contestants *all* gathered at the judges' bench.

## Indefinite Pronouns

Unlike most pronouns, except perhaps the universals, the reference of these pronouns is semantically more often to indefinite rather than to definite quantities. Furthermore, indefinite pronouns do not carry many of the features, such as case or distance, that other pronouns do. In order that those having similar characteristics may be compared, we present the indefinite pronouns in groups.

Group I: *some, any,* and *none.*

Two of these indefinite pronouns, *some* and *any,* can combine with *-one, -body,* and *-thing* to form compounds (the word *no* is substituted for *none* in these compounds). *Some* usually indicates an unspecified quantity. *Any* can indicate "any" quantity—one or more. *None* is often used as the negative counterpart of *any* and *some.* Typical uses are shown in the following sentences:

I don't have *any,* but I'd like *some.*
There's *none* in the house.
I saw *someone* (*somebody, something*) in those bushes.
I'll talk to *anyone.*
*Anyone* (*anybody*) can do it.
*Anything* can happen.
*No one* (*nobody*) saw me.
*Nothing* is happening.

Group II: *either, neither.*

*Either* and *neither* are a positive/negative pair. Although they usually refer to two, they are considered grammatically singular when used as subjects, so the verb takes the singular form:

*Either* (Clark or David) has done it.
*Neither* (Clark nor David) has done it.
*Either* (of the two) is acceptable to me.

The word *one* is sometimes used after these pronouns:

*Either* (one) could have done it.
*Neither* (one) likes licorice.

Group III: *one.*

Although singular, the pronoun *one* is often used to represent an indefinite number:

> *One* should always do *one's* duty. (Any number of people could be meant.)
> *One* could easily drown in this swamp. (Any number of people could who got caught in it.)

It can also be used to refer specifically to one of an indefinite number, however:

> You have shirts on sale and I'd like *one.*

## Archaic Pronouns

Although archaic pronouns like *thou, thee, thy/thine,* and *ye* are used today only by a few individuals belonging to certain religious groups, you have almost certainly encountered these forms while studying sixteenth- and seventeenth-century literature, reading various versions of the Bible, or reciting certain prayers. *Thou* meant singular "you" (subject) and *thee* meant singular "you" (object). By the thirteenth century these singular forms were used for (1) addressing those of lesser social rank, as when a person of high station addressed a servant; and (2) speaking to intimates, such as loved ones and close personal friends. A conversation between intimates might therefore include sentences like "*Thou* bringst me joy" (i.e., "You bring me joy"), "What dost *thou* seek?" ("What do you seek?"), "*Thou* shouldst know it" ("You should know it"), "I must leave *thee*" ("I must leave you"), "He loves *thee*" ("He loves you"), and "I thank *thee*" ("I thank you"). Those who held a higher position in society, were older, or for some other reason merited deference, however, were addressed with *you,* rather than *thou* or *thee.* A servant addressing his or her employer, an artisan addressing a member of the aristocracy, a member of the nobility addressing the king, or even a child addressing a parent in a formal setting would say things such as "If *you* will hear me," "that it may please *you,*" "I'll follow *you,*" "*You* gave it me," and so forth. The deferential pronoun *you* was also used between equals of very high rank, especially in formal circumstances. *Thy* and *your* constitute a similar pair, *thy* generally being used with *thou* and *thee,* and *your* with *you.* Thus a father would command his son, "Say *thy* prayers," but the same sentence addressed to a member of the royal court would come out as "Say *your* prayers." *Ye* originally meant plural "you" (subject form), as in "Ye (more than one) may find rest," but eventually *ye* came to mean singular "you" (subject), and, like the pronoun *you*, signaled respect.

Unfortunately, many people today who read Shakespeare and other early writers are not aware of these nuances in pronoun usage and therefore miss much of what is going on in the dialogues of these authors. Early writers frequently relied on pronoun usage to provide insights into character and relationships. A low-born soldier who suddenly begins addressing an earl with *thou*'s and *thee*'s is being impudent and insulting. A switch to *ye*'s and *you*'s between lovers who have previously employed *thou*'s and *thee*'s most likely means that a warm relationship has chilled considerably. The use of *ye* and *you* by an aristocrat addressing a clerk indicates an extremely great respect for the clerk, that the two are very close personally, that the aristocrat is mentally disturbed, or that the aristocrat may be using deferential pronouns for very calculated reasons. The point is that shifts in pronoun usage usually meant *something*, and early English literature is the richer for it.

# OUR NEXT-TO-THE-LAST WORD ON PRONOUNS

Even our brief review should have made it clear that pronouns provide a wealth of semantic information and perform a variety of functions.[2] Given this complexity and their abundance,[3] you might predict that they cause problems at times. And you would be right. Problems with case and agreement are especially common. The next section will discuss the most important variations in the use and form of pronouns.

# PRONOUNS IN THE EVERYDAY WORLD

Some of the problems people have with pronouns are simply spelling or punctuation errors. Who, for example, has not sometime or

[2] Many of these functions have not been explained in this chapter (pronouns as *determiners*, for example) because by doing so we would have raised matters best left for other chapters.

[3] Although we have given you many words that can be called pronouns, we have left out words like *few*, *both*, *other*, and *another*, which usually function as *determiners* or *quantifiers*, but see occasional use as pronouns:

*Few* could survive his wrath.
*Both* appeared distraught.
*Others* have trod these paths.
*Another* could have done as well.

another written the adverb *there* instead of the pronoun *their* or the contracted form *they're*? Such mistakes as *"I saw *there* new house" happen because most speakers pronounce all three *there*'s the same. To mistakenly use the contracted forms of the pairs *whose/who's* and *its/it's* instead of the possessive forms is also common:

*Who's* book is that?
*The robin laid an egg in *it's* nest.

The *its/it's* confusion is particularly common because the apostrophe is associated with possessive forms of nouns (John's bike, my father's car, etc.). Therefore, students sometimes carry the apostrophe over to the possessive form *it's. Since context, both in speech and writing, provides the intended meaning, these errors are not serious. However, their constant occurrence on themes can eventually cause even the most gentle teacher to go into a pedagogical rage.

More serious are pronoun usages that cause people to judge (without basis, we repeat) the user's intelligence or literacy. Some of the most blatant "errors" that almost every speaker of Standard English would condemn include the following:

1 Putting object pronouns in subject position:
*Me* and *her* did it.
2 Combining the possessive form of a third person personal pronoun with -*self* (or -*selves*):
*He cut *hisself*.
3 Substituting *youse* for plural *you*:
*Youse* guys should leave now.[4]
4 Using *nothing* in a negative sentence rather than *anything*:
*He don't know *nothing*.

All these nonstandard expressions are common and widespread, and many people are comfortable using them in their speech and occasionally even in their writing. Bringing them forth at the wrong time, however, can result in some strongly negative reactions.

One nonstandard pronoun variation which is not quite so apt to be regarded negatively is the "double subject" construction so often found in Southern speech. This construction is being heard more and more in Northern and Western cities as residents of the South who have migrated to Northern and Western urban areas bring this construction with them. The "double subject" is a noun +

[4] Seeing our *youse* example, you may think, "What about *you-all* (*y'all*, etc.) as a plural form? Isn't that nonstandard, too?" Whether it is partly depends on whom you ask. Many Southerners would not only say "No," but would be indignant that you raised the question. Speakers in other parts of the country might reject *you-all*, only because they would not use it themselves.

pronoun construction found in subject position, with the noun being the antecedent of the pronoun. In other words, the subject of the clause is stated twice in succession—once as a noun and again as a pronoun. This construction is illustrated as follows:

*Wilbur and Otis, they* hate to see her go.
*Linda, she* don't have no trouble at all.
*The reverend, he* told 'em 'bout it.
*A. J., he* won that race without no trouble.

Some pronoun forms exist that are unlikely to bring any censure to their user, although some speakers, especially teachers, might not like to see or hear them used in formal contexts. For example, for years students have had it drilled into them that "It is *I*" is right and "It is *me*" is wrong. If an explanation is offered, it is that the nominative or subjective form of the pronoun should be used after the verb *be*, a rule that conflicts with the standard rule requiring the objective form after other verbs. The result for students has often been confusion and a feeling that "the rules don't mean anything," or that "they're just arbitrary." Some even grow hypersensitive about using "good" English and make mistakes like *"between you and I," where *me* after a preposition would be standard. Almost no grammarian would consider the "It is *I*" (or *he*, *she*, etc.) issue an important one, and most speakers of Standard English are perfectly content to accept "It is *me*." In fact, since many people consider the "It is *I*" construction to be stilted or affected, it is seldom really expected or required, except in very formal speech or writing.

More upsetting to most people are situations in which the antecedent of a pronoun is unclear. This problem is referred to as *ambiguous pronoun reference*. A few examples should help illustrate it:

Tom told Don that *he* should be the one to do it.
Betty began to miss her mother after *she* moved to New York.
The cowboys managed to water the horses that night, but *they* were too exhausted to go on.

In the first example, it is not clear whether *he* refers to Tom or Don. In the second, *she* could mean either Betty or her mother, so that we are not sure who it was that moved to New York. In the third example, it is unclear whether *they* refers to the cowboys or the horses, or to both. Ambiguous pronoun reference is remedied simply by rewording sentences to eliminate any confusion:

Tom felt Don should be the one to do it, and told him so.
After Betty moved to New York, she began to miss her mother.
Even though they managed to water the horses that night, the
    cowboys were too exhausted to go on.

Another fine point in pronoun usage concerns agreement with some of the universal and indefinite pronouns. Almost everyone has at one time or another been bothered by uncertainty over whether some of the indefinite pronouns take a singular or plural verb form. The most troublesome of the indefinite pronouns are *each, either, neither,* and *none,* and the prescriptive rule states that all these pronouns should take the singular form of the verb, as shown in the following list:

*Each* of the boys *is* content.
*Either* of the plans *is* fine with us.
*Neither is* fit for duty.
*None* of the ideas *is* acceptable.

When two or more nouns or pronouns or a plural noun follow the indefinite pronoun, this rule is sometimes broken, even by very educated and literate speakers. Such "violations" of the prescriptive norm bring no dire consequences—in fact, most are not even noticed. Thus we often accept sentences such as "*Either* Ted or I *are* going to win" and "*None* of the ideas *are* acceptable" without giving them a second thought, even though both are "technically" incorrect.

By this time you might be thinking, "But wait a minute! You've left out the matter of gender and sex discrimination entirely, even though it could have been raised in half of your examples." All right, what about the practice of using masculine *his* in a sentence where sex is not specified but the antecedent is singular and human? It is true that sentences like "Each person has his own desk" and "Everyone likes to be his own master" can seem awkward and sexually biased. But the problem is not the same as others we have looked at (standard versus nonstandard), since Standard English has accepted such sentences without reservation for years. Rather it is a matter of questioning social and personal values. If a person writes sentences like those just given, he or she might be considered chauvinistic or socially unaware by some, but not unintelligent or illiterate. The grammatical reality, of course, is that we do not have a third person singular pronoun unmarked for sex except *it.* In at least one nonstandard dialect speakers do use *it* rather than *he* or *she,* though not for reasons that have anything to do with what we have been talking about. Sentences like "A person should work hard if it wants to succeed" are hardly likely to be generally accepted, however, partly because, though sexless, *it* has nonhuman reference. One partial solution has a chance of occurring naturally since, as some grammarians have noted, the problem might encourage more extensive use of *they* to refer to a singular antecedent. This practice can now be seen and heard in such sentences as "Everyone has a right to *their* (rather than *his*) own opinion," "Someone called you but *they* didn't leave a message" (a usage already fairly common), and "I saw someone leave the house but *they* weren't carrying anything" (when the observer was not able to identify the sex of the "someone"). Whether teachers, editors, and grammarians will lend their support to such a practice, however, remains to be seen. Other solutions to the problem have also been suggested, but to date none has gained favor. One suggestion—to use *s/he* rather than "he or she" in writing—appears doomed because *s/he* is as awkward as the construction it is meant to replace. Another suggestion is to add a new pronoun to the language. *Em* has been recommended for a couple of reasons: *em* is a neutral term that could be used to refer to humans, and people are already familiar with expressions like "I saw 'em (from "I saw him" or "I saw them"). *Em* would be recommended, then, in all expressions where either *he* or *she* could appear, as in the following examples:

A student must study if *em* is to pass.
Will each person pick up *em's* coat?

That *em*, or *any* new pronoun, could be accepted is doubtful, however, because adding a new pronoun to any language is extremely difficult. Pronouns are used so frequently that they usually constitute as closed a class as any to be found in the most exclusive society—and they admit new members just as grudgingly. We can hardly imagine the matter of language-based sex discrimination being resolved quickly or easily either. But the entire controversy has raised significant questions and led people to take a close look at their language and values. These are important benefits. Hopefully, more will follow.

Finally, one more observation about pronouns in the everyday world, this time having to do with case. The deployment of Standard English subjective and objective pronoun forms is one of the aspects of English grammar that many children learn late. It is not unusual for grammarians to encounter troubled parents whose kindergarten-age children typically place objective-case pronouns in subject position, so that sentences such as the following result:

*Him* told me it.
*Them* don't got any.
*Me and Julie* are going to her house.

The truth of the matter is that many children are well beyond kindergarten age when they finally get pronoun case straightened out, so case problems in the early school years are normal and no cause for concern. If the problem persists for several years, then parents and teachers might do well to give it some special attention.

# Exercises

I Identify the underlined pronouns as demonstrative, indefinite, interrogative, personal, reciprocal, reflexive, relative, or universal.

*Example:* Those two teams hate <u>each</u> <u>other</u>.   <u>reciprocal</u>

1 <u>She</u> does too much.   _____

2 <u>Who</u> forgot the salt?   _____

3 <u>Everyone</u> loves an underdog.   _____

4 You don't have to accept <u>that</u>.   _____

5 Joan really enjoyed <u>his</u> cooking.   _____

6 Rachel shouldn't punish <u>herself</u> so.   _____

7 <u>No one</u> could miss that sign.   _____

8 <u>Whose</u> is that?   _____

9 He adopts every stray cat <u>that</u> comes his way.   _____

10 <u>Why</u> do you ask that?   _____

11 <u>These</u> are very good grapes.   _____

12 Did you get <u>some</u>?   _____

13 I witnessed his success <u>myself</u>.   _____

14 I said I didn't have <u>any</u>.   _____

15 <u>Neither</u> has convinced me.   _____

16 He envied people <u>who</u> improved themselves.   _____

17 Jordan seems to know <u>everything</u>.   _____

18 They considered <u>one</u> <u>another</u> friends.   _____

**19** They praised Harriet, <u>whose</u> quick thinking had _____
saved them.

**20** Safety should be <u>our</u> first concern. _____

**21** They gave <u>me</u> a second chance. _____

**22** The trainer treated <u>it</u> with kindness. _____

**23** <u>Nothing</u> could please me more. _____

**24** <u>This</u> is much too big. _____

**25** <u>We</u> wish you a Merry Christmas. _____

**II** Fill in each blank with the appropriate pronoun. If more than one
pronoun may be used, circle the alternative(s).

> *Example:* _____ (all, one, each) of the guests were present.
>
> <u>All</u> (all, one, each) of the guests were present.
>
> A good test is one _____ (that, which) is fair.
>
> A good test is one <u>that</u> (that, (which)) is fair.

**1** _____ (whose, who's) red boat is sailing up the channel?

**2** _____ (she, her) and Laurie shared the expenses.

**3** If _____ (one, someone, somebody) wants more, just yell.

**4** The reporter _____ (who, that, which) wrote the report is biased.

**5** The price of fame is the same for _____ (all, everyone, everybody).

**6** The cat chased _____ (it's, its) tail.

**7** They should do it _____ (theirselves, themselves).

**8** That was between you and _____ (I, me).

**9** Her parents respected _____ (each other, one another).

**10** _____ (their, they're) not sure of the outcome.

**III** Change the following sentences where necessary to put them into
Standard English. Put a check in the box after those sentences where
no change is necessary.

> *Example:* He don't know nothing. [ ]
>
> He doesn't know anything. _____

1 He cut hisself. ☐

2 Charlotte and her mother, they left this morning. ☐

3 If you have a question, ask them guys. ☐

4 Neither the American nor the Russian wants

to sign the treaty. ☐

**5** Him and me caught the biggest fish that summer. ☐

**6** Each citizen should cherish his right to vote. ☐

**7** I want that there piece of cake. ☐

**8** I don't think it's appropriate. ☐

**9** Neither boy swims as well as they should. ☐

# THIRTEEN

# The Determiner System

## INTRODUCTION

*Determiners* constitute a rather small though important category of words in English. Coming from several different parts of speech, their defining characteristic is their dependency upon the existence of a following noun. In fact, many determiners cannot be used unless they are followed by a noun. The determiners include articles, demonstrative pronouns, possessive pronouns, and other words as well. A few determiners are shown in the following phrases:

*the* albatross
*an* obese rhinoceros
*a* beautiful sunset
*our* younger cousin
*my* keys
*those* plastic raincoats

You will notice that most of the determiners in these phrases would never be used without a following noun. Every speaker of English would find sentences such as *"I saw *the*," *"We found *an*," and *"She has *our*" to be unacceptable. This is not true of the adjectives in the preceding phrases, however. In "The sunset was beautiful," "This cousin is *younger*," and "Those raincoats are *plastic*," the adjectives are no longer followed by nouns, yet the sentences are perfectly acceptable. One difference between determiners and adjectives, then, is that determiners are usually (*not always*) required to have a noun follow them, whereas adjectives are not.

A second distinction between determiners and adjectives involves their relative word order. When both a determiner and an adjective modify the same noun, the determiner will always precede the adjective. The following phrases illustrate:

| *Det.* | *Adj.* | *Noun* |
|--------|--------|--------|
| an | old | friend |
| the | helpful | librarian |
| her | yellow | pillow |
| those | anxious | parents |

Determiners are classified as *regular determiners, predeterminers,* and *postdeterminers*. We will look at regular determiners first.

# REGULAR DETERMINERS

*Regular determiners* can be divided into two groups: the *articles* (*a, an,* and *the*), and the *demonstrative pronouns* and various *possessives*, including *possessive personal pronouns*. In many ways the articles are the most important of the determiners, which is why we discuss them first.

## The Articles: *A, An,* and *The*

Among the articles there is a clear difference in usage. *The* is definite, while *a* and *an* are indefinite. For example, "the boy" indicates a particular boy, but "a boy" could mean any boy. Most of the time this definiteness is established by using *the* with a noun that has already been mentioned. For example, the noun *truck* may be used in one sentence with the indefinite article and repeated in a second sentence with the definite article:

> A truck appeared on the crest of the hill. *The* truck was carrying a load of vegetables.

At times the earlier reference to the noun can be a matter of presupposition rather than explicit statement. Consider the following sentences:

*The* weather was changeable.

He opened *the* door and headed for *the* kitchen.

*The* traffic light was about to change.

In all of these sentences, presuppositions based on our knowledge of the world allow the definite article to be used without prior mention of the noun. In other words, we know that there is such a thing as weather, that houses have doors and kitchens, that street corners have traffic lights. Knowing these things, we are free to use *the*, avoiding awkward sentences like "There was a door and he opened *the* door."

In the foregoing examples both the definite and the indefinite articles were used *specifically*, i.e., to refer to a member or members of a class. They can also be used *generically* when we want to refer to an entire class itself. The following sentences will illustrate:

| | |
|---|---|
| Specific Reference: | *The lion* was eating. |
| | *A lion* was eating. |
| | *An apple* is on the table. |
| Generic Reference: | *The lion* is the king of beasts. |
| | *A lion* is a magnificent creature. |
| | *An apple* contains vitamins. |

With plural nouns, *specific* reference can be conveyed both with and without the definite article:

| | |
|---|---|
| Specific Reference: | *Lions* were eating. |
| | *The lions* were eating. |
| | *Apples* are on the table. |
| | *The apples* are on the table. |

The definite article *cannot* be used with plural nouns for *generic* reference, however:

| | |
|---|---|
| Generic Reference: | *Lions* are magnificent creatures. |
| | *Apples* contain vitamins. |
| | but not: |
| | *\*The lions* are magnificent creatures. |
| | *\*The apples* contain vitamins. |

Other important distinctions that the articles help us make will be discussed when we talk about count and noncount nouns, but one last point should be made before we leave articles. This concerns the alternation of *a* and *an*. *A* is used before words that begin with a consonant sound, and *an* is used before words that begin with a vowel sound, as in the following examples:

| | |
|---|---|
| *an* apple | *a* tree |
| *an* umbrella | *a* yokel |
| *an* egg | *a* river |
| *an* hour (*h* silent) | *a* cocker spaniel |

Since the distinction is based on the way a word is pronounced and pronunciation can vary, you can expect to find both used before certain words, as in the following example:

    *an* historical account    *a* historical account

Here the *h* is not pronounced by some speakers, leading to the possibility of their saying or writing *an* rather than *a*. Furthermore, words which begin with a consonant sound are sometimes spelled with a vowel letter, which explains why we say "*a* one o'clock appointment," or "*a* unique design." The initial sound in *one* is *w*, while the initial sound in *unique* is *y*.

## Demonstrative Pronouns and Possessives

When they appear before a noun or an adjective + noun combination, the demonstrative pronouns and various possessives can be considered determiners. Included among the possessives are possessive personal pronouns and the possessives of indefinite pronouns and nouns. Examples of all are given in the following lists:

| *Demonstrative Pronouns* | *Possessive Personal Pronouns* |
|---|---|
| *this* book | *my* revenge |
| *that* problem | *his* appetite |
| *these* ruffians | *her* regrets |
| *those* artichokes | *its* characteristics |
| | *your* insolence |
| | *their* meringue pie |

| *Possessive Indefinite Pronouns* | *Possessive Nouns* |
|---|---|
| *someone's* dog | *Juan's* little sister |
| *one's* opportunity | *Chicago's* size |
| *somebody's* elbow | *propaganda's* value |
| *no one's* fault | etc. |
| *either's* book | |
| *neither's* riches | |
| *anybody's* chair | |

One point concerning word order should be made here. Although most regular determiners do not usually co-occur, i.e., appear successively in a noun phrase, this is not true of possessive common nouns, which can be immediately preceded by other determiners:

a *child's* game
the *cow's* stall
his *brother's* clothes
this *man's* abilities

In these examples you can see that two determiners precede each of the nouns.

# PREDETERMINERS

*Predeterminers* are able to precede regular determiners in a noun phrase. They include the words *all*, *both*, and *half*. These predeterminers may be followed by an optional *of* if the noun phrase contains a noun; if the noun phrase contains only a personal pronoun, however, the *of* is obligatory. The following sentences illustrate the various characteristics of these predeterminers. Notice that when both a predeterminer and a regular determiner are present, the predeterminer comes first:

*All* (*of*) the food was eaten.   (noun in noun phrase)
*All* (*of*) my apple was eaten.   (noun in noun phrase)
*Both* (*of*) the babies wore blue.   (noun in noun phrase)
*Half* (*of*) those apples were rotten.   (noun in noun phrase)
*Half* (*of*) a day was wasted.   (noun in noun phrase)
*All of* it was eaten.   (pronoun in noun phrase)
*Both of* them wore blue.   (pronoun in noun phrase)
*Half of* them were rotten.   (pronoun in noun phrase)
*Half of* it was wasted.   (pronoun in noun phrase)

Aside from *all*, *both*, and *half*, there are no agreed-upon words that grammarians call predeterminers.

# POSTDETERMINERS

*Postdeterminers* include numbers, both *cardinals* (numbers used in simple counting, like *three*, *four*, and *five*) and *ordinals* (numbers indicating the place of something in a series, like *first*, *second*, and *third*). In a noun phrase, postdeterminers occur after all other determiners, though usually before adjectives. Unlike most of the other determiners, postdeterminers can co-occur; that is, a cardinal may follow an ordinal in the same noun phrase. Typical examples of postdeterminers are as follows:

her *two* brothers
these *three* pictures
the *tenth* annual reunion
a *second* chance
the *first three* customers
the *four* white shoes

# THE IMPORTANCE OF COUNT AND NONCOUNT NOUNS

The basic difference between *count* and *noncount* nouns is simple but important. *Count nouns* have referents that can be counted, like *tree*, *rabbit*, *dish*, *missile*, and *orange*. They can be either singular or plural. Noncount nouns have referents that cannot be counted, like *water*, *money*, and *tennis*. The fact that certain nouns are "uncountable" may seem difficult to comprehend at first. It is often helpful to contemplate the unacceptability of sentences such as *"The doctor told me to drink *eight waters* a day," *"You owe me *twelve monies*," or *"I played *six tennises* this morning." These sentences sound strange because we do not count *water*, *money*, or *tennis* directly. We measure these things, it is true, but only through countable units. Thus it is acceptable to talk of *"eight pints* of water," *"twelve dollars," "six sets* of tennis." *Pints*, *dollars*, and *sets* are countable nouns; *water*, *money*, and *tennis* are not.

Some nouns are capable of being used in both a count *and* a noncount sense. When this happens, the meaning of the noun changes according to which way it is being used. Observe how this happens in the following sentences:

Raymond likes *beer*.   (noncountable sense)
George drank two *beers*.   (countable sense)
The workbench was covered with *metal*.   (noncountable sense)
Iron and copper were the two *metals* they needed.   (countable sense)
*Love* is beautiful.   (noncountable sense)
Serena had two *loves*.   (countable sense)

The distinction between these two classes of nouns is important because it helps dictate which determiners are permitted to be used in given situations. First, the words *many* and *few* (which some grammarians include among the determiners) are almost always used with count nouns, while the words *much* and *little* (meaning "not much") almost always go with noncount nouns. This restriction is illustrated in the following sentences:

*Count Nouns*
*Many pets* are abandoned.
*Few pets* are abandoned.
**Much pets* are abandoned.
**Little pets* are abandoned.

*Noncount Nouns*
*Much gasoline* is wasted.
*Little gasoline* is wasted.
**Many gasoline* is wasted.
**Few gasoline* is wasted.

Second, the distinction between count and noncount nouns is important in determining how articles are used. Noncount nouns and plural count nouns may be preceded by the article *the*, but they can also occur without any article whatsoever. Thus we can have the following:

*The ice* in the drinks was dirty.  (noncount with *the*)
*Ice* has covered the highway.  (noncount without article)
*The students* asked many questions.  (plural count with *the*)
*Students* are often destitute.  (plural count without article)

The articles *a* and *an* will never precede noncount or plural count nouns, however:

**An ice* in the drinks was dirty.
**An ice* has covered the highway.
**A students* asked many questions.
**A students* are often destitute.

With singular count nouns, the situation is different. Singular count nouns must be preceded by *a, an, the*, or some other determiner; the absence of determiners before singular count nouns is not permitted in English. In the first of the following sentences, each singular count noun is preceded by an article or other determiner, as required by the rules of English. In the second sentence, these determiners have been removed, resulting in a sentence that is no longer acceptable:

*My friend* used *a broom* to clean *the driveway*.
*\*Friend* used *broom* to clean *driveway*.

A final word about count and noncount nouns concerns agreement. Since the referent of a noncount noun is typically viewed as a mass, not as a set of individual items, most of the time the noncount noun takes a singular verb. Notice this contrast in the following examples:

(The) *bread is* on the table. (noncount noun)
(The) *pennies are* on the table. (count noun).

This feature of agreement sometimes holds even when the noncount nouns have a "plural" suffix:

*Statistics is* my favorite subject.

This brief discussion covers what we think are the most important facts about count and noncount nouns. With it and our previous discussions of nouns, you now have information that will help you understand and analyze noun phrases and the determiners that can be included in them.

# DETERMINERS IN THE EVERYDAY WORLD

Now that we have taken a brief look at some aspects of the complex determiner system, it will probably not surprise you to learn that considerable variety exists in the ways determiners are used in the everyday world.

One kind of variation is found among speakers whose first language is not English. Because the rules for using articles differ from language to language, many non-native speakers inadvertently apply the article rules of their mother tongue when they use the English language. For example, the sentence "At home, *dinner* is served at six o'clock" might, when spoken by a French person, become "At home, *the dinner* is served at six o'clock." In like manner, "She studies *French*" might become "She studies *the*

*French.*" This would happen because the equivalent sentences in French would require the use of the definite article before the word for "dinner" and the word for "French."

The requirement that every singular count noun in English be preceded by a determiner raises havoc for other speakers, particularly Asians, as the grammatical rules in many Asian languages *permit* the use of singular count nouns without determiners. With the habits of a lifetime behind them, many Asians find it particularly difficult to remember to insert a determiner every time they use a singular count noun in English. For this reason, sentences like those following are often spoken or written by Asians who have not yet mastered English:

> *I have *test* tomorrow.
> *She has *appointment* with *teacher*.
> *He put *briefcase* in *living room*.
> *I buy *doughnut* every morning.
> *Could I borrow *wrench*, please?

This stumbling block sometimes remains even after an Asian has mastered virtually every other aspect of the English language. There are doubtless similar stumbling blocks which plague English speakers trying to master one of the Oriental languages.

One need not turn to other languages to find differing determiner constructions, however, as determiner usage differs even among varieties of English. Speakers of British English, for example, would say "He's in *hospital*," an expression that can only be "He's in *the hospital*" in American English.

Demonstratives come in for their share of variation, too. One usage, common to many nonstandard speakers, involves the substitution of a personal pronoun form for the standard demonstrative:

> Standard:  *Those* books are expensive.
> Nonstandard:  *Them* books are expensive.
> Standard:  She likes *those* Fred Astaire movies.
> Nonstandard:  She likes *them* Fred Astaire movies.

A second variation, sometimes called the "redundant demonstrative," is illustrated as follows:

> Standard:  *This* map is wrong.
> Nonstandard:  *This here* map is wrong.
> Standard:  *That* car is sold.
> Nonstandard:  *That there* car is sold.

*Here* and *there* are redundant because *this* already indicates "nearness" in the first example, while *that* indicates "farness" in the second.

Possessives are also used differently at times. One variation heard mainly in poor inner-city areas involves the loss of the possessive marker. "What's that *fellow's* name?" might become *"What's that *fellow* name?" This loss also occurs in phrases that contain possessive pronouns, especially in dialects whose speakers regularly do not pronounce the *r* after vowels, and results in expressions like *"They brothuh" and *"You cah" rather than "*their* brother" and "*your* car." Expressions such as *"I cah," *"she cah," and *"we cah" seldom appear, but *"he cah" can occasionally be heard in the speech of some young children.

Moving to *much* and *many*, we find a different situation. Children learning the language often take some time to learn the *much/many* distinction when they use these words before count and noncount nouns. Such expressions as *"I have *much* pennies" or *"There are *much* ants on the ground" are not infrequent. Parents and teachers should be forewarned that "correcting," explaining, scolding, and pleading are usually equally ineffective in changing this and many other childhood speech forms. Happily, children seem to have little difficulty in adopting adult forms on their own, when they are good and ready.

Our next item concerns the indefinite articles and, mainly, written English. People will sometimes write *a* when *an* is called for, as in the sample errors which follow:

*A umbrella hung on the rack.
*A orchid grew in the garden.
*A effort was made to improve.

At other times people will not know which form to use. This might happen when the article precedes an abbreviation, such as *M.A.* (Master of Arts degree). As long as a person remembers to use *an* before a vowel *sound* and *a* before a consonant *sound*, such uncertainty is quickly resolved. We say "*an* M.A." because the first sound in *M.A.* is the vowel *e*, as in the word *enter*.

Finally, children occasionally make an entirely different and somewhat humorous mistake when first learning new words. For example, their mother or father might ask "Do you want *an orange*?" and they might respond by saying, "Give me *a norange*," indicating that they have not learned the word *orange* yet. Such mistakes might seem funny and inconsequential, but once in a while the "mistake" sticks and the English language is then given a "new" word. Historically this happened with the word *apron*, which was once *napron*, but at some time the *n* moved to the article (*a napron* became *an apron*) and we have been stuck with the new form ever since.

# Exercises

I Determiners.

    A. In the spaces provided, list all of the *regular* determiners present in each of the following sentences.

       *Example:* His dog has half the stamina Jim's two dogs have.

          His, the, Jim's

      **1** Both of the parents objected to their marriage.

      **2** Good citizens support that initiative.

      **3** Myron's five tortoises performed a slow mazurka.

      **4** My aunt loves an artful pickpocket.

      **5** Half her allowance went for pretzels in the park.

      **6** The first clown was funnier than the second comic.

      **7** That hurricane caused widespread damage.

      **8** Simple Simon wondered if his name was significant.

**9** Those children are playing with great enthusiasm.

_____

**10** All of the players were content with their salary increase.

_____

B. In the spaces provided, list the *predeterminers* and the *postdeterminers* in each of the sentences given in the previous section. If a sentence did not contain any, leave the space blank.

*Example:* His dog has half the stamina Jim's two dogs have.

| Predeterminers | Postdeterminers |
|:---:|:---:|
| half | two |

| Predeterminers | Postdeterminers |
|:---:|:---:|
| 1 _____ | 1 _____ |
| 2 _____ | 2 _____ |
| 3 _____ | 3 _____ |
| 4 _____ | 4 _____ |
| 5 _____ | 5 _____ |
| 6 _____ | 6 _____ |
| 7 _____ | 7 _____ |
| 8 _____ | 8 _____ |
| 9 _____ | 9 _____ |
| 10 _____ | 10 _____ |

C. Write two sentences whose noun phrases contain only regular determiners, two sentences whose noun phrases contain both predeterminers and regular determiners, and two sentences whose noun phrases contain predeterminers, regular determiners, and postdeterminers.

1 _____

2 _____

3 _____

4 _____

5 _____

6 _____

II  Specific and Generic Reference.
Each of the nouns underlined in the following sentences has either specific or generic reference. In the spaces provided, state whether the reference is specific or generic in each case.

*Examples:* Cows were grazing in the <u>pasture</u>.  <u>specific</u>
<u>Cows</u> were among the first animals to be
domesticated.  <u>generic</u>

1  Roxann directed the <u>play</u> with flair.  _____

2  <u>Moths</u> are attracted by lights.  _____

3  A <u>politician</u> is one who promises much but delivers
little.  _____

4  The treacle <u>soup</u> laid Benjamin low.  _____

5  <u>Skunks</u> can release a terrible odor.  _____

6  The <u>mechanics</u> worked on the car until midnight.  _____

7  A <u>storm</u> devastated farms in the lowlands.  _____

8  Bread sustains people, but <u>love</u> elevates them.  _____

**III** Count and Noncount Nouns.

Identify the count and noncount nouns in each of the following sentences by underlining the nouns and writing "C" or "NC" above them.

$$\begin{array}{ccc} & \text{C} & \text{NC} \end{array}$$

*Example:* The <u>miners</u> badly needed fresh <u>air</u>.

1 The hurricane wreaked havoc everywhere.

2 Debris was scattered throughout the streets.

3 Paramedics and rescue workers rushed to the scene.

4 Free milk, bread, and meat were distributed.

5 Bulletins provided hourly information to the public.

6 Reconstruction began, and the area returned to normal.

7 Time passed, and the destruction was forgotten.

8 The significance of weather was no longer discussed.

9 Months later they heard more bad news.

10 They prepared for the new storm with vigor.

11 His cousin never does his homework.

12 The peak was covered with the new snow.

13 Dust blew against the burned-out tank.

14 Equipment was rusting away in one corner of the factory.

15 The workers badly needed extra instruction.

# FOURTEEN

# Direct and Indirect Objects

The terms *direct object* and *indirect object* are two of those "basic" grammatical terms, along with *subject, verb, preposition,* and a few others, that almost all educated speakers of English have heard of at one time or another. While most could probably identify the subject of a given sentence, or name a few specific prepositions, not as many would be able to tell you exactly what a direct or an indirect object is, or point to the direct and indirect objects in a particular sentence. In this chapter we will take up these two objects and consider the role they play in English grammar.

## DIRECT OBJECTS

The term *direct object* ordinarily refers to the person or thing being acted upon in a sentence, in other words, to the person or thing receiving the action described by the verb. For example, consider the sentence "Jack kicked the football." The thing being acted upon in this sentence is "the football"—it is receiving Jack's kick. You might think of the action of kicking as originating with the subject "Jack" and being passed along to the recipient, "the football." "The football," then, is the direct object in this sentence. Or consider the sentence "Jessie painted the house." The thing acted upon in this sentence is "the house." The action of painting originated with Jessie, and the thing which was on the receiving end of her action was "the house." The phrase "the house," then, is the direct object in this sentence. You will find other sentences in the following list. Observe how the direct objects are the recipients of the actions in these sentences—notice the sense in which they are the persons or things being acted upon.

Patty opened *the door*.
Hans repaired *the faucet*.
The Kaiser shot *an elk*.
Greta kissed *her husband*.
Four scholars translated *the ancient Norse manuscript*.
The boss fired *him*.

One very practical test which can usually help you identify direct objects is called the "what got" or "who got" test. To see whether a noun phrase is really serving as a direct object, just ask "What (or Who) got _____?" and insert the past participle form of the verb from the sentence in the blank. For the first four of the preceding sentences, you would ask "What got opened?", "What got repaired?", "What got shot?", "Who got kissed?", and so forth. The answer, when there is one, will be the direct object of the sentence. In these cases, "the door" got opened, "the faucet" got fixed, "an elk" got shot, and "her husband" got kissed. These, then, are the direct objects of the sentences in question.

# TRANSITIVE AND INTRANSITIVE VERBS

The term *transitive* is derived from a Latin word meaning "passing over," and we have seen how the action described by a verb can originate with the subject of a sentence and be passed along to a direct object. The verbs in the preceding examples, because they are all followed by direct objects, are called *transitive* verbs.

Verbs that do not take a direct object are called *intransitive* verbs. With these verbs, there is no sense of an action originating with a subject and then being passed along to another person or thing. The verbs in the following sentences are all intransitive:

The elderly monk *laughed*.
Melissa *sang* beautifully tonight.
We *run* every afternoon at five.
The children *slept* in the barn.
The terrible chieftain finally *died*.
Tony *sneezed* loudly.

A few verbs, such as *die* (in the sense of "to cease living") and *sneeze*, are mainly intransitive. Others, such as *repair* (in the sense of "to fix"), are mainly transitive. The overwhelming majority of verbs, however, can be used both transitively *and* intransitively:

Pablo *returned* before sunset. (intransitive)
Doris *returned* the shovel. (transitive)

Lois *painted* in the attic. (intransitive)
Eric *painted* the table. (transitive)
Jennifer *drives* now. (intransitive)
Spenser *drives* a truck. (transitive)

# INDIRECT OBJECTS

In sentences which contain direct objects, there is sometimes an additional noun phrase which names the *beneficiary* of the action being described in the sentence. Such a noun phrase is referred to as an *indirect object*. Consider the sentence "Sylvia built a greenhouse for her husband." The direct object in this sentence is "a greenhouse," since it directly receives the action of building; i.e., it is what got built. The beneficiary of the act of building a greenhouse, however, is Sylvia's husband, so "her husband" is the indirect object of the sentence. In the sentence "John sent the recipe to Carla," we know that "the recipe" is the direct object, since it is what got sent. The beneficiary of the action, however, was "Carla," so "Carla" is the indirect object. The grammatical term *beneficiary* means "the one for or to whom something is done," and need not imply that the beneficiary profits from the action. In "That man made a threatening phone call to Cynthia," "Cynthia" is the beneficiary of the call in the grammatical sense, though she is certainly not "benefiting" in the sense of anything positive happening to her.

In the following sentences, both direct and indirect objects have been labeled:

The priest sent <u>a letter</u> to <u>his sister</u>.
                       direct     indirect
                       object     object

Mayor Robinson gave <u>an award</u> to <u>the heroic policeman</u>.
                            direct        indirect
                            object        object

The colonel ordered <u>extra rations</u> for <u>his exhausted troops</u>.
                         direct         indirect
                         object         object

The eager young executive presented <u>his ideas</u> to
                                       direct
                                       object

<u>the board of directors</u>.
    indirect
    object

From these and earlier examples, you can see that a sentence with an indirect object will normally also contain a direct object. You have probably also observed that indirect objects usually represent either people or animals—in other words, animate things. This is not always true, however. In the sentence "The remodeling provided extra space for the family room," the beneficiary is "the family room"—therefore, it is possible to have an inanimate indirect object.

## INDIRECT-OBJECT INVERSION

In the examples you have seen so far, a direct object has always preceded the indirect object. It is usually possible to switch the order of these two objects by employing a grammatical operation known as *indirect-object inversion*. This operation places the indirect object in front of the direct object, and deletes the preposition *to* or *for* which typically precedes the indirect object. This operation *in no way changes the meaning* of the sentence, however. The form of the sentence is the only thing affected. The indirect-object inversion operation, which you have used countless times, is illustrated as follows:

*Original Sentence Form:*

John sent the recipe to Carla.
           direct      indirect
           object      object

*Step 1:* The preposition and indirect object are placed in front of the direct object.

John sent to Carla the recipe
        indirect   direct
        object    object

*Step 2:* The preposition is deleted.

John sent to Carla the recipe.
        indirect   direct
        object    object

Here is a second example, this time involving the preposition *for*:

*Original Sentence Form:*

Wilbur bought a rose for his wife.
           direct    indirect
           object    object

*Step 1:* The preposition and indirect object are placed in front of the direct object.

Wilbur bought for <u>his wife</u> <u>a rose</u>.
                 indirect direct
               object  object

*Step 2:* The preposition is deleted.

Wilbur bought ~~for~~ <u>his wife</u> <u>a rose</u>.
               indirect direct
               object  object

It must be understood that indirect-object inversion is an optional procedure—sometimes we apply the procedure and sometimes we do not. We might say "I gave a message to Helen" on one occasion, but "I gave Helen a message" on another. We might say "I bought candy for the kids" one week and "I bought the kids candy" the next. The reason why we jump back and forth between these forms is not clear, but the fact is that we do.

There is one time when the rules of English do *not* permit indirect object inversion to take place. This occurs when the *direct object* is present in *pronoun* form. Consider the following sentence:

Paolo gave <u>it</u> to <u>the child</u>.
          direct   indirect
          object   object

Since the direct object is the pronoun *it*, indirect-object inversion cannot be successfully applied. You can *try* to apply it to sentences like this, but the resulting sentences always appear very awkward or unacceptable. If we applied indirect-object inversion to the preceding example, the resulting sentence would be the following:

*Paolo gave <u>the child</u> it.
           indirect direct
           object  object

Forcing the inversion operation on a sentence such as "I sent *it* to *her*" would yield *"I sent *her it*," and so forth.

Before leaving indirect-object inversion, we should point out that this grammatical operation can be useful in determining whether a given element is (or is not) an indirect object. Consider, for example, the following two sentences:

**1** She bought a steak for *her husband*.
**2** She bought a steak for *five dollars*.

"Her husband" seems to be the beneficiary of the purchase in the first sentence, but this could hardly be said for the "five dollars" in the second. It seems, therefore, that "her husband" is an indirect-object and that "five dollars" is not. Application of the indirect-object inversion confirms this impression, for in the first case we obtain a perfectly acceptable sentence—"She bought *her husband* a steak"—while in the second we end up with the ungrammatical (or at least nonsensical) *"She bought *five dollars* a steak." This practical test is not infallible, alas, as you will occasionally encounter legitimate indirect objects which, for reasons not fully understood, fail to invert successfully. When this happens, you will have to rely strictly on the semantic definition involving the concept of "beneficiary."

# OBJECTS IN THE EVERYDAY WORLD

Objects do not seem as marked by variation in the everyday world as do many other aspects of English grammar. One variation that is frequently encountered, however, is a childhood version of the indirect-object inversion operation. This variation is used by children who have learned inversion but have not yet learned the restriction concerning direct objects in pronoun form. As a result, these children switch the positions of the objects even when the direct object is a pronoun. This leads to sentences like *"I gave Billy it," *"Marjorie told her mommy it," and *"We sold Mark it." Often years will pass before a child who has learned indirect-object inversion also learns when not to use it: when the direct object is in pronoun form. As a result, you may hear this variation coming from children who are well along in their school years.

A second variation is found in British English, where it is acceptable to omit the preposition *to* when the direct object is *it* and the verb is *give*. This rule permits sentences such as "He gave it me," which in American English would have to appear as "He gave it *to* me."

# Exercises

I Underline all direct objects in the following sentences once, and all indirect objects twice. Some of the sentences might not contain any objects.

*Example:* Gertrude sent <u>Martha</u> <u>an invitation</u>.

1 The Curtis family harvested apples.
2 This dog is content.
3 The sheriff issued Tom a weapon.
4 Benjamin delivered flowers to Sandra.
5 Gustaf laughed loudly.
6 Elizabeth signed the contract.
7 The butcher set aside a roast for the elderly man.
8 Bill's father flew bombers during the war.
9 I bought the dog a bone.
10 Tenzing and Hillary climbed Mount Everest.
11 Mr. Goss fed the parrot.
12 Caesar conquered Gaul.
13 The new quarterback faked beautifully.
14 Bjorn was tired.
15 Switzerland sent relief to the stricken country.
16 Donelle left her sister a note.
17 The well ran dry.
18 Mr. Willsboro hid the knife.

II  Identify the underlined verbs in the following sentences as transitive (T) or intransitive (I).

*Examples:* Peter <u>cut</u> his finger.     <u>T</u>

            The crew <u>quit</u> early.     <u>I</u>

1 The irate customer <u>spoke</u> angrily.     _____

2 Little Jennifer <u>found</u> the missing key.     _____

3 Wilhelmina <u>collects</u> tropical fish.     _____

4 That horrible man just <u>chuckled</u>.     _____

5 Patty and Frank <u>danced</u> in a corner.     _____

6 Tony <u>washed</u> the dishes.     _____

7 I will <u>master</u> calculus yet.     _____

8 Almost everyone <u>hates</u> forest fires.     _____

9 The appointees <u>accepted</u> without protest.     _____

10 The Hernandez family <u>eats</u> outdoors in the summer-time.     _____

11 Dr. Schiller <u>treats</u> stroke victims.     _____

12 Forty villagers <u>harvested</u> the olives.     _____

**III** Apply indirect-object inversion to the following sentences and write the result. Where the inversion is not possible, write "not possible" and explain why.

*Example:* Julia sent some wine to her boyfriend.
Julia sent her boyfriend some wine.

1 Mrs. Henderson gave a new dress to her daughter.

2 Ed handed a hundred dollars to his bookie.

3 The coach bought dinner for the whole team.

4 Mabel always sends presents to her nieces.

5 The President sent it to the new champion.

6 Mr. Tracy offered a job to me.

7 Gregory bought it for his secretary.

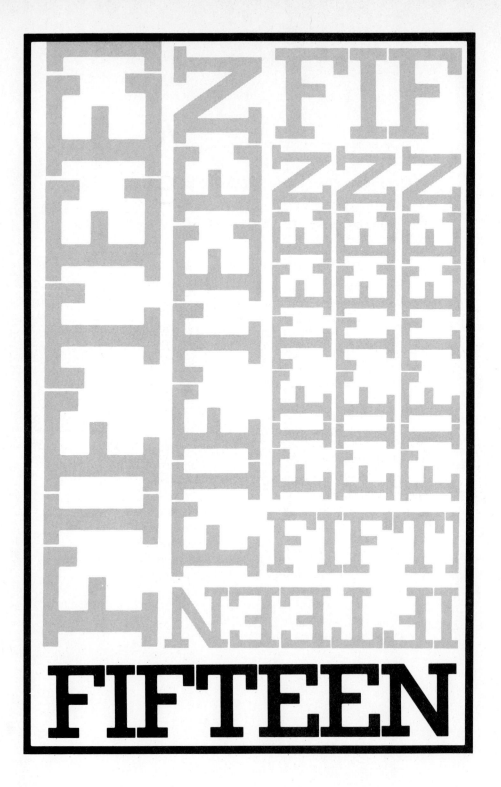

# Complements: Easier to Give than to Perceive

## COMPLEMENTS DEFINED

Many students of English grammar have trouble identifying complements, partly because they cannot distinguish them from objects. Since you have just finished a chapter on objects, some of these problems might not exist for you. Those that do, however, will be resolved once you have gained a clearer understanding of just what complements are.

First, some grammarians use the term *complement* to include direct and indirect objects, structures that follow transitive verbs. For now we will limit the term *complement* to:

1 adjectives in a predicate that *modify* either the subject or direct object of the sentence. Such adjectives are traditionally called *predicate adjectives*.
2 noun phrases in a predicate that *describe* (in different words) the same person or thing denoted by the subject or the direct object (you might even say they "rename" the subject or object). These noun phrases are called *predicate nouns*.

Let us first look at adjectives functioning as complements. They are illustrated in the following sentences.

## Adjectives which modify the subject

| Subject | Predicate |
|---------|-----------|
| Olaf | is irascible. |
| That old truck | was green. |
| My sister | is rich. |
| Clifford | becomes enraged easily. |

## Adjectives which modify the direct object

| Subject | Predicate | | |
|---------|-----------|--------|------------|
| | verb | object | complement |
| Jerome | called | them | idiotic. |
| Sandra | considered | her boss | very fair. |

Noun phrases functioning as complements can be seen in the next set of sentences. Note that in each example the noun phrase in the predicate renames the person or thing described by the subject or object.

## Noun phrases which refer to the subject

| Subject | Predicate |
|---------|-----------|
| Joseph | is my accountant. |
| A Pittsburgh teenager | is the current golf champion. |
| Rachel | was a great success. |
| Their leader | remained a tyrant. |

In the first example, "Joseph" and "my accountant" refer to the same individual, in the second sentence "A Pittsburgh teenager" and "the current golf champion" are one and the same person, and so forth. This kind of "shared reference" is the principal defining characteristic of noun-phrase complements.

**Noun phrases which refer to the direct object**

| Subject | Predicate | | |
|---|---|---|---|
| | verb | object | complement |
| The workers | considered | their boss | a fraud. |
| General Hayes | made | him | a colonel. |
| They | elected | her | president. |

In the first sentence, "their boss" and "a fraud" constitute two different ways of referring to the same individual. This is also true of "him" and "a colonel," and "her" and "president."

The complements that we have just presented may all be called *predicate complements*, since they occur in the predicate. Those that relate back to the subject are more specifically designated as *subject complements;* those that relate to the direct object, as *object complements*. We will now look at each of them in turn.

# SUBJECT COMPLEMENTS

*Subject complements* occur after *linking verbs* (also called *copulas*). You were introduced to *be*, one of the most common of the linking verbs, in Chapter 5. Others that occur frequently are *appear, feel, look, seem, smell, sound,* and *taste* (the "verbs of the senses"), and *become, get, go, grow, make, remain, turn,* and *weigh*. The following sentences are typical examples of how these linking verbs are used with subject complements. (The abbreviation "NP" stands for "noun phrase.")

Ruby was *ill*.   (adj.)
Ruth is *a monster*.   (NP)
The teacher appeared *grouchy*.   (adj.)
The teacher appeared *a grouch*.   (NP)
The surface felt *smooth*.   (adj.)
Rosemary looked *pregnant*.   (adj.)
Harry looked *a sight*.   (NP)

That problem seems *trivial.*   (adj.)
Carol seemed *his every desire.*   (NP)
The children grew *excited.*   (adj.)
She remained *a member of the board.*   (NP)
He weighs *150 pounds.*   (NP)
Manchester became *industrial.*   (adj.)
The sky became *a screeching demon.*   (NP)
Timmy got *sick.*   (adj.)
The invalid turned *green.*   (adj.)
That couple make *a perfect team.*   (NP)

Two verbs, *weigh* and *make*, can usually be followed only by complements that are noun phrases, while *smell, sound, taste, get, go,* and *turn* can usually be followed only by complements that are adjectives. Notice that the subject and the predicate noun must refer semantically to the same person or thing. If not—if the noun phrase in the predicate *cannot* be said to be the same as or in some way equivalent to the subject—then it is probably a direct or an indirect object. In a sentence such as "Someone smelled a skunk," for example, "someone" and "skunk" have no semantic identity. In this sentence "skunk" is the object of the action (smelling), so that "skunk" must be considered a direct object and "smelled" a transitive verb.

In addition to semantic identity and modification, subject complements have a number of other interesting characteristics. As you went through our list of sentences, perhaps you realized that the infinitive *to be* could be inserted between the verb and the subject complement in a few sentences. Doing so would lead to such sentences as the following:

The teacher appeared *to be* grouchy.
The teacher appeared *to be* a grouch.
That problem seems *to be* trivial.
Carol seemed *to be* his every desire.

In fact, two or three of these sentences probably sound better with the *to be*. That *to be* can be inserted before some complements will assume even more significance when we discuss object complements, for this characteristic of *to be* insertion can sometimes be helpful in distinguishing objects from complements. *To be* can *never* be inserted before objects.

Another characteristic of subject complements is that the sentences in which they occur cannot be passivized, since linking verbs do not take the passive voice. You cannot say *"A sight was looked by Harry," *"A screeching demon was become by the sky," or *"Green was turned by the invalid," for example. This passivization "test" will help you distinguish predicate adjectives from constructions that are actually past participles following some form of the auxiliary *be*. Consider these sentences:

The cake was *baked*.
The clothes were *pressed*.
The soldiers are *tired*.

The first two of these sentences can easily be considered passives that have undergone "subject deletion," since you can easily add an indefinite agent to them, giving "The cake was baked *by someone*" and "The clothes were pressed *by someone*." It is a different matter with the next sentence, however. *"The soldiers are tired *by someone*" is not a very acceptable passive, and we can conclude that *tired* is an adjective functioning as a complement.

There is yet another "test" that can help you distinguish these predicate adjectives from other constructions. It consists of placing the word *very* before what you suspect is a predicate adjective. Doing so with the first two sentences gives *"The cake was *very* baked" and *"The clothes were *very* pressed," which are not really good, idiomatic sentences. They are not good sentences because, although the word *very* can precede adjectives, it sounds awkward between an auxiliary and a past participle. Our judgment that *baked* and *pressed* are past participles rather than adjectives is again confirmed. In contrast, "The soldiers are *very* tired" is perfectly acceptable, confirming our earlier conclusion that *tired* is a subject complement (predicate adjective).

# OBJECT COMPLEMENTS

One of the major differences between subject complements and object complements is that the latter occur in predicates containing transitive verbs—after the object of that verb. Other than that, the two constructions act in very similar ways. The following sentences will illustrate:

| Subject | Predicate | | |
|---|---|---|---|
| | **verb** | **object** | **complement** |
| The boss | considered | him | obnoxious. (adj.) |
| The public | judged | the accused | guilty. (adj.) |
| Who | elected | him | president? (NP) |
| Madeline | called | Joan | the best contralto in the state. (NP) |

Notice that in these sentences modification or semantic identity relates to the object rather than the subject. Further, in all but the last of these sentences, it is possible to insert *to be* between the object and the complement. Both of these characteristics of object complements are important to remember, since they can help you distinguish object complements from other constructions that resemble them. For example, at first glance you might think these sentences contain object complements:

Ms. McGill teaches them *mathematics*.
Randolf resembles Mike *the most*.
Tom confronts matters *head-on*.
Jacob always drives the car *slow*.

It would be difficult to argue that "them" and "mathematics" refer to the same person or thing in the first sentence, or that "Mike" and "the most" share semantic identity in the second. Nor can you insert *to be* between the noun phrases:

*Ms. McGill teaches them *to be* mathematics.
*Randolf resembles Mike *to be* the most.

We must conclude, then, that the first sentence has two objects in the predicate, while the second has an object, "Mike," followed by an adverbial, "the most." In the final two sentences we have object noun phrases, "matters" and "the car," followed by manner adverbials, "head-on" and "slow," with the latter lacking the *-ly* suffix that it often takes.

Since object complements follow a transitive verb and an object, sentences containing them can be passivized, unlike those containing subject complements:

He was considered *obnoxious* by *the boss*.
He was elected *president* by *whom*?

Notice that in the passive versions of these sentences the object complement, whether it is a predicate adjective or a predicate noun, directly follows the verb, while the object now functions grammatically as the subject. In no instance, however, could the object complement be made to function as the subject. *"President was elected him by whom?" is not a possible sentence.

# OUR NEXT-TO-THE-LAST WORD ON COMPLEMENTS

In the description of complements that we just provided, we deliberately gave examples with adjectives or noun phrases as complements. In actuality, you can find a number of different constructions functioning as complements, including infinitives, gerunds, and clauses. Some of these complements will be looked at in later chapters.

# COMPLEMENTS IN THE EVERYDAY WORLD

Perhaps the most obvious fact about complements in the everyday world is their frequency of occurrence. Linking verbs are frequently used because they are so necessary for talking about the world around us (at least so far as the English language is concerned). Furthermore, many of the verbs that take complements are the very ones that allow us to voice opinions, raise objections, or air our feelings. Think about how often during any one day you are likely to hear or make statements like the following:

You make me *happy*. (object complement)
She's becoming *hard-to-handle*. (subject complement)
I consider that *rude*. (object complement)
Why, your sauce is *delicious!* (subject complement)
The boss sounds *mad*. (subject complement)
You seem *restless*. (subject complement)
That test was *hard*. (subject complement)

As you can see, complements are an important part of regular, day-to-day conversation.

# Exercises

Underline the complement in each of the following sentences, and write "SC" for a subject complement or "OC" for an object complement in the space to the right. If the sentence has no complement, write "NC."

*Examples:* Shirley is <u>ambitious</u>.       <u>SC</u>

             Amos considered the problem <u>trivial</u>.       <u>OC</u>

             Ben felt the material.       <u>NC</u>

1 The guide thought the stream impassable.       _____

2 The loser was furious.       _____

3 Strangers make Lucy uneasy.       _____

4 Eric called the suggestion dumb.       _____

5 Walter became an electrician.       _____

6 The clerk read the message.       _____

7 Louis mixed a drink.       _____

8 The bettors made the gray horse the favorite.       _____

9 Sandra is very upset.       _____

10 Her uncle was a billiards player.       _____

11 He looks peculiar.       _____

12 The new customer ordered a ham sandwich.       _____

13 Martin was tricked.       _____

14 The Spaniards were victorious.       _____

**15** We believed him incompetent.          _____

**16** Janice is a straight-A student.          _____

**17** The artist completed the mural quickly.          _____

**18** Our star player is extremely thin.          _____

**19** The problem was solved.          _____

**20** This exercise was easy.          _____

# Gerunds and Infinitives

## GERUNDS AND INFINITIVES DEFINED

Speakers of English will often take a verb form that has an *-ing* ending and use it as a noun instead of as a verb. When this happens, the form is called a *gerund*. We say that gerunds are "used" as nouns because they are made to perform some of the same functions that nouns perform—they act as subjects of sentences, as direct objects, and as complements. The *meanings* they communicate, however, are always those of verbs, since gerunds describe actions and states rather than name persons, places, things, or ideas, as nouns do. Several gerunds are shown in the following sentences:

> *Dancing* is good exercise. (subject)
> *Fishing* relaxes the soul. (subject)
> His *snoring* disturbed everyone. (subject)
> We enjoyed her *singing* very much. (object)
> Their *meddling* infuriated us. (subject)
> Pamela practices *juggling*. (object)
> Ray's hobby is *skiing*. (subject complement)

The *infinitive* is the simple or base form of a verb. Like a gerund, it does not carry tense or the third person singular *-s*, nor does it serve as the predicate of a sentence. Because it is used as a noun, an infinitive can function as the subject of a sentence, an object, or a complement. An infinitive retains the *meaning* of a verb, just as a gerund does, describing actions and states rather than naming persons, places, things, and ideas. Unlike gerunds, however, infinitives cannot be preceded by possessive pronouns. Sentences such as *"His to snore disturbed everyone" are unacceptable.

While the infinitive is technically considered the simple form of the verb (e.g., *begin, jump, see, wonder*), infinitives are so frequently preceded by the preposition *to* (e.g., *to begin, to jump, to see, to wonder*) that in practice the *to + verb* combination is usually called "the infinitive." In this chapter, following custom, we will refer to the *to + verb* combination by that term. A sampling of infinitives can be seen in the following sentences:

*To travel* is fun. (subject)
*To forgive* is divine. (subject)
*To know* her is *to love* her. (subject and subject complement)
Sandra learned *to swim*. (object)
The pilot decided *to speak* Swahili. (object)
Bruno's intention is *to win*. (subject complement)

# GERUNDS AND INFINITIVES AS SUBJECTS

A *gerundive phrase*, composed of the gerund and any words associated with it, can act as the subject of a predicate, as in the following examples:

*Losing* infuriated the coach.
*Playing tennis* is very good exercise.
*Knowing one's limitations* can reduce frustration.
*His cutting class* eventually caught up with him.

An *infinitive phrase*, composed of the infinitive and any words associated with it, can also act as the subject of a predicate:

*To quit* would have been foolish.
*To climb mountains* requires courage.
*To accept the job* would mean moving to Florida.
*To eat well* is all he asks.

# GERUNDS AND INFINITIVES AS DIRECT OBJECTS

Both gerunds and infinitives are used as nouns in another way, too: they can serve as direct objects of transitive verbs. You can see gerundive and infinitive phrases playing this role in the following sentences:

She admits *cheating*.
We missed *living on the old farm*.

Ted Williams practiced *hitting* for several hours each day.
She tolerates his *gambling*.
Trevor forgot *to call*.
We arranged *to meet them*.
Carol promised *to try*.
Mayor Channing undertook *to streamline city government*.

# CHOOSING THE CORRECT DIRECT-OBJECT FORM

When you have a sentence containing a transitive verb, it is often necessary to decide which form—the gerund or the infinitive—to use as the direct object. With many verbs, the two *cannot* be interchanged. *Deny, enjoy,* and *finish*, for example, take the gerund but not the infinitive:

Acceptable:   Tony denied *stealing* the money.
Unacceptable:   *Tony denied *to steal* the money.
Acceptable:   I enjoy *playing* badminton.
Unacceptable:   *I enjoy *to play* badminton.
Acceptable:   We will finish *painting* soon.
Unacceptable:   *We will finish *to paint* soon.

A few other verbs that require the gerund are *avoid, consider, imagine, practice, resent, suggest,* and *understand*.

Some verbs, like *need, promise,* and *want*, accept only the infinitive—they cannot take the gerund:

Acceptable:   I need *to see* you.
Unacceptable:   *I need *seeing* you.
Acceptable:   She promised *to call* at six.
Unacceptable:   *She promised *calling* at six.
Acceptable:   They want *to try* Moroccan food.
Unacceptable:   *They want *trying* Moroccan food.

Other verbs in this category are *agree, decide, expect, forget, hope, pretend, refuse, tend,* and *wish*.

A few verbs, such as *let* and *make*, permit neither the gerund nor the *to* infinitive, requiring instead a sequence of *direct object + short infinitive* (the *short infinitive* is the infinitive without *to*). Thus, we have the following:

Acceptable:   My uncle made *me do* it.
Unacceptable:   *My uncle made *me to do* it.
Unacceptable:   *My uncle made *me doing* it.

Unacceptable: *My uncle made *to do* it.
Unacceptable: *My uncle made *doing* it.

At this point you may well wonder whether there is any rule that can predict which verbs take the gerund, which the infinitive, and which the object + short infinitive. The answer, regrettably, is "no." Grammarians have been unable, so far, to discover any semantic or formal property common to all and only the verbs which take just one of these three constructions. It appears that as children **we** learn the right combinations "by ear" and can therefore distinguish those combinations that sound "good" from those that do not.

The situation is not all bad, however. Some verbs will take both the gerund and the infinitive. *Begin, continue,* and *like* are in this category:

I began *thinking*.
I began *to think*.
Jan continued *working*.
Jan continued *to work*.
Her brother likes *playing* baseball.
Her brother likes *to play* baseball.

Some other verbs which behave in this way are *hate, love, prefer,* and *start*.

# GERUNDS AND INFINITIVES AS COMPLEMENTS

You have seen in Chapter 15 how nouns may serve as subject complements. Since gerunds and infinitives can be used as nouns, it should not surprise you that they can serve as subject complements as well.[1] In the following sentences, notice how the gerundive and infinitive phrases, like true noun complements, are equivalent to the subject:

Simon's need was *knowing that someone cared*.
Beth's hobby is *collecting butterflies*.
Inspector Berg's greatest joy is *arresting jewel thieves*.
Our only hope is *to beg for mercy*.
My father's greatest wish is *to see Cleveland win a World Series*.

_____
[1] Note that this chapter expands the list of constructions cited as complements in Chapter 15.

# GERUNDS AND INFINITIVES DO OTHER THINGS TOO

Besides functioning as subjects, objects, and complements, gerunds and infinitives frequently perform other jobs as well. Both gerunds and infinitives can be used in an adjectival sense to modify a noun. (True nouns can function adjectivally, also, as in "the *fire* department," where the noun *fire* modifies *department* by ruling out reference to the police, sanitation, or other kinds of departments). Gerunds become part of a prepositional phrase which functions adjectively; infinitives, on the other hand, are able to modify nouns directly. Observe in the following sentences how the gerunds and infinitives function to limit the meaning of a noun:

> Her knowledge *of typing* made college work much easier. ("Of typing" modifies the noun *knowledge*.)
> Carl's talent *for picking winners* became well known. ("For picking winners" modifies the noun *talent*.)
> Our intention *to visit Mexico* was complicating our plans. ("To visit Mexico" modifies the noun *intention*.)
> The attempt *to find witnesses* proved futile. ("To find witnesses" modifies the noun *attempt*.)

Gerunds and infinitives are also used in an adverbial sense; that is, they modify verbs, adjectives, and adverbs. Again, gerunds become part of a prepositional phrase which functions adverbially, while infinitives perform this modification directly. A few examples are given as follows:

> He suffered *without complaining*. ("Without complaining" modifies the verb *suffered*—it tells *how* the person suffered.)
> Aspirin is useful *for reducing fever*. ("For reducing fever" modifies the adjective *useful*—it tells in what manner the drug is useful.)
> We are ready *to leave*. ("To leave" modifies the adjective *ready*—it tells what the people are ready to do.)

# GERUNDS AND INFINITIVES
# IN THE EVERYDAY WORLD

If you have ever heard non-native speakers of English form sentences such as, *"I suggested to go to the store," *"I refused listening to him" or *"He made me to do it," you know that gerunds and infinitives can cause problems in the everyday world. Errors such as the ones just mentioned are caused by an inadequate working knowledge of which verbs take the gerund, which the infinitive, and so on. It is possible, of course, for non-native speakers to memorize lists explaining which verbs take which forms, and many textbooks dealing with English as a second language contain such lists. Being forced to refer to memorized lists while engaging in spontaneous conversation, however, is like trying to eat an apple while playing a flute, and most non-native speakers simply develop a sense of what sounds right and allow their "ear" to be their guide. The more exposure to English the non-native speaker experiences, the faster this sense of how to use gerunds and infinitives develops.

Then there is the issue of the "split infinitive," a problem not confined to non-native speakers of the language. "Thou shalt not split the infinitive" was a commandment articulated for centuries by prescriptivist teachers, grammarians, and other authorities on "proper" English. The act of splitting an infinitive is, like most other sins, easily committed—the transgressor merely places one or more modifiers between the preposition *to* and the simple form of the verb. The following sentences all contain split infinitives, but we warn you now that some of the sentences may sound just fine:

1 We planned to $\boxed{\text{thoroughly}}$ enjoy it. (*Thoroughly* splits the infinitive *to enjoy*.)
2 Dr. Hodges wanted to $\boxed{\text{seriously}}$ pursue the matter. (*Seriously* splits the infinitive *to pursue*.)
3 The President promised to $\boxed{\text{quickly}}$ name a successor. (*Quickly* splits the infinitive *to name*.)
4 Karen wants to $\boxed{\text{before the end of next month}}$ quit. ("Before the end of next month" splits the infinitive *to quit*.)
5 Pedro wanted to, $\boxed{\text{in spite of his shyness,}}$ ask Susan to the dance. ("In spite of his shyness" splits the infinitive *to ask*.)

You probably reacted to the first three sentences by thinking, "Golly, those don't sound bad at all." You are right, of course, and most modern grammarians recognize this fact. Contemporary prescriptive grammarians usually concede that there is nothing wrong with splitting an infinitive *provided that* doing so does not lead to awkwardness or confusion. By today's standards, then, the first three examples are acceptable Standard English sentences. The fourth and fifth examples, however, illustrate the kinds of problems that splitting an infinitive can give rise to. In both sentences, the infinitive is split not by a single word but by several. This "gross" splitting usually results in awkwardness and often in confusion. Such sentences would be improved by placing the modifiers entirely outside of the infinitive, as has been done in the following sentences:

4 Karen wants *to quit* before the end of next month.
5 In spite of his shyness, Pedro wanted *to ask* Susan to the dance.

# Exercises

I Underline and identify all gerundive, infinitive, and prepositional phrases in the following sentences.
Name the function (e.g., subject, direct object, subject complement, object of preposition, adjectival, or adverbial) that each phrase performs.

|  | Type of Phrase | Function |
|---|---|---|
| *Examples:* | | |
| Camping is an increasingly popular pastime. | gerundive | subject |
| Jennifer decided to call Mark. | infinitive | direct object |
| The couple dined without conversing. | prepositional | adverbial |

1 Larry tried selling the bicycle. _____ _____
2 Taking inventory requires three days. _____ _____
3 To continue seemed foolish. _____ _____
4 His reputation for screaming at employees was justified. _____ _____
5 The movement to declare independence gained strength. _____ _____
6 Maria's greatest pleasure is to help the young. _____ _____
7 Teaching requires sacrifice and dedication. _____ _____
8 The audience loved Michael's singing. _____ _____
9 Marcel was good at scoring goals. _____ _____

**10** Karen learned by making
mistakes. _____ _____

**11** An old Irish law prohibits fishing
in that stream. _____ _____

**12** The chief danger there is your
getting lost. _____ _____

**13** The old soldier had chosen to
remain in India. _____ _____

**14** To live comfortably costs money. _____ _____

**15** His whining drove Joan crazy. _____ _____

**16** Gregory enjoys acting. _____ _____

**17** That old judge is difficult to
outsmart. _____ _____

**18** Half the students threatened to
sue. _____ _____

**II** Place either the gerund or infinitive form of the verb *try* in·each of
the following blanks. Where both forms are possible, write "both."

*Examples:* They risked <u>trying</u> it.

Carol wants <u>to try</u> it.

We continued <u>both</u> it.

1 She managed _____ .

2 I will volunteer _____ .

3 We considered _____ it at night.

4 Joanne admitted _____ to steal the papers.

5 Sue promised _____ harder.

6 We prefer _____ it by ourselves.

7 The frightened students denied _____ it.

8 The executive mentioned _____ to find a replacement.

9 I am tempted _____ .

10 Paul and Gilbert started _____ seriously.

11 Everyone began _____ .

Exactly what determined whether the infinitive, the gerund, or both could be used in each sentence? _____

_____

_____

# SEVENTEEN

200

# Prepositions and Particles

## PREPOSITIONS AND THEIR USES

Prepositions are words like *at*, *for*, *from*, *in*, *of*, *to*, *under*, and *with*. Their primary function is to describe relationships that exist between elements in sentences. In the sentence "Geraldine went to the game *with* Robert," the preposition *with* indicates that the relationship between Geraldine and Robert was one of accompaniment. In "Hillary jumped *off* the train," the preposition *off* shows that the relationship between jumping and the train was one of direction, the jumping being away from the train rather than toward it or parallel to it. In the sentence "Stella died *from* fright," *from* tells us that the relationship between Stella's death and fright was one of causation—i.e., *from* makes clear that fright caused her death.

Some of the most common relationships described by prepositions are illustrated in the following sentences.

### Place Relationships

The family was *at* the church.
The dictionary is *on* the desk.
Our money stays *in* the bank.
Bill's new restaurant is *opposite* City Hall.
Your keys are *by* the vase.

### Direction Relationships

Our plane flew *toward* St. Louis.
We drove *past* Central Park.
Some people walked *out of* the theater.
Sam is bicycling *to* Portland.
The boat sailed *through* the channel.

## Time Relationships

> Dinner is served *at* six o'clock.
> We must finish *before* dark.
> T. S. Eliot was born *in* 1888.
> I'll meet you *on* Tuesday.

## Comparative Relationships

> This bread is *as* hard *as* a rock.
> My cousin looks *like* Gary Cooper.

## Accompaniment Relationships

> Phyllis went *with* Jane.
> White wines go *with* fish and poultry.

## Source Relationships

> This letter is *from* the Registrar's Office.
> Kathryn is *from* Ireland.
> That butterfly came *from* a tropical rain forest.
> The solution came *out of* the class discussions.

## Instrumental Relationships

> The infection was treated *with* penicillin. (Penicillin was the instrument used to treat the infection.)
> Enemy movements were monitored *by* radar. (Radar was the instrument used to monitor the enemy movements.)

## Purpose Relationships

> I have a device *for* measuring angles.
> Walter uses a gun *for* protection.
> Eight people applied *for* the job.

## Partition Relationships

> Some *of* my friends are agnostics. (The group of friends is divided, or "partitioned," into those who are agnostics and those who are not.)
> Many *of* us are worried. (The group is partitioned into those who are worried and those who are not.)
> A few *of* the horses show genuine promise. (The horses are partitioned into those with promise and those without it.)

## Attachment Relationships

The tip *of* the wing is painted blue.
The front *of* the book was stained.
The wind damaged a branch *of* the tree.

These are only a few of the many relationships which can be described by prepositions.

Prepositional phrases play various grammatical roles, the most common being adverbial, as in "Dorothy drove *toward the gate*," where the prepositional phrase modifies the verb *drove* by stipulating the direction of travel; and adjectival, as in "The man *with the golden umbrella* was here," where the prepositional phrase helps describe the noun *man*. Frequently both functions can be observed in the same sentence. In "She walked *to the end of the road*," "to the end" functions adverbially to modify the verb *walked*, while "of the road" functions adjectivally by modifying the noun *end*.

Prepositional phrases are frequently tied together in strings, probably because doing this yields a progressively more exact description. Examples of increasingly lengthy strings of successive prepositional phrases are shown as follows:

It was cold *at night*.   (one prepositional phrase)
It was cold *at night in the forest*.   (two successive prepositional phrases)
It was cold *at night in the forest near Basel*.   (three successive prepositional phrases)
It was cold *at night in the forest on the estate near Basel*.   (four successive prepositional phrases)

# PARTICLES

Some words in English look like prepositions but do not act the part, either semantically or grammatically. These words are called *particles*. To understand the difference between particles and prepositions, it is helpful to compare the two directly. As you study the following sentences, pay particular attention to the role played by the word *in*:

Mary studied *in* the library.
The police kicked *in* the door.

Many people, after a bit of thought, will remark that *in* seems more closely associated with the verb in the second sentence than it does in the first. The words "kicked in" seem to constitute a kind of semantic unit, to "belong together" in a way that the words "studied in" do not. This feeling is confirmed when people are asked to divide the two sentences into their natural constituents. Most feel comfortable with an analysis of the first sentence which yields the following:

| Mary | studied | in the library. |

If the second sentence is divided in the same way, however, the result is not as satisfying:

| The police | kicked | in the door. |

Since *in* is felt to be associated with the verb, a better analysis would be the following:

| The police | kicked in | the door. |

Because of this strong association with the verb, the word *in* is classified as a *particle* in the second sentence. In the first sentence *in* does not have the same semantic tie to the verb, and for this reason it is a preposition.

There is more to the distinction between particles and prepositions than this, however. A second difference is that particles, unlike prepositions, can be moved to the other side of the direct object, through an operation known as *particle movement*. This operation is illustrated as follows:

Before Particle Movement:   The police kicked in the door.
After Particle Movement:   The police kicked ⎯⎯ the door in.

Through particle movement, the sentence "The police kicked in the door" may be transformed into the sentence "The police kicked the door in." Both forms are entirely acceptable; and both mean exactly the same thing.

By contrast, prepositions cannot be moved to the other side of the noun phrase, as the following demonstration illustrates:

Before Movement:   Mary studied in the library.
After Movement:   *Mary studied ⎯⎯ the library in.

The resulting sentence, *"Mary studied the library in," is obviously unacceptable. Here are some more examples. It is apparent from each that the particle can be moved successfully, whereas the preposition cannot:

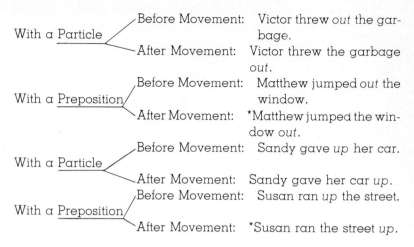

With a Particle
   Before Movement:   Victor threw *out* the garbage.
   After Movement:   Victor threw the garbage *out*.

With a Preposition
   Before Movement:   Matthew jumped *out* the window.
   After Movement:   *Matthew jumped the window *out*.

With a Particle
   Before Movement:   Sandy gave *up* her car.
   After Movement:   Sandy gave her car *up*.

With a Preposition
   Before Movement:   Susan ran *up* the street.
   After Movement:   *Susan ran the street *up*.

Remember, then, that particles are semantically bound to the verb and can be moved to the other side of the direct object. In addition, we might point out that particles are usually pronounced with greater emphasis than prepositions. For example, *in* is more heavily stressed in "The police kicked in the door" than it is in "Mary studied in the library."

Before leaving the subject of particles, a last observation should be made. In the examples given so far, the particle movement has been entirely optional; in other words, the sentences with particles have been acceptable regardless of whether the particle has been moved or not. There is one exception, however, and that occurs when the direct object happens to be a pronoun. In this circumstance, the particle movement *must* take place in order to make the sentence acceptable. The following examples will illustrate:

Particle Not Moved:   *The police kicked *in* it.
Particle Moved:   The police kicked it *in*.
Particle Not Moved:   *Rosemary threw *out* him.
Particle Moved:   Rosemary threw him *out*.
Particle Not Moved:   *Jack helped *up* her.
Particle Moved:   Jack helped her *up*.

# PREPOSITIONS AND PARTICLES IN THE EVERYDAY WORLD

Non-native speakers probably have more trouble mastering prepositions than any other aspect of the English language. This is partly because the rules governing prepositions are quite complex—far more complex than they appear to native speakers, who use prepositions easily and frequently and scarcely give them a second thought. To see just how involved the preposition rules can become, however, consider a few of the rules for relationships of time. We must use *in* when we refer to a year or month (*in* 1942, *in* July), but shift to *on* for days (*on* Monday, *on* April 11), then switch to *at* when referring to minutes or hours (*at* 9:00 A.M., *at* noon). As for relationships of place, we use *in* for our city (*in* San Francisco), *on* for our street (*on* Birch Avenue), and *at* for our numbered address (*at* 114 Birch Avenue).

A different set of rules affects prepositional use with verbs and adjectives. We say things like "I got *to* Denver at noon," but we cannot say *I arrived *to* Denver at noon." With *arrive*, we must use the preposition *at* or *in*. We say we are impatient *with* someone but never *at* someone, even though we do say we are impatient *at* things and situations. We can also be angry *at* or happy *for* someone, but never angry *for* or happy *at* someone. And so it goes, with literally thousands of these fine points waiting to trip up any user of our language.

Prepositions are also troublesome for non-native speakers in that they do not always mean what the standard dictionary definitions say they mean. For example, a standard definition of *on* is "in contact with the surface of something," as in "The book is *on* the desk" or "The picture is *on* the wall." Yet in the sentence "We have supplies *on* hand," the supplies are certainly not on the surface of the hand and may not even be within reach of the hand. Or take the preposition *up*. This preposition usually refers to a higher position, as in "The girls are walking *up* the hill." But in the sentence "Harry is *up* to something," no reference is being made to height at all. As you might imagine, non-native speakers often assign standard meanings to prepositions at times when these meanings are not applicable, with misinterpretation the result.

Furthermore, prepositions are often a part of entire constructions which are not intended for literal interpretation. Unsuspecting non-native speakers sometimes accept these constructions at face value with, once again, misinterpretation resulting. Just think how confused *you* would become if you interpreted the following constructions literally:

Stay *on your toes.*
He won't *hold it against you.*
She'd like *to get in touch with you.*
They will *bend over backwards* to help you.
*Take hold of yourself.*

Take this *with a grain of salt*.
I really *put my foot in it*.
He really *takes after* his mother.
I *don't think much of* him.
They'll try *to pull the wool over your eyes*.

The authors have personally witnessed many such instances of misinterpreted idiomatic expressions, but two of them may be worth describing in detail here. The first involved a student from Asia whose American friend had invited him to "drop over sometime." This remark was interpreted literally, in the sense that he should physically keel over, as in "drop dead." Needless to say, the friendship was greatly strained until the idiomatic meaning of "drop over" was finally made clear. The other concerned a female university student still in the process of learning English. One of this student's professors, during an advising session, told her that he thought she was "in good shape." Taking this comment literally, the student thought this a bold compliment about her body. As she learned later, the professor was actually referring to her grades.

Where particles are concerned, the most apparent deviation from standard usage is probably found among young children, who frequently make statements such as *"She knocked down it," *"He threw up it," or *"They threw away it." Children speak like this when they have not yet mastered particle movement, or when they have not learned that particle movement is mandatory when the direct object is a pronoun. Eventually, of course, these children do learn to use particle movement correctly.

We could not end this chapter on prepositions without commenting, however briefly, on the persistent belief that it is not "proper" to end a sentence with a preposition. This belief stems from a now defunct prescriptive rule, and while the rule is no longer a part of prescriptive grammar, it is still faithfully followed by some members of the public. Today's prescriptive grammarians realize that there is nothing inherently awkward about ending a sentence with a preposition, and they also know that the attempt to avoid terminal prepositions can actually encourage awkwardness as, for example, in the sentence "For what are you looking?" The act of writing well is difficult enough without being further complicated by prescriptive rules that are no longer "on the books."

# Exercises

I Underline the prepositions in the following sentences, and indicate whether the relationship being described is one of place, direction, time, comparison, accompaniment, source, instrument, purpose, partition, or attachment.

*Example:* Manuel drove <u>around</u> the block.                                     direction

1 We started a club for bridge players.                                          _____

2 The motorcycle gang raced through the town.                              _____

3 Quite a few of the cars were damaged.                                        _____

4 That phone booth is near my father's office.                              _____

5 The top of the mountain is almost flat.                                       _____

6 Call me after lunch.                                                                  _____

7 We sampled a wine from Madeira.                                               _____

8 He runs like a penguin.                                                            _____

9 The demolition crew leveled the old bridge with dynamite.                                                               _____

10 Mr. Lim traveled with his secretary.                                          _____

11 The huge diamond was cut by a special chisel.                         _____

12 The battle occurred at Sharpsburg.                                           _____

13 A card came with each gift.                                                      _____

14 The frightened children ran from me.                                        _____

15 Molly received a small yacht on her birthday.                          _____

16 The door of the house was wide open.                                       _____

**17** Our teacher is as mad as a hornet.    _____

**18** Many of the children love their music teacher.    _____

**19** Mr. Harris donated a million dollars for a new civic center.    _____

**20** The invaders came from outer space.    _____

**II** Apply particle movement to each of the following sentences. Indicate whether the movement is optional or required in each case.

*Example:* The amateur boxer knocked out his opponent.

The amateur boxer knocked his opponent out.    optional

**1** Aimee put on her new dress.

_____    _____

**2** The bandits tied up him.

_____    _____

**3** I will hand in the assignment.

_____    _____

**4** Karen made up an excuse.

_____    _____

**5** The young policeman turned in his badge.

_____    _____

**6** Roger decided to look up his old roommate.

_____    _____

**7** Four hikers put out the fire.

_____    _____

**8** Please let in them.

_____    _____

**9** We covered up it.

_____    _____

**10** The aides sent in some refreshments.

_____    _____

In some of the preceding sentences, particle movement was required. Why? _____

_____

_____

_____

**III** Using the semantic and grammatical tests described in this chapter, determine whether the underlined words in the following sentences are prepositions or particles.

*Examples:* The young couple strolled <u>up</u> the avenue.     <u>preposition</u>

     Peter made <u>up</u> the story.     <u>particle </u>

1 We have sent <u>out</u> all the letters.     _____

2 Several people brought <u>up</u> that subject.     _____

3 Shawn slid <u>off</u> the chair.     _____

**4** The bomber flew <u>over</u> Labrador.   _____

**5** The soldier struggled <u>up</u> the steep embankment.   _____

**6** Scott tried <u>on</u> a pair of Italian shoes.   _____

**7** John returned <u>in</u> an hour.   _____

**8** Everyone rushed <u>out</u> the door.   _____

**9** Please turn <u>off</u> the water.   _____

**10** I will leave <u>on</u> the third of April.   _____

# EIGHTEEN

212

# Expletives: Much Ado about Nothing

## EXPLETIVES DEFINED

Although English requires that a grammatical subject physically precede the predicate in all declarative sentences, it does not require that the subject possess any intrinsic meaning. Meaningless grammatical subjects occur frequently and they are known as *expletives*.[1] Two words function as expletives in English—*it* and *there*—both of which are also used in other ways (*it* as a pronoun and *there* as an adverb and noun). In the following examples, *it* and *there* function as expletives. Observe how these words by themselves do not convey any particular meaning:

> *It*'s noisy in here.
> *It*'s getting dark now.
> *It* was raining yesterday.
> *There*'s a shipment on the way.
> *There* was joy in their hearts.
> *There*'s always hope.

In the next set of examples, you will find these expletives contrasted with the pronoun *it* and the adverb and noun *there*. It should be clear that, unlike the expletives, the pronoun, adverb, and noun possess a specific, definable semantic content:

[1] This constitutes the grammatical definition of an expletive, but the term is also used to refer to any profane or obscene exclamation.

Expletive *It*:   *It* is chilly in here. (*It* has no specific reference.)

Pronoun *It*:   That car is Julie's. *It* cost her $10,000. (*It* means "the car.")

Expletive *There*:   *There* was joy in their hearts. (*There* has no specific reference.)

Adverb *There*:   I asked her to meet me *there*. (*There* means "at that location.")

Noun *There*:   *There* is where we will build our dream house. (*There* means "that place.")

Though both expletives are essentially meaningless, this does not mean that they are freely interchangeable. The expletive *it* is used primarily before adjectives and verbs to describe environmental conditions, as in "*It*'s quiet here at night," or "*It* always snows in Minnesota." *There*, on the other hand, is usually followed by a noun phrase, and this noun phrase need not refer to the environment, although, of course, it can, as in "*There*'s a mouse in the pantry," "*There*'s a chance of rain," or "*There* exist certain problems that defy solution."

# *THERE* INSERTION

The expletives *it* and *there* differ in yet another way. Unlike *it*, the presence of *there* in a sentence can be explained by a grammatical procedure called *there insertion*. This operation does not change the meaning of a sentence; it simply alters the form. Since the operation is also optional, the new sentence may be regarded as a stylistic variation of the original.

Specifically, *there* insertion may be applied to most sentences which contain the sequence indefinite subject + *be* + verb or prepositional phrase. Predictably not all sentences of this configuration are subject to *there* insertion, and some sentences which lack the verb or prepositional phrase take *there* insertion anyway. As with passivization, the only way we can be certain whether *there* insertion will apply to a particular sentence is to try it and see.

To perform *there* insertion, one simply moves the subject of the sentence to the other side of *be* and inserts *there* in the subject position. This procedure is illustrated as follows:

Before *There* Insertion:    A skunk          is          on the porch.
                              indefinite       *be*        prepositional
                              subject                      phrase

*There* Insertion:

Step 1:  The subject is moved to the other side
of *be*.

—————— is <u>a skunk</u> on the porch.

Step 2:  The expletive *there* is inserted in the
original subject position.

<u>There</u> is a skunk on the porch.

By employing *there* insertion, we have recast "A skunk is on the porch" into the synonymous form "There is a skunk on the porch." Here is another example:

Before *There* Insertion:  <u>A famous countess</u> <u>was</u> <u>attending</u> that
        indefinite       *be*     verb
        subject
    night.

*There* Insertion:

Step 1:  The subject is moved to the other side of
*be*.

—————— was <u>a famous countess</u> attending that
night.

Step 2:  The expletive *there* is inserted in
the original subject position.

<u>There</u> was a famous countess attending that
night.

Here we have converted the sentence "A famous countess was attending that night" into "There was a famous countess attending that night." More conversions are shown in the following examples:

Before *there* insertion:   A dictionary is on the desk.
After *there* insertion:   There is a dictionary on the desk.
Before *there* insertion:   Several police officers were directing
        traffic.
After *there* insertion:   There were several police officers directing
        traffic.
Before *there* insertion:   A client is with Mr. Jones now.
After *there* insertion:   There is a client with Mr. Jones now.

The choice of whether we wish to express a sentence one way or the other is strictly ours to make, though the decision is usually made unconsciously. When deliberate decisions are called for, as, for example, in formal writing, the achievement of both variety and smoothness is apt to be an important consideration.

Not all sentences which contain the expletive *there* are the direct result of the *there* insertion operation. Sentences like "There are two possibilities" and "There was a large explosion" probably derive from "Two possibilities exist" and "A large explosion occurred." A preliminary step is required to substitute *be* for the verbs *exist* and *occur*, after which *there* insertion applies in the normal manner.

It is also important to realize that definite subjects rarely undergo *there* insertion. Consider the sentence "The student is one of a kind." Following the first step of *there* insertion would give the following:

is *the student* one of a kind

The second step would give the following:

*There is the student one of a kind.

The result is obviously not an acceptable English sentence because "the student" is a *definite*, not an indefinite, subject.

# AGREEMENT AND THE EXPLETIVE *THERE*

In sentences with the expletive *there*, *be* agrees with the original subject, even though this subject appears after *be* rather than before it. This agreement can be seen operating in the following examples:

There is a cat outside. (i.e., "A cat is outside.")
　　　　original
　　　　subject

There were six judges in the building. (i.e., "Six judges were in the building.")
　　　　original
　　　　subject

There are several flies on the screen. (i.e., "Several flies are on the screen.")
　　　　original
　　　　subject

There was a telephone ringing. (i.e., "A telephone was ringing.")
　　　　original
　　　　subject

# EXPLETIVES IN THE EVERYDAY WORLD

It is not unusual to hear people employing the expletive *it* in sentences where Standard English requires the expletive *there*. A usage most common in the South, it can also be heard in other regions, particularly in inner-city areas where large numbers of residents have roots in the South and continue to use Southern speech forms. This feature is illustrated in the following examples, together with the Standard English equivalents:

Standard Form:  *There*'s a man downstairs.
*It* Form:  *It*'s a man downstairs.
Standard Form:  *There*'s nothing to it.
*It* Form:  *It*'s nothin' to it.
Standard Form: *There*'s another tree behind the house.
*It* Form: *It*'s another tree behind the house.
Standard Form: *There* were some fish in the freezer.
*It* Form: *It* was some fish in the freezer.

Another observation concerning expletives pertains to English as it is sometimes used by Spanish speakers. Spanish does not require that a visible subject or expletive invariably precede the predicate in declarative sentences; therefore, Spanish speakers may use verbs to begin declarative sentences *if* the context, the verb ending, or a specific reference later in the sentence makes the intended subject clear. A Spanish speaker who does not have complete control of English will sometimes carry the Spanish pattern into English, creating sentences such as *"Is raining," *"Was a man at the door," and *"Is so much to do." This kind of error usually begins to disappear when the speaker realizes that English requires that either a subject or an expletive be *physically* present (not just "implied") before the predicate of every declarative sentence.

Finally, some people make the mistake of using the singular verb with the expletive in situations where Standard English requires the plural. This practice leads to incorrect sentences such as *"There *was* several cars parked in the driveway," *"There *was* thirty people standing in line," or *"There's several things we've got to buy." The notion that the verb must agree with the actual subject rather than with the expletive is not difficult to grasp once it is pointed out, however. After that, a bit of coaching generally solves the problem.

# Exercises

I Identify each of the underlined words in the following sentences as an adverb, a noun, a pronoun, or an expletive.

*Example:* We saw him <u>there</u> last night.　　　　<u>adverb</u>

1 <u>It</u>'s becoming unbearably hot outside.　　　_____

2 <u>There</u> is where I left my purse.　　　　_____

3 Let's go outside. <u>It</u>'s stuffy in here.　　　_____

4 I bought this desk yesterday. <u>It</u>'s beautiful, isn't it?　_____

5 A new storm is on the way. <u>It</u>'s going to arrive tonight.　_____

6 <u>There</u>'s a new tenant next door.　　　_____

7 Get out your skis. <u>It</u>'s going to snow this weekend.　_____

8 George Washington stayed <u>there</u> all winter.　_____

9 <u>There</u> was some dissatisfaction with the verdict.　_____

10 <u>There</u> were hundreds of otters playing amid the seaweed.　_____

**II** Apply *there* insertion to the following sentences.

*Example:* A glass is on the counter.

There's a glass on the counter.

1 A small dog is inside that car.

_____

2 A ship is leaving tonight.

_____

3 A stork is nesting on their chimney.

_____

4 A rattlesnake is directly in front of you.

_____

5 A good restaurant is just around the corner.

_____

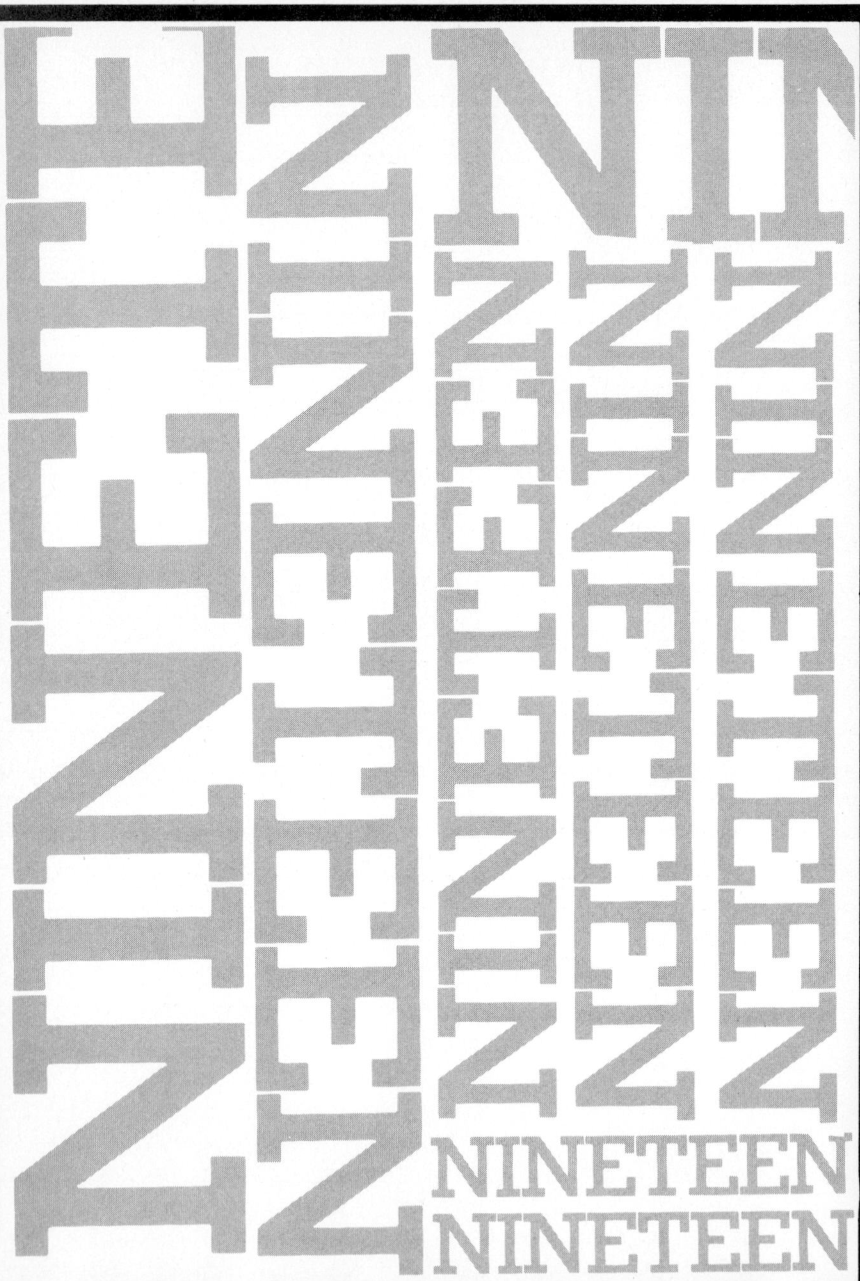


# NINETEEN

# Clauses: Variations on a Common Theme

## WHAT IS A CLAUSE?

A *clause* is any grammatical construction which contains a subject-predicate relationship. Several clauses are shown in the following list. Note that while some of these clauses can function as complete sentences and some cannot, all are alike in possessing both a subject and a predicate.

|  | *Subject* | *Predicate* |
|---|---|---|
| before | the dance | ended |
| whom | I | visited |
|  | the new boss | pleased everyone |
|  | Karen | danced all night |
| that | tickets | went on sale |
| because | my sister | speaks Finnish |
|  | our coach | is a perfectionist |

## INDEPENDENT AND DEPENDENT CLAUSES

Some clauses are capable of standing alone as sentences. Of the preceding examples, "the new boss pleased everyone," "Karen danced all night," and "our coach is a perfectionist" share this ability. Clauses like these are called *independent* (or *main*) clauses. Other clauses cannot stand by themselves as complete sentences. Clauses such as "before the dance ended," "whom I visited," "that tickets went on sale," and "because my sister speaks Finnish" are of this type. These are called *dependent* (or *subordinate*) clauses and must always be attached to an independent clause, as shown in the following examples:

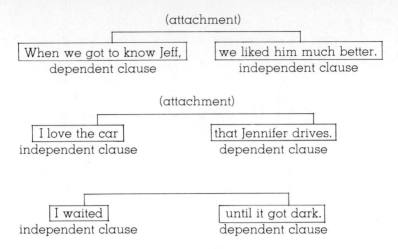

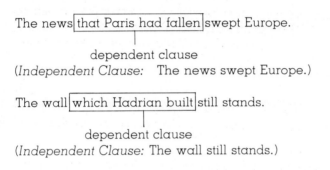

Sometimes the dependent clause is attached by being placed in the middle of an independent clause, as in the following examples:

The news that Paris had fallen swept Europe.

dependent clause

(*Independent Clause:* The news swept Europe.)

The wall which Hadrian built still stands.

dependent clause

(*Independent Clause:* The wall still stands.)

The important thing to remember is this—independent clauses can stand by themselves as complete sentences, while dependent clauses cannot. Consequently, dependent clauses are always attached to independent clauses.

# TYPES OF DEPENDENT CLAUSES

## The Adverbial Clause

There are three main kinds of dependent clauses in English. One is the *adverbial* clause, which modifies either the entire independent clause or its predicate. It is easy to spot an adverbial clause, since it always begins with a word called a *subordinator*. The most common subordinators are *after, although, as soon as, because, before, by the time, even though, ever since, if, just as, since, when, whenever, while, unless,* and *until*. The following sentences all contain adverbial clauses. Observe that the adverbial clauses may precede or follow the independent clause, and that it is even possible to place them in the middle of the independent clause.

*Unless she shows some interest*, he will never ask her out.
*Although the game was over*, the fans remained at the stadium.
*Whenever it rains*, this street becomes flooded.
Derek became a new person *after he met Ann*.
We were late *because we had a flat tire*.
The woman succeeded, *even though her friends had said success was impossible*.
My father, *when he was a student in Canada*, came to appreciate that nation's immense resources.

## The Noun Clause

The second principal type of dependent clause is the *noun clause*. Noun clauses begin with the introductory conjunction *that*, and receive their name from the fact that they perform the same functions that nouns do. In the following examples, you will see noun clauses performing as subjects, direct objects, and subject complements.[1]

### NOUN CLAUSE AS SUBJECT

*That Margaret chose to marry Felix* was a real surprise.
*That the horse was totally outclassed* did not seem to bother its owner.

Sentences which have noun clauses functioning as subjects are usually alternate forms of sentences such as these:

It was a real surprise *that Margaret chose to marry Felix*.
It did not seem to matter to the owner *that the horse was totally outclassed*.

Through a process known as *extraposition*, the noun clauses can be brought forward to replace the word *it*, with the result that the noun clauses themselves become the subjects of the sentences.

### NOUN CLAUSE AS DIRECT OBJECT

I think *that most people are basically kind*.
Dominic said *that the vaccine was only partially effective*.
We believe *that Dick did it*.

[1] Note that this chapter expands the list of constructions cited as complements in Chapter 15.

When a noun clause functions as a direct object, the introductory conjunction *that* can usually be omitted, provided that no confusion results. Omitting the conjunction would give our examples the following alternative forms:

I think *most people are basically kind*.
Dominic said *the vaccine was only partially effective*.
We believe *Dick did it*.

## NOUN CLAUSE AS SUBJECT COMPLEMENT

My opinion is *that we should grant the request*.
His idea was *that each of us should contribute $5*.

A noun clause can also function as an *appositive*; i.e., it can be placed immediately next to the subject:

The belief *that money brings happiness* motivates many people.

# The Relative Clause

The *relative clause* is the third type of dependent clause. These clauses begin with one of the relative pronouns: *that, which, who, whom,* and *whose.* The following are a few sentences containing relative clauses:

The watch | that Joyce bought | cost $200.

The song | which Harold wrote | is becoming popular.

The man | who hired me | knows my father.

Dr. Jones is a person | whom my family respects |

I pitied the man | whose car had been stolen |

The most important fact about relative pronouns is that they *always* refer to the same person or thing named by a noun phrase elsewhere in the sentence. Partly because of this fact, many grammarians view sentences with relative clauses as if they were actually *two* complete sentences, one inserted within the other, with each sentence containing a noun phrase that is identical in reference to a noun phrase in the other. According to this approach, the sentence "The watch *that Joyce bought* cost $200" would be analyzed as two separate sentences: "The watch$_①$ cost $200" and "Joyce bought the watch$_①$"—with the symbol $①$ standing for "identity" and indicating that the watch which cost $200 is the same watch that Joyce bought. If you carefully consider the combined meaning of the two shorter sentences, you will find that this meaning is identical to the meaning of the longer sentence, "The watch that Joyce bought cost $200." It is this synonymity which leads some grammarians to believe that sentences with relative clauses are really derived from a combination of shorter sentences. Furthermore, this analysis is consistent with another apparent property of the English language, which is that most long and complex sentences are actually made up from combinations of shorter, simpler sentences. You will hear more of this idea in the next chapter.

Using the approach just described, the meaning of the sentence "The song *which Harold wrote* is becoming popular" would be viewed as a combination of these sentences:

**a**  The song$_i$ is becoming popular.
**b**  Harold wrote the song$_i$.

The same can be said for our third example, "The man *who hired me* knows my father." The meaning here is obtained by combining these sentences:

**a**  The man$_i$ knows my father.
**b**  The man$_i$ hired me.

In each case, the **a** sentence will end up as the independent clause, while the **b** sentence will become the relative clause.

By this time you may be thinking, "OK, I see that the two shorter sentences say the same thing as the longer sentence with the relative clause. But what's the point? Why bother with the two shorter sentences?" The answer here is that sentences with relative clauses constitute a complexity in the grammar of English, and on occasion this complexity causes problems for people as they write or speak the language. By using the two shorter sentences as a starting point, individuals can be shown, step by step, how to construct the longer sentences that contain relative clauses, and they can learn to get them right every time. The longer, more complex sentences are obtained by using a grammatical operation known, simply enough, as *relative-clause construction*. We shall look at this procedure now.

Sentences with relative clauses are constructed in three simple steps. Each step is illustrated as follows:

## RELATIVE-CLAUSE CONSTRUCTION PROCEDURE

*Illustrative Shorter Sentences:*
  **a**  The watch$_i$ cost $200.
  **b**  Joyce bought the watch $_i$

*Step 1:* Insert the second sentence (i.e., the **b** sentence) after the identical noun phrase in the first sentence (**a** sentence).

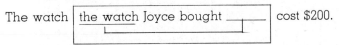

The watch ① | Joyce bought the watch | cost $200.

*Step 2:* Find the noun phrase in the **b** sentence which is identical with the noun phrase in the **a** sentence (in this case it is the watch). Move this noun phrase to the front of the **b** sentence.

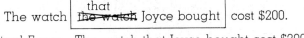

The watch | the watch Joyce bought _____ | cost $200.

*Step 3:* Replace the noun phrase at the front of the **b** sentence with the appropriate relative pronoun. (In this case either *that* or *which* is appropriate.)

The watch | ~~the watch~~ that Joyce bought | cost $200.

*Final Form:* The watch that Joyce bought cost $200.

As this procedure is probably new to you, we will go through it once more, using two other "shorter" sentences:

*Illustrative Shorter Sentences:*
    **a**   The song ① is becoming popular.
    **b**   Harold wrote the song ①.

*Step 1:* Insert the second sentence (**b** sentence) after the identical noun phrase in the first sentence (**a** sentence).

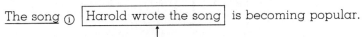

The song ① | Harold wrote the song | is becoming popular.

*Step 2:* Move the identical noun phrase in the **b** sentence to the front of the **b** sentence.

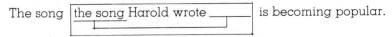

The song | the song Harold wrote _____ | is becoming popular.

*Step 3:* Replace the noun at the front of the **b** sentence with the appropriate relative pronoun. (The relative pronoun *that* is also appropriate in this sentence.)

The song | ~~the song~~ which Harold wrote | is becoming popular.

*Final Form:* The song which Harold wrote is becoming popular.

Often, the identical noun phrase is already at the front of the **b** sentence. In such a case, Step 2 is simply omitted.

*Illustrative Shorter Sentences:*

**a** The man ⓘ knows my father.
**b** The man ⓘ hired me.

*Step 1:* The man ⓘ | the man hired me | knows my father.

↑

*Step 2:* (omitted)

*Step 3:* The man | who ~~the man~~ hired me | knows my father.

*Final Form:* The man who hired me knows my father.

Sometimes the identical noun phrase in the **a** sentence functions as a direct object. When this happens, the **b** sentence ends up at the end of the **a** sentence, as in the following example:

*Illustrative Shorter Sentences:*

**a** We saw the mechanic ⓘ.
**b** The mechanic ⓘ gives free estimates.

Observe that the mechanic ⓘ functions as a direct object in the **a** sentence.

*Step 1:* Insert the second sentence (**b** sentence) after the identical noun phrase in the first sentence (**a** sentence).

We saw the mechanic ⓘ | the mechanic gives free estimates |

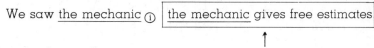

↑

*Step 2:* (omitted)

*Step 3:* Replace the noun phrase at the front of the **b** sentence with the appropriate relative pronoun. (The relative pronoun *that* is also appropriate in this sentence.)

We saw the mechanic | who ~~the mechanic~~ gives free estimates |

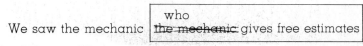

*Final Form:* We saw the mechanic who gives free estimates.

We will go through this procedure one more time, using another example:

*Illustrative Shorter Sentences:*

**a** I enjoyed the soup ⓘ.
**b** You made the soup ⓘ.

Observe that *the soup* ① functions as a direct object in the **a** sentence. The fact that it also functions as a direct object in the **b** sentence is not relevant.

*Step 1:* Insert the second sentence (**b** sentence) after the identical noun phrase in the first sentence (**a** sentence).

I enjoyed <u>the soup</u> ① | you made <u>the soup</u> |

*Step 2:* Move the identical noun phrase in the **b** sentence to the front of the **b** sentence.

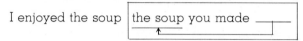

I enjoyed the soup | the soup you made ____ |

*Step 3:* Replace the noun phrase at the front of the **b** sentence with the appropriate relative pronoun. (The relative pronoun *which* is also appropriate in this sentence.)

I enjoyed the soup | that ~~the soup~~ you made |

*Final Form:* I enjoyed the soup that you made.

The third step in relative-clause construction calls for the selection of an "appropriate" relative pronoun. If the noun phrase being replaced refers to a person, then *who* or *whom* and *that* are appropriate choices (the *who/whom* distinction is dealt with later in this chapter). If the noun phrase being replaced refers to a thing, the choice must be either *which* or *that*. Only one relative pronoun, therefore, may refer either to persons or things. This is the pronoun *that*, and it is shown being used both ways in the following examples:

The teacher *that* I like best is Mrs. Marks. (*That* refers to a person.)
The house *that* we bought has a sauna. (*That* refers to a thing.)

The relative pronoun *whose* is used to replace an identical noun phrase indicating possession:

*Illustrative Shorter Sentences:*
    **a**  I pitied the man ①.
    **b**  The man ①'s car had been stolen.

*Step 1:* I pitied <u>the man</u> ① | <u>the man's</u> car had been stolen |

*Step 2:* (omitted)

Step 3:   I pitied the man whose car had been stolen

> *Step 3:*   I pitied the man | whose ~~the man's~~ car had been stolen |

*Final Form:*   I pitied the man whose car had been stolen.

The relative-clause construction procedures may seem a little strange to you at first, and for this reason they are covered extensively in the exercises at the end of this chapter. With a little practice, the procedures will become automatic, and you will be able to easily follow the relative clause presentations given in some of the elementary- and secondary-school texts (if you teach), and to help individuals who might benefit from perceiving relative clauses in this light.

## RESTRICTIVE AND NONRESTRICTIVE RELATIVE CLAUSES

The relative clauses we have used as examples in this chapter so far have all been *restrictive*, because they have "restricted" (i.e., limited) the identity of a noun phrase outside the relative clause. In order to focus on this concept of identity restriction, consider the sentence "The explorer who discovered Greenland was a Viking." The relative clause in this sentence, "who discovered Greenland," serves to restrict the identity of the noun phrase "the explorer," since it excludes from possible reference the explorer who discovered South America, the explorer who discovered Alaska, the explorer who discovered the Mississippi River, and so forth. The noun phrase "a Viking," which occurs at the end of the sentence, serves to restrict the identity of the explorer also, because it rules out Portuguese explorers, French explorers, English explorers, and others. But this is beside the point. As long as a relative clause helps to narrow down the identity of a noun phrase, it is considered a restrictive clause, even though other restricters may be present in the same sentence. As a further example, consider the sentence "The team which won the championship celebrated all night long." In this sentence, the relative clause "which won the championship" restricts the identity of "the team" by specifying which team we are talking about. We are referring to the championship team, not the second-place team, or the third-place team, or the cellar dweller. For this reason, the relative clause in this sentence is restrictive. As a final example, think about the sentence "The cars that Michael owns are all British imports." The relative clause "that Michael owns" narrows down the identity of "the cars" because it excludes reference to any cars *except* the ones which Michael owns. This, then, is another restrictive clause.

Restrictive relative clauses, you will note, are *not* set off by commas.

*Nonrestrictive* relative clauses, on the other hand, do not restrict (i.e., limit) the identity of a noun phrase outside the relative clause. In these clauses, the specific identity of the noun phrase is made sufficiently clear before the reader or listener sees or hears the relative clause. Observe how this is true in the following sentences:

> The state of Colorado, *which offers some of the best skiing in North America*, earns millions of tourist dollars annually.
> Louis Pasteur, *who discovered a means for preventing rabies*, was a careful and energetic researcher.

In the first example, the noun phrase "the state of Colorado" is so specific that the relative clause "which offers some of the best skiing in North America" does nothing to make the identity of Colorado any clearer. True, the relative clause provides us with additional information about Colorado, but *identity* is the crucial factor here, and since the relative clause does not help to narrow down the identity of "the state of Colorado," the clause must be considered nonrestrictive. The same is true of the relative clause "who discovered a means for preventing rabies" in the second sentence. This clause provides information about Louis Pasteur, but the information is not essential in identifying Mr. Pasteur. He has already been identified *by name* at the beginning of the sentence. The clause, therefore, is nonrestrictive.

Sometimes the identity of a noun phrase is sufficiently established in an earlier sentence. When this occurs, subsequent relative clauses which refer to this noun phrase will be nonrestrictive, a situation illustrated in the following sequence of sentences:

> When I was sixteen, I used to help repair my father's tractor. The tractor, *which was already ancient*, seemed to break down once or twice a week.

In the preceding example, the tractor is specifically identified in the first sentence, where it is made clear that the tractor being discussed is the one which belonged to the writer's father. The relative clause in the second sentence, then, does not serve to further restrict the identity of the tractor; therefore, it is nonrestrictive.

Nonrestrictive relative clauses cannot use *that* as a relative pronoun, and they are *always* set off by commas.

## REDUCING RELATIVE CLAUSES

Under certain well-defined conditions, it is possible to delete parts of a relative clause so that a shorter, *reduced* relative clause results. These deleting procedures change the form of a relative clause but do not change its meaning.

The first operation we will consider permits us to optionally delete the relative pronoun if (and *only* if) it is followed by the subject of the verb in a *restrictive* relative clause. This condition, plus the deletion itself, is shown in the following examples:

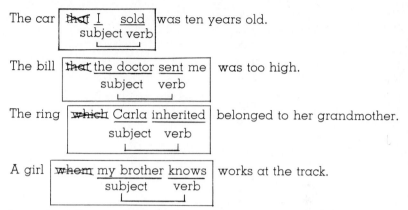

In each of these sentences, the relative pronoun is followed by the grammatical subject of the relative clause. In other words, a subject noun or pronoun exists between the relative pronoun and the verb in the relative clause. In the first sentence, the subject "I" stands between the relative pronoun *that* and the verb *sold*, in the second sentence the subject "the doctor" stands between the relative pronoun *that* and the verb *sent*, and so forth. Because of this condition, all the relative pronouns in the preceding examples are subject to deletion. Applying this deletion would leave us with the following sentence forms:

The car <u>I sold</u> was ten years old.
The bill <u>the doctor sent me</u> was too high.
The ring <u>Carla inherited</u> belonged to her grandmother.
A girl <u>my brother knows</u> works at the track.

The underlined part of each sentence is called a *reduced relative clause*, since the relative pronoun is missing. In conversation, the option to delete the relative pronoun is frequently taken, but in writing deletion is less common.

Whenever a grammatical subject is *not* present between the relative pronoun and the verb in the relative clause, the relative pronoun cannot be deleted:

The car | which | struck | me | was moving slowly.
relative | verb
pronoun

| The person | who | signed | the report | has left. |
|---|---|---|---|---|
| | relative pronoun | verb | | |

| A drug | which | costs | less | will soon be developed. |
|---|---|---|---|---|
| | relative pronoun | verb | | |

Deleting the relative pronoun under these conditions would result in the unacceptable sentences *"The car struck me was moving slowly," *"The person signed the report has left," and *"A drug costs less will soon be developed."

Another kind of relative-clause reduction may occur when a restrictive relative clause has the form relative pronoun + present tense of *be* + verb-*ing*, as in the following:

| The fire | which | is | burning | over there |
|---|---|---|---|---|
| | relative pronoun | present tense of *be* | verb-*ing* | |

is dangerous.

| The teacher | who | is | talking | to him now |
|---|---|---|---|---|
| | relative pronoun | present tense of *be* | verb-*ing* | |

is really mean.

In this situation, both the relative pronoun *and* the form of *be* may be deleted, leaving the following sentences:

The fire *burning over there* is dangerous.
The teacher *talking to him now* is really mean.

Another type of reduction operates on nonrestrictive relative clauses of the form relative pronoun + be + subject complement. Sentences which illustrate this pattern follow:

Admiral Ollo, *who was a great navigator*, served in three navies.
Linda Bast, *who is my dentist*, collects Brazilian butterflies.
Her uncle arrived in Montana aboard the *Empire Builder*, *which was a famous old passenger train*.
My father, *who was completely exhausted*, fell asleep at once.
The airplane, *which was white with red polka dots*, was the darling of the photographers.

Under these conditions, both the relative pronoun and *be* may be deleted, leaving the following:

Admiral Ollo, *a great navigator*, served in three navies.

Linda Bast, *my dentist*, collects Brazilian butterflies.

Her uncle arrived in Montana aboard the *Empire Builder*, a famous old passenger train.

My father, *completely exhausted*, fell asleep at once.

The airplane, *white with red polka dots*, was the darling of the photographers.

Such reduced nonrestrictive relative clauses are often called *appositives*.

All these optional reduction procedures allow us to shorten sentences and vary syntax without changing the meaning of our sentences in any way.

# CLAUSES IN THE EVERYDAY WORLD

When a person does not fully understand the essential facts about clauses, he or she can easily fall into the habit of writing *sentence fragments*. Sentence fragments occur whenever someone uses a dependent clause or part of an independent clause as if it were a complete sentence. This is one of the most common writing errors, and it can be found in student compositions at all educational levels. One type of sentence fragment is seen in the example *"Because I needed more money." Here the writer has used a single adverbial clause as if it constituted a complete sentence. Fragments like this can be remedied by attaching the dependent clause to an independent clause, so that a truly complete sentence results, such as *"Because I needed more money*, I took a second job" or "I took a second job *because I needed more money*."

Another kind of fragment is found in the example *"The man who phoned me." Here a relative clause, "who phoned me," is attached to the subject of what should be an independent clause. The predicate of that clause, however, is missing. In other words, the predicate of the **a** sentence has been omitted. This kind of fragment can be corrected by adding a predicate, as in "The man who phoned me *told a lie*." Because the predicate of the **a** sentence is now present, the sentence is truly complete. Both subject-predicate relationships are labeled in the following illustration:

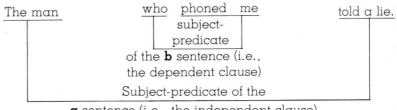

The man    who phoned me    told a lie.
subject-predicate
of the **b** sentence (i.e.,
the dependent clause)
Subject-predicate of the
**a** sentence (i.e., the independent clause)

Students who write this type of fragment are frequently helped by the relative-clause construction approach used in this chapter. In fact, sometimes the mere realization that two complete sentences underlie the meaning of sentences which contain relative clauses is sufficient to eliminate the problem.

Some writers of fragments will not use any clauses whatsoever in their fragments, their "sentences" being composed of phrases such as *"Being late for dinner," *"The teacher in the cafeteria," and so forth. Writers of these fragments are often helped by understanding that a sentence *must* (except for the imperative) contain both a visible subject and a complete verb tense. Once this concept is thoroughly grasped, these people can check each of the sentences they write to make sure that both the subject and complete verb tense are present.

It might be that sentence fragments appear frequently in writing because it *is* permissible to use fragments when answering questions orally. If asked, "Why did you do it?" it is perfectly acceptable to answer "Because I needed more money." If asked, "Who told you a lie?" we can answer "The man who phoned me." The answer to "Who gave you that?" might well be "The teacher in the cafeteria." Students must understand that while these constructions are permissible as oral responses, they cannot be treated as complete sentences in writing.

A second problem involving clauses concerns the matter of choosing between the relative pronouns *who* and *whom*. If you become a teacher, or if for other reasons people see that you are knowledgeable about English grammar, you will almost certainly be asked about this. The distinction between *who* and *whom* can be explained in several ways, but since most people are looking only for a simple test that will provide the correct pronoun each time, we suggest that you give them just that—a simple test—and try to avoid reference to "direct-object functions" and other more theoretical approaches, at least initially. The simplest test we know of is to determine whether a subject noun (or subject pronoun) follows the relative pronoun. If it does, then *whom* should be used; if not, the correct pronoun is *who*. In the following examples, you will see that a subject noun or pronoun *is* present, and that therefore the correct pronoun to use is *whom*.

The attorney *whom* $\boxed{I}$ *contacted* refused my case.

$\uparrow$
subject
pronoun

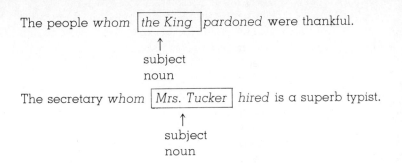

The people *whom* [the King] *pardoned* were thankful.

↑
subject
noun

The secretary *whom* [Mrs. Tucker] *hired* is a superb typist.

↑
subject
noun

In the next three sentences, you will find that a subject noun or personal pronoun does *not* follow the relative pronoun. Consequently, *who* is used.

The doctor *who treated me* is from India.
The person *who tutored Jim* charges very little.
The woman *who wrote this book* lives in Des Moines.

In practice, many people find it sufficient just to see what kind of word follows the relative pronoun. If a noun or pronoun immediately follows the relative pronoun, they use *whom*; if a verb follows the relative pronoun, they use *who*. This version of the test is extremely simple and will almost always provide the correct answer.

If the test just described does not satisfy the individual who is questioning you, then try to explain that *whom* represents the direct object in the relative clause (I contacted *the attorney*; the King pardoned *the people*; Mrs. Tucker hired *the secretary*), while *who* represents the subject (*the doctor* treated me; *the person* tutored Jim; *the woman* wrote the book). If this fails, have the individual make a question out of the relative clause (Who or whom did I contact? Who or whom did the King pardon? Who or whom did Mrs. Tucker hire?). If the answer to the question can contain an objective-case personal pronoun, such as *him, her, them,* or *us,* then *whom* is the correct relative pronoun for that relative clause. Since the answers to the preceding questions would be "I contacted *him*" (i.e., the attorney), "The King pardoned *them*" (i.e., the people), and "Mrs. Tucker hired *her*" (i.e., the secretary), *whom* is in fact the correct choice. On the other hand, the questions "Who treated me?", "Who tutored Jim?", and "Who wrote this book?" would be answered with *subject* pronouns—"*He* (or *she*) treated me," "*He* (or *she*) tutored Jim," and "*She* wrote the book." When this happens, the correct relative pronoun for the clause in question is *who.*

# Exercises

I  Draw boxes around the clauses found in the following sentences. Indicate beneath each box whether the clause is independent (I) or dependent (D). For dependent clauses, indicate in parentheses whether the clause is an adverbial clause (adv. c.), a noun clause (noun c.), or a relative clause (rel. c.).

*Examples:*

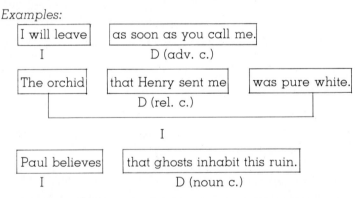

(Dependent clauses which begin with *that* are either noun clauses or relative clauses. If the sentence can be broken down into **a** and **b** sentences which share an identical noun phrase, the clause is a relative clause. Otherwise it is a noun clause. You might also try substituting *which*, *who*, or *whom* for *that*. If any of these substitutions work, then the clause is a relative clause. If all three substitutions result in unacceptable sentences, then the clause is a noun clause.)

**1** Even though Helen likes yellow, all her clothes are blue.

**2** While Judy sculpted, her husband continued to write.

**3** The lawyer argued that the motion was out of order.

**4** My mother likes the house that we bought.

**5** I will believe it when I see it.

**6** The radio which Lois fixed works perfectly.

**7** Wilbur climbs mountains because he enjoys the exercise.

**8** The salesperson who helped me gave me too much change.

**9** The idea that practice makes perfect can be very useful.

**10** Gloria lived in Texas before she came here.

**11** That no one was killed seemed miraculous.

**12** The course that Doris teaches is always well attended.

**13** The pipe that broke was very old.

**14** Gary fishes for trout whenever he visits Idaho.

**15** The agent hinted that his client might accept the offer.

**16** When Mark turned twenty, he was one of the most accomplished violinists in the country.

**17** The airport that Fernando designed has become famous.

**18** The dog which guards the house is really quite affectionate.

**19** Mary suspects that the car will soon quit running.

**20** The game will be canceled if it rains.

**II** Rewrite each of the following sentences so that the adverbial clause occupies a different position in the sentence.

*Example:* Before she left, Jackie bolted the rear door.
Jackie bolted the rear door before she left.

**1** Until we hear something definite, let's remain here.

_____

**2** Brenda toured the Middle East after she graduated.

_____

**3** Patty had dreamed of being a professional golfer ever since she was a child.

_____

_____

**4** If he really wanted to, he could do much better.

_____

**5** Whenever it rains, the chimney leaks.

_____

**6** The man was fully conscious by the time help arrived.

_____

**7** Until I see it myself, I'll never believe it.

_____

**8.** The children were busy raiding the refrigerator while their parents were playing cards.

_____

_____

**III** Use each of the following pairs of **a** and **b** sentences to construct a longer sentence which contains a relative clause. Remember to insert the **b** sentence into the **a** sentence, except when the identical noun phrase in the **a** sentence functions as a direct object. When this happens, you should place the **b** sentence after the **a** sentence.

_Examples:_ **a** The farm ⓘ is very profitable.
        **b** Frank sold the farm ⓘ.
        The farm that (or which) Frank sold is very profitable.

        **a** The crows ate the cornⓘ.
        **b** You planted the corn ⓘ.
        The crows ate the corn that (or which) you planted.

   **1 a** The truck ⓘ needs new tires.
      **b** Martin drives the truck ⓘ.

_____

**2 a** The fisherman ⓘ was ecstatic.
  **b.** The fisherman ⓘ caught the gigantic salmon.

---

**3 a** A book ⓘ contains fascinating photographs.
  **b** Peter found a book ⓘ.

---

**4 a** The computer ⓘ cannot be repaired.
  **b** The computer ⓘ broke down.

---

**5 a** The team ⓘ will return in April.
  **b** The team ⓘ beat us badly.

---

**6 a** I cherish the recipes ⓘ.
  **b** You sent me the recipes ⓘ.

---

**7 a** Karen installed the drapes ⓘ.
  **b** Her mother made the drapes ⓘ.

---

**8 a** The school ⓘ encourages the study of languages.
  **b** Sylvia attends the school ⓘ.

---

**9 a** The lieutenant ⓘ lives in Little Rock.
  **b** Julie likes the lieutenant ⓘ.

---

**10 a** The artist ⓘ understood human frailty.
  **b** The artist ⓘ painted this picture.

---

**11 a** A movie ⓘ is playing downtown.
  **b** A movie ⓘ sounds interesting.

---

**12 a** The person ⓘ received no thanks.
  **b** The person ⓘ helped them.

---

**13 a** Everyone respected the quarterback ⓘ.
  **b** The quarterback ⓘ refused to give up.

---

**14 a** The dog ⓘ became a champion.
  **b** Charlene trained the dog ⓘ.

---

**15 a** The comet ⓘ was truly spectacular.
  **b** Dr. Okada discovered the comet ⓘ.

_____

**16 a** I favor the solution ⓘ.
  **b** Dorothy suggests the solution ⓘ.

_____

**17 a** The wine ⓘ tastes delicious.
  **b** This island produces the wine ⓘ.

_____

**18 a** The building ⓘ had a weak foundation.
  **b** The building ⓘ collapsed.

_____

**19 a** The craftsman ⓘ received the contract.
  **b** The craftsman ⓘ did the best work.

_____

**20 a** Jean met the man ⓘ.
  **b** The man ⓘ wrote the book.

_____

**21 a** I met the woman ⓘ.
  **b** The woman ⓘ's husband knows the President.

_____

**22 a** We visited the captain ⓘ.
  **b** The captain ⓘ's ship had been saved.

_____

**IV** Reduce the relative clauses in the following sentences by applying the reduction rules cited in this chapter. Where a reduction is not possible, write "not possible" on the line. Remember that your deletions must not alter the meaning communicated by the relative clause in its full form.

_Examples:_  The street th~~at~~ they paved yesterday is still closed to traffic. _____

Any person w~~ho~~ ~~is~~ having a birthday will receive a free dinner. _____

The lion that roars loudest is usually hungriest. _not possible_

  **1** The problem which is bothering them now has no quick solution. _____

  **2** The violin that sounded best was from Austria. _____

**3** The dinner that Jill prepared was sensational. _____

**4** The film which we saw yesterday lasted five hours. _____

**5** The people who are living here seem exceptionally friendly. _____

**6** The horse which won the race belongs to Terry. _____

**7** The man who gave us directions seemed well informed. _____

**8** The coach, who was anxious about the welfare of his players, insisted that a physician travel with the team. _____

**9** The patient whom she treated recovered rapidly. _____

**10** An umbrella that someone forgot is on the desk. _____

**11** Dr. Cardin, who is the chairman of the Thoracic Surgery Committee, believes that the complaints are groundless. _____

**12** Anna always felt a longing for the village that she had left. _____

**13** Karen, who is my next-door neighbor, knows all the important people in town. _____

You should review the text, if necessary, to be sure you understand why the deletions above were possible.

**V** Copy each of the following sentences and insert the required commas around any relative clause that is nonrestrictive.

*Examples:* The door that Elmer installed is beginning to squeak.

The door that Elmer installed is beginning to squeak.

The planet Mars which appears red can be seen in the morning sky.

The planet Mars, which appears red, can be seen in

the morning sky.

**1** The Empire State Building which attracts thousands of tourists each year is located in New York.

_____

_____

**2** Mount Everest which was first climbed in 1953 has claimed the lives of many mountaineers.

_____

_____

**3** The building which my father owns does not have elevators.

_____

_____

**4** The mountain which we see to the south is called Old Grayback.

_____

_____

**5** Yesterday we went shopping for a new television set. The set which we liked best had a 25-inch screen. The price which includes delivery and installation is $900.

_____

_____

_____

_____

**6** I read a great book last night. The book which is only 200 pages long tells the story of a determined young hog farmer. The part which enthralled me the most described the complex psychology of hogs.

_____

_____

_____

_____

**VI** Insert either _who_ or _whom_ into each of the following sentences.

_Examples:_ The architect __who__ designed this building lives in Phoenix.

The singer __whom__ she prefers usually works in Las Vegas.

**1** The actor _____ he interviewed was very courteous.

**2** The electrician _____ checked the wire said it was all right.

**3** The fighter _____ won the match had a cut over one eye.

**4** The golfer _____ the oddsmakers favored was soundly beaten.

**5** Someone ＿＿＿＿ sells real estate left you a message.

**6** We visited a woman ＿＿＿＿ had known Queen Victoria.

**7** I talked with the computer analyst ＿＿＿＿ we had just hired.

**8** The man ＿＿＿＿ Nancy married is extremely handsome.

# Putting It
# All Together

In previous chapters we presented some of the most basic, important, and useful facts about the grammatical system of English. With this knowledge, you are now in a position to go a step beyond words, phrases, and clauses in order to look at how these elements and constructions can be arranged and combined into various kinds of sentences.

## COMPLEX SENTENCES

A *complex sentence* is one that contains an independent clause and one or more dependent clauses. The following sentences will illustrate:

1. Complex Sentences with One Dependent Clause:

   <u>After the Deluge had ended</u>, Noah released a dove.
              adverbial clause

   The story <u>that intrigued Tom</u> was about a pet lion.
              relative clause

   A cynic once said <u>that a sucker is born every minute.</u>
              noun clause—direct object

2. Complex Sentences with More than One Dependent Clause:

   Jane coveted the house <u>that Jack bought from the one-eyed</u>
              relative clause

   <u>man</u> <u>who trained monkeys.</u>
              relative clause

Although it rained heavily, little damage was done to the dam
      adverbial clause

that had burst the preceding year.
         relative clause

The man who came to dinner said that he was glad to be
       relative clause       noun clause—direct object

there.

As you can see from these few examples, an independent clause can be preceded or followed by a dependent clause or have a dependent clause embedded within it. Such sentences can become difficult to analyze, but by breaking them down into separate components, you can see their structure more clearly. Here is a previous sentence with the clauses separated:

Although it rained heavily,
     dependent clause

little damage was done to the dam
      independent clause

that had burst the preceding year.
      dependent clause

In the examples thus far, the verb in the independent clause has been in the active voice. Clauses can contain verbs in the passive voice, too, as the independent clause does in the following sentence:

The pitcher who beaned our star player was tossed out
       dependent clause

of the game by an irate umpire

who always reacted immediately to such misconduct.
      dependent clause

In this sentence, the independent clause is the passive sentence "The pitcher was tossed out of the game by an irate umpire." Were we to restore the sentence to the active voice, we would have the following complex sentence:

An irate umpire who always reacted immediately to such mis-
      dependent clause

conduct tossed the pitcher <u>who beaned our star player</u> out of the
dependent clause
game.

If the passive version sounds better to you than its active counterpart, you have just learned one benefit of experimenting with sentence variety: variety offers us a chance to attain maximum clarity. Furthermore, complex sentences, as one part of this variety, can lead to conciseness and away from boredom. Imagine what the preceding sentence would have become if each of its clauses had been made independent:

> The pitcher was tossed out of the game by an irate umpire. The pitcher beaned our star player. The irate umpire always reacted immediately to such misconduct.

Lacking coherence and sounding awkward, these three simple sentences read much worse than the passive version of the complex sentence.

# COMPOUND SENTENCES

A *compound sentence* is one that contains two or more independent clauses usually linked together by a coordinating conjunction (*and, but, or, nor, for, yet* or *so*). Consider the following examples:

> Matilda sang, *and* Jessica danced.
> Thorndike scored the first goal, *but* Brandon saved the day.
> They visited Philadelphia, *for* they had never seen the Liberty Bell.
> Barry caught a cold, *so* he had to miss class.
> Marge made faces, Bill stood on his head, *and* the baby laughed.

Notice that a coordinating conjunction appears in each of these sentences. It is not absolutely necessary in any of them, however. We could remove the conjunction, add appropriate punctuation, and have essentially the same meanings:

> Matilda sang; Jessica danced.
> Thorndike scored the first goal; Brandon saved the day.
> They visited Philadelphia; they had never seen the Liberty Bell.
> Barry caught a cold; he missed class.
> Marge made faces; Bill stood on his head; the baby laughed.

This dropping of the conjunctions demonstrates that the two clauses in each of the preceding sentences are independent. Notice also that we have replaced the commas with semicolons. A punctuation rule says that a semicolon must be used in a compound sentence if a coordinating conjunction is not.

# BRANCHING OUT

If you want to branch out, to go beyond complex and compound sentences, you have many choices. Add a second independent clause to a complex sentence and you get what is called a *compound-complex sentence*. This is a sentence containing two independent clauses and at least one dependent clause. The following is an example:

<u>After they won the pennant,</u> the Dodgers celebrated, but
      dependent clause          independent clause

their rest was short.
independent clause

You could add still another dependent clause to this compound-complex sentence and have the following:

<u>After they won the pennant,</u> the Dodgers celebrated, but
      dependent clause          independent clause

their rest was short <u>as the World Series was less</u>
  independent clause         dependent clause

<u>than a week away</u>.

It is also possible to build a compound-complex sentence another way, by beginning with two independent clauses and ending with a series of dependent clauses:

Henry purchased an antique shotgun, and Martha bought an
      independent clause          independent clause

old sewing machine <u>which someone had found in a house</u>
              dependent clause

<u>that had been abandoned</u> <u>when the Union Army surrounded</u>
  dependent clause         dependent clause

<u>Vicksburg</u>.

With these examples we leave you to your own devices and inventiveness—with these words of encouragement: when you find yourself becoming hopelessly entangled in the briar patch of your own words, remember that sometimes "branching out" does end in failure, but that more often it eventually leads to better writing.

# MORE NOTES ON GRAMMAR
# IN THE EVERYDAY WORLD

Choices unlimited can lead to "mistakes unlimited" if the writer-speaker is not careful. In fact, the mere act of reaching out for greater syntactic complexity *will* lead to some mistakes. A writer going beyond simple sentences, venturing into the syntactic jungle of gerunds, infinitives, compound-complex sentences, and so forth, will find every now and then misplaced modifiers, disruptive sentence fragments, or ambiguous phrases to trip over. In this section we will consider a few common problems, looking at written English, but remaining fully aware that a person speaking can also get lost in his or her own verbiage.

## Misplaced Modifiers

A *misplaced modifier* occurs when a modifier is not properly attached to the independent clause. The most common misplaced modifiers are prepositional phrases, gerundive phrases, and infinitive phrases, as illustrated in the following sentences:

> *With the taste of victory in his mouth*, an ankle twisted and John lost the race. (misplaced prepositional phrase)
> Her cooking over, the guests were fed by Joan. (misplaced gerundive phrase)
> *To be truly tasty*, you should broil lobster, then dip it in butter. (misplaced infinitive phrase)

These mistakes in modification can be corrected by changing the subject of the independent clause so that it appears closer to the phrase which modifies it:

> With the taste of victory in his mouth, *John* twisted an ankle and lost the race.
> Her cooking over, *Joan* fed the guests.
> To be truly tasty, *a lobster* should be broiled, then dipped in butter.

## Sentence Fragments

A *sentence fragment* is a construction intended as a sentence (other than an imperative) that lacks a complete subject and/or predicate. They can be effective in the hands of a competent writer, but too often they are only annoying, as in the following narrative:

> John woke suddenly. *Startled but groggy. Hearing a noise outside.* He jumped out of bed. *Immediately slipping on an innocent-looking throw rug that lay on the floor. Screaming.*

Many times fragments can simply be added to a sentence they precede or follow; if they cannot, they should be rewritten as complete sentences:

> John woke suddenly, *startled but groggy. Hearing a noise outside,* he jumped out of bed, *immediately slipping on an innocent-looking throw rug that lay on the floor.* He screamed.

## Ambiguity

*Ambiguity* can creep into any conversation or piece of writing. Listeners can always ask a speaker for clarification, but readers seldom get such a chance. It is up to the writer, then, to make sure that the writing is clear and precise. Ambiguity can be present for many reasons. Consider the following examples:

> Jeff saw a man on a horse *with a patch over one eye.*
> *When he was 20,* his father began graduate school.
> He didn't care to attend Harvard, because it was *an old men's college.*

In the first example, the reader cannot be sure whether the man or the horse has the patch. In the second, the pronoun *he* could refer to a son of the man who went to graduate school or to the father himself. In the last example, the "he" might not want to attend Harvard because he believes it is for "old" men, but he might also just want to attend a "new" men's college. These ambiguous sentences could be made clear with just a little rewriting:

> Jeff saw a man *with a patch over one eye* riding a horse.
> When *Hildon* was 20, his father began graduate school.
> He didn't care to attend Harvard, *preferring a newer men's college.*

Our selection of problems has certainly not exhausted the supply of those that you might encounter. Once you become aware that they exist, however, they will be easier to spot in your own writing and in the writing of others.

# Exercises

Mark each of the following sentences as simple (S), complex (CX), compound (CD), or compound-complex (CC).

*Example:* Max said that his dog gave him great comfort.    __CX__

1 Driving through the Oregon countryside pleased Jennifer greatly.                              _____

2 The problem arose because people were so disorganized.                                      _____

3 If winter comes, can spring be far behind?        _____

4 Early purchasers received the best tickets.       _____

5 Spencer improvised on the cello, and everyone loved it.                                          _____

6 After the party was over, Milton reminisced until he fell asleep.                                   _____

7 Millions of ants completely spoiled the Smiths' picnic.   _____

8 They looked and they looked, but Ponce de Leon and his men couldn't find the Fountain of Youth.     _____

9 Pick people who think for themselves, and you'll have a better committee.                        _____

10 Ellen passed the written exam, but she failed the oral.                                           _____

11 Beverly loved Clint passionately, but she suspected that he would make a lousy husband.           _____

12 The young lieutenant, even though he had never seen combat, proved to be a calm and courageous leader. _____

13 The story which interested her most concerned an unmarried millionaire who would soon be visiting the city. _____

14 The young couple built a home on the cliffs overlooking the tiny village of St. Ives. _____

15 Bring me your plans, but don't bring me your problems. _____

16 This may sound mean, but I hope that Mildred stays home. _____

# TWENTY-ONE

# Usage: Bringing Judgment to Bear

## WHAT IS USAGE?

As we write or speak, all of us make certain decisions concerning word choice, grammatical form, and sometimes pronunciation. It is our selection from among various possible alternatives that we refer to as *usage*.

## USAGE JUDGMENTS

When anyone becomes too "critical" of our speech or writing, we tend to react negatively. Yet these critics may only be making well-intentioned *usage judgments*, saying, "This pronunciation is better than that," "This word is more fitting here," or "Your grammar is incorrect at this point." Knowing the judgments are well-meant does not help our feelings, of course, and we might think or even say, "How do you know? What is good usage anyway? And who are *you* to tell *me*?"

## WHAT IS GOOD USAGE?

Definitions of *good* usage abound. Here is one that we think is useful and reasonable. Since usage refers to standards of correctness or acceptability that bear on choices we make among various items of pronunciation, vocabulary, and grammar, *good* usage means those choices that are especially fitting for the occasion, the audience, the speaker, and the speaker's intentions. *Good* usage, then, is not necessarily *formal* usage, since not all occasions require a formal response. For example, few instructors give formal lectures in the classroom today, even though this practice was followed in the past, at least in some schools, with the instructor even putting the lecture into written form before delivering it to the class. Nor would formal usage be tolerated for long in the average home by *any* members of the American family—children or adults. In the classroom, *informal* usage might be best, while in the home either informal or *casual* usage might be preferred.

If we are going to develop a reasonably clear idea of good usage, then, it is necessary to understand how the concepts *formal*, *informal*, and *casual* apply to language, and to realize that these three concepts pertain to the spoken as well as to the written language.

*Formal* usage occurs in situations that demand the most care and precision in the use of language, situations where a person is most conscious of the effect his or her speech or writing will have on others. It is called *educated* usage by some, and consists of choices that the average person would consider "correct," even though that person might not use those forms in his or her own speech and writing. For example, included among the requirements of formal usage would be the following:

1 That *whom*, the objective form of *who*, be used as the object of verbs and prepositions, as in "You saw *whom?*" and "To *whom* do you wish to speak?"
2 That singular personal pronouns be used with singular indefinite pronouns, even though the common inclination is to use plural personal pronouns:
This: *Anybody* could do that if *he* or *she* tried.
*Not* this: *Anybody* could do that if *they* tried.
3 That the subject form of personal pronouns be used after the verb *be*, as in "It was *I* who did it."
4 That subjunctive *were* be used in statements contrary to fact, as in "If I *were* you, I'd leave."

The requirements would apply to both written and spoken formal English.

Were we to move from formal to *informal* usage, however, the forms previously denied would now be allowed us. Not only would the *m* probably be dropped from *whom* in the first example, but a different word order and even different words might be used, possibly giving "*Who'd* you see?" and "*Who* do you *want* to speak to?" The second example might become "Anybody could do that if *they* tried," whether the sentence was written or spoken. The next examples would most likely become "It was *me that* did it" and "If

I *was* you, I'd leave." In informal situations, where people are generally more at ease, less guarded in their speaking or writing, few would reject these expressions. Indeed, chances are that many of the forms required by formal usage would be rejected instead. They would be considered stiff, cold, or just not appropriate.

*Casual* usage, common when we are speaking or writing to family, relatives, and close friends, is usually characterized by shorter utterances, lexical items with special, often private meanings, more nonstandard forms than either of the other two *levels* (or varieties) of usage, and the dropping of auxiliaries and subjects, especially pronouns.

The following might be considered one kind of casual speech (not the only kind, of course) commonly heard in home or other intimate situations:

> Parent: Where'd you go, Tiger?
> Child: Out.
> Parent: Wha'd you do?
> Child: Nothin'.

Here is another example:

> Parent 1: Wanna do something this weekend?
> Parent 2: How 'bout a movie? Haven't seen one in a while.
> Parent 1: Anything good playing?
> Parent 2: Donno. I'll check the paper.

As you can see, the language in the preceding examples is less "guarded" (one might even say it is more "condensed") than that usually found in either formal or informal situations. One reason is that there are generally more shared or tacitly assumed values, facts, and beliefs present in intimate situations than in others. People do not have to explain themselves so often or strive so consciously for clarity. They are also more certain of being accepted by their listeners, regardless of the language they use. The speech or writing of people reflects that situation. It follows that nicknames, terms of endearment, slang, and other forms that might not be considered appropriate either in formal or in informal situations can also occur. Finally, in more casual, intimate situations, *ain't*, "he don't" and similar nonstandard expressions are likely to occur. You can probably verify this by listening carefully as you talk with your friends. Expressions similar to "I been studyin' all night and still *don't know nothin'*" and "I *ain't never gonna* take another load this heavy" will probably appear more often than you had thought. The frequency of their appearance forces us to list such forms as components of casual language, even though they are nonstandard.

The preceding discussion should not lead you to the conclusion that there are no standards or that anything goes. There definitely are standards. Every language community has them, just as every society has rules governing other forms of behavior and the way that behavior can vary from situation to situation. It is no different with language, and violating usage rules can sometimes lead to results every bit as unpleasant as the results of breaking rules governing other types of behavior (refer to Chapter 1 again).

Before moving on, we should make two last points. The first is that the three levels of usage cannot always be clearly distinguished. Unlike countries, they do not have borders that can be patrolled and protected (although some people treat them as though they do). Rather, the three levels "fade" into one another. Formal English will contain informal usages at times, just as informal will contain formal usages. Casual English may even contain forms characteristic of formal English. The second point is that you should distinguish dialects from levels (or varieties) of usage. All dialects, whether or not they are standard, have forms that speakers recognize as more formal than others, and most nonstandard speakers will vary their speech to fit the situation and audience, just as standard speakers will. A person living in a small, rural town and speaking a nonstandard dialect, for example, might refer to nonadults as *children* at a school-board meeting, as *kids* to neighbors, and as *younguns* to an older relative.

## WHO DECIDES?

When we ask "who decides" what good usage is, we are probably talking about *Standard English* and *formal usage*, since to most people formal Standard English is good English—*period*. The question is not always easy to answer, but if one *is* talking about formal Standard English, then a reasonably accurate answer might be: those people in a speech community who have the most education and the most social prestige. Such people are able to make judgments (and have them listened to) primarily because they are also the ones who use written language a great deal, and have the opportunity and the power to influence education (through school policy, curricula, etc.) and the media (printed matter, television, etc.). This group dictates formal usage directly by its example, and indirectly through the teachers, writers, editors, publishers, dictionary makers, and authors of grammar books who officially "instruct" the public as to educated, formal usage.

# GOOD USAGE CHANGES WITH TIME

Complicating the picture somewhat is the fact that good usage changes slowly through time. A passive form possible in the eighteenth century was "The body *was carrying* downstairs," though today we would have to say "The body *was being carried* downstairs." In the late sixteenth and early seventeenth century, Shakespeare used double superlatives ("the *most* beautiful*est*"), and Chaucer, in the fourteenth century, was comfortable with double and even quadruple negatives ("He nevere yet no vileynye ne sayde/ In al his lyf unto no maner wight"—The General Prologue to *The Canterbury Tales*, lines 70–71). In like manner, perhaps one day adults as well as children will be able to utter a sentence such as "I *gots* two pencils," as many young children do today, and think of it as "good" English. If the "gots" sentence gets to you, remember that (1) usage is basically a value judgment, and (2) change is not necessarily corruption. As a further example, consider that only a few years ago *Time* magazine (and others) berated two Presidents for using the word *finalized*, as in "They've *finalized* the agreement." Today the word meets little if any opposition.

# CAN WE AGREE?

The question is sometimes asked, "Can we agree as to what good usage is?" If this question means can we agree as to what *formal usage* is in Standard English, we can usually say "Yes." Few people will call "He *don't* know *nothing*," "He *swum* today," or "*Him* and *her done* it" good formal Standard English. But there are forms that educated speakers who consider themselves good writers and speakers will disagree about. Some will use *dived* as the past tense of *dive*, others will use *dove*; some will pronounce *aunt* the same as *ant*, others so that it rhymes with *gaunt*; some will abhor the word *sweat*, while others will use it, thinking *perspiration* affected. So we must say that some items of pronunciation, vocabulary, and grammar have *divided usage* and that neither the one form nor the other can be said to be better.

Usage—it is an interesting if complex topic. In summary, perhaps the best statement that can be made is to say that there *are* standards, that they do *change* from time to time, that they are set by the users of the language, especially by the influential and educated users, and that these standards must be looked at as covering a scale that goes from the most to the least formal speech and writing. Such a statement allows us to accept, with grace, the mistakes that we and others make from time to time.

# THOSE THAT MATTER, THOSE THAT DO NOT

Before leaving usage, we will offer some practical advice. Some usage items matter more than others. The following usages are judged harshly by many speakers, often regardless of the situation or context in which they occur, and should be particularly avoided in formal contexts (unless you do not want the job, do not care about the person or people making the judgment, etc.):

1 *Double negatives.* They *never* appear in formal, are frowned upon in informal, but do appear in casual English.

2 *Ain't.* Although used by even educated speakers as late as the Victorian period, it *never* appears in formal English today, except in dialogue. It occurs frequently in the casual speech of some people, particularly younger speakers.

3 *Subject and verb agreement.* Dropping the third person singular present-tense suffix is not allowed in either formal or informal Standard English. Saying or writing "He *don't*" rather than "He *doesn't*" can even leave you branded illiterate, regardless of how unjust the charge would be. Although this form appears mainly in dialects other than Standard English, it sometimes occurs in casual conversation, even in that of educated speakers.

4 *Cases of pronouns.* Using object forms in subject position is not allowed in either formal or informal Standard English. Whether written or spoken, "*Me* and *her* saw them" would be condemned (unless the speaker were a young child).

5 *Past tense and past participles.* Using the past-tense form when the past participle is called for (and vice versa) is a practice condemned by most speakers of Standard English. Such usage occurs among standard speakers, of course, but infrequently and usually in casual conversation. The incorrect use of past-tense and past participle forms is mainly a feature of nonstandard dialects. Examples of forms that are frequently misused include the following:

> *Past Tense:*
> I *seen* it.
> I *swum.*
> He *done* it.
>
> *Past Participles:*
> I've *went* there.
> I've *swam* here.
> They've *ran* that course before.

The preceding are five of the most important usage items that *matter*. Unless you really do not care or do not need to care about having your speech or writing judged harshly by others, avoid them (and pass on the advice to your students). These grammatical "mistakes" can prevent you from getting jobs or from being promoted. They can exclude you from certain social groups and even make it difficult or impossible for you to meet certain people. All of this is unfortunate but true.

The following items cause few problems:

1 *Split infinitives*. Do not worry about splitting the infinitive unless doing so leads to an awkward construction. If it does, throw out the split infinitive and revise.

2 *Who/Whom*. Formal Standard written English requires *whom* in the object function (see Chapter 19). Although many people use only *who*, they often feel uncomfortable in not knowing how to use *whom*.

3 *It's I/me*. Except for some English teachers, the employees of certain businesses or expensive shops, etc., very few people use *I* after *is* when speaking. In fact, many good writers and speakers consider expressions such as "It was *I* who did it" as correct but too formal, preferring "It was *me* who did it," even though *me* in this context is "technically" incorrect. *He* and *she* appear more often, perhaps because to some speakers they sound better after *is* than does *her* or *him*. It is hardly a problem in written English, since the construction would appear mainly in dialogue or as a quotation; hence "It's *me* (*her*, *him*)" is usually appropriate.

4 *Shall/Will*. Although the standard rule still says that in declarative sentences *shall* should be used with first person pronouns ("*I* shall," "*we* shall") and *will* with all others, the distinction is not maintained in speech and is even being ignored in formal written English. This is not a problem.

5 *Ending a sentence with a preposition*. This is definitely not a problem in speech. In writing, despite the rule, trying not to end a sentence with a preposition can lead to awkward sentences, as Winston Churchill demonstrated with his intentionally ludicrous sentence "There are some things *up with* which I will not *put*."

The preceding two sets of so-called "usage problems" are only a handful of those that you could find discussed in handbooks on the subject. When you do have questions and no answers, consult one of the sources listed in the usage section of our bibliography. Do not forget how helpful a good desk dictionary can be, either.

# TWENTY-TWO

# Where Do You Go from Here?

Right now you should be feeling more comfortable and confident with English grammar than when you first opened this book. But if you are like the rest of us, eventually you will find yourself in situations where your knowledge will not seem so great after all, or, conversely, where your knowledge of grammar has the effect of intimidating others. When difficult situations arise, do not panic or lose your composure. There are certain things you can do to ease yourself through these crises.

The first situation we will postulate is not a major crisis, but it does happen, especially to English teachers. You are at a party and someone walks up to you, engages in conversation, and eventually says, "And what do you do?" You answer, with rightful pride, "I'm an English teacher (or English major)." Sometimes a slight but very noticeable pause will occur, followed somewhat later, perhaps after a few other "polite" remarks, by "I'm not very good at English" or "English was my worst subject." What do you do? Do you say, "Oh, I'm sure you're better than you think" or "Well, isn't that too bad?" No. Nor do you have to slip into a nonstandard dialect or break a few usage rules just to show the person that you are human, too, regardless of your strange proclivities. Remember, first of all, that most Americans are linguistically insecure. In other words, they believe that they don't write or speak as well as they should. What you might say in this situation depends on whether you believe the person is insecure with English but nonetheless interested in it, or whether the person is so ill at ease that you had better change the topic of conversation entirely (after all, even English teachers go "off duty," and if the person is too ill at ease, doing so would probably help both parties). In the case of the interested individual, however, you might reassure the person and discuss the near universality of linguistic insecurity and the fact that it is so often unwarranted. As often as not, the other person will share his or her ideas on the subject, and an interesting and rewarding conversation can result (as you have probably already realized, interesting opinions about language are not the exclusive property of college students and college graduates).

The second situation revolves around your own accessibility as an "expert" on the English language. Especially if you become a teacher, you will be regarded by your neighbors, friends, and family as an accessible "authority" on English, and may find the telephone and doorbell ringing with questions about Johnny's schoolwork, the punctuation of someone's job resume, the proper grammar for use in a report that is due the next day, and so forth. These questions are usually of the "which is correct" variety, and you are expected to know the answers.

Our belief is that you *ought to* be prepared with most of the answers. Knowing the answers to the most frequently asked questions will do wonders for your professional self-confidence and will also help the public have confidence in you. Many answers to the commonly asked questions have already been provided in this text. The answers to some other frequently asked questions are given in Appendix 1 at the end of this book.

Sometimes there will be more than one acceptable answer, as when someone asks what the correct past-participle form of *prove* is (both *proved* and *proven* are acceptable). Our advice is to acknowledge that two or more correct answers are possible, but then to go ahead and make a specific recommendation anyway, perhaps the grammatical usage, pronunciation, or word choice that you would make yourself. Always try to avoid saying that a clear answer is not possible. You may confuse the person or, worse yet, cause your qualifications to be doubted. After all, you expect your doctor, dentist, gardener, mechanic, and so on to be knowledgeable and confident. Their expectations of you are no less.

The final situation we present is slightly different. It could happen whether you became a secretary, a business manager, an engineer, a doctor, or a teacher. One morning a bright, sunny day will dawn only to be clouded over by what you feel is the linguistic stupidity (backwardness, sloppiness, etc.) of an associate. When you catch yourself wondering why little Johnny, big Benny, or elegant Ellen can not handle the language worth a darn and does not seem willing or able to learn, stop a minute before letting the storm of abuse break. Is it really stupidity? Or is it a matter of dialect interference, second-language interference, poor spelling, or lack of knowledge of the rules of formal English? If it is any of these things, you can not call it a matter of stupidity; rather, it is a matter that warrants your attention, understanding, and patience. Remember that losing patience or becoming overly critical could just compound the linguistic insecurity that the other person might already be laboring under. On the other hand, by trying to help the person, you will learn, too, making it easier to get through those times when you yourself may have forgotten some of the facts of English that you once felt so confident about.

Finally, we want to remind you that one course, if that is all you have had, is not going to make you familiar with every facet of English grammar. You may even doubt your knowledge when you begin to teach (if that is what you plan to do), but the very act of teaching will make you learn more. You will find it helpful to review the contents of this book occasionally, and since you will probably be asked the same questions about English over and over again, you might memorize the information given in Appendix 1 at the end of this book. Being able to give immediate and correct answers to these commonly asked questions will save you from having to "check" every time before giving authoritative answers, and both you and your students will appreciate this. You might also find the information in Appendix 2 helpful, especially if you use sentence diagraming to explain the structure of sentences to students.

We know you will enjoy your future work with English grammar. In this book you have seen how people and grammar go hand in hand. If you are interested in the one, you cannot help but find pleasure in the other.

# APPENDIX 1

# Helpful Answers to Ten Commonly Asked Questions

The following questions are not the only ones that you might be asked, but they are among the most frequent. We strongly urge you to memorize the answers. Doing so will increase your confidence and eliminate the need to "check the facts" all the time. Bear in mind that these rules apply mainly to American English; the rules of British English may differ.

1  When do I double the final consonant of a word to which a suffix beginning with a vowel has been added?

*Answer:*  **1** For a one-syllable word, double if the final consonant is immediately preceded by a *single* vowel.

*Examples:*  put—putting, drop—dropping, hop—hopped, tap—tapped, plan—planner, bat—batter.

*But:*  sleep—sleeping, fail—failed, send—sender.

   **2** For a multisyllable word, double if the preceding conditions are met *and* the primary stress falls on the final syllable.

*Examples:*  occúr—occurring, refér—referring, outwít—outwitted.

*But:*  recóver—recovering, bénefit—benefited.

**2** When does *i* come before *e* and vice versa?

*Answer:* Use *i* before *e*, except after *c* or when the sound is *a* as in *neighbor* or *weight*.

*Examples:* relieve, believe, reprieve.

*But:* perceive, receive, feign.

**3** When do I drop the final *e* on words?

*Answer:* **1** Drop the *e* when adding a suffix that begins with a *vowel*.

*Examples:* love—loving, hope—hoping, desire—desirable, blaspheme—blasphemous.

*But:* arrange—arrangement, love—lovely, hope—hopeful.

    **2** After *c* or *g*, the *e* is *retained* if the suffix begins with *a* or *o*.

*Examples:* courage—courageous, salvage—salvageable, notice—noticeable.

**4** When do I change final *y* to *i*?

*Answer:* When adding a suffix other than *-ing*, unless the *y* is preceded by a vowel.

*Examples:* speedy—speedily, friendly—friendliness, mercy—merciful, crazy—crazier.

*But:* marry—marrying, modify—modifying, study—studying, monkey—monkeys, Monday—Mondays.

**5** When do I underline titles and when do I put quotation marks around them?

*Answer:* **1** Underline the titles of separate publications: books, magazines and newspapers, bulletins, pamphlets, musical productions (symphonies, operas, etc.), and long poems.

*Examples:* War and Peace (the title of a book), Time (the title of a magazine).

*Note:* In professional printing, italics replace underlining.

**2** Use quotation marks around any part or subdivision of a printed publication: short poems, chapters, essays, magazine and newspaper articles, and songs.

*Examples:* "Owning a Boston Terrier" (the title of a magazine article),
"Because I Could Not Stop for Death" (the title of a short poem).

**6** How do I use the apostrophe to show possession?

*Answer:* **1a** With a *singular* noun add an apostrophe and s unless the word already ends in s:

*Examples:* girl—girl's, brother—brother's.

**1b** If the singular noun ends with s, add an apostrophe and s if the apostrophe plus s is pronounced. Otherwise, just add the apostrophe:

*Examples:* Bess's hat (apostrophe plus s pronounced),
Bill Fitzsimmons' hat (apostrophe plus s not pronounced).

**2a** With a plural noun ending in s, add only the apostrophe.

*Examples:* sisters—sisters',
employers—employers',
birds—birds'.

**2b** With a plural noun not ending in s, add an apostrophe and s.

*Examples:* children—children's, sheep—sheep's.

**7** When do I use ellipsis?

*Answer:* Use three periods to indicate the intentional omission of words in a passage that you are quoting. Any punctuation marks *preceding* the ellipsis are retained if they serve a purpose, and when an ellipsis ends a sentence, a fourth period (the writer's own) is added.

*Example:* Quotation *without* ellipsis:
"Now we are engaged in a great civil war, testing whether that nation, or any nation so

conceived and so dedicated, can long endure. We are met on a great battlefield of that war. We have come to dedicate a portion of that field, as a final resting place for those who here gave their lives that that nation might live."

    Abraham Lincoln, "Gettysburg Address"

Quotation *with* ellipsis:
". . . we are engaged in a great civil war, testing whether that nation . . . can long endure. We are met on a great battlefield of that war. We have come to dedicate a portion of that field, as a final resting place for those who here gave their lives. . . ."

    Abraham Lincoln, "Gettysburg Address"

**8** How do I punctuate dialogue (direct quotations)?

*Answer:* You enclose all of the speaker's words within the quotation marks, using commas to set off dialogue guides such as "he said" or "she asked." A new paragraph is begun each time the speaker changes.

*Example:* "Who," she asked, "are you?"
"I'm the caretaker here," the man answered. Her escort said, "I don't believe this man. I've never seen him here before."

*Note:* Commas and periods are always placed *inside* the closing quotation marks. Question marks and exclamation points are placed inside the closing quotation marks if they are part of the quoted passage, outside if not.

**9** How do I punctuate a quotation within a quotation?

*Answer:* The usual practice is to place *single* quotation marks around the inner quotation and *double* quotation marks around the outer quotation.

*Example:* Benjamin said, "I believe the line 'To be, or not to be—that is the question' occurs in Shakespeare's *Hamlet*."

**10** When do I use a semicolon?

*Answer:* You use a semicolon:

**1** To separate independent clauses that are *not* joined by a conjunction.

*Example:*    Cecil enjoys greyhound racing; his wife hates it.

**2** Before certain adverbs (*however, moreover, besides, consequently, also, furthermore, therefore, thus, hence,* and *nevertheless*) when they introduce independent clauses.

*Example:*    She wanted to leave; however, they persuaded her to stay.

**3** Between independent clauses that are joined by conjunctions *if* the independent clauses contain commas.

*Example:*    John, the minor poet, arrived late; but Pierre, who was the main attraction, came early.

**4** Between items in a series when those items contain commas:

*Example:*    Jason wrote three books: *Helmuth,* the story of an orphan; *Gorgeous Times,* a novel about the 1950s; and *All Who Came,* a history of immigrants in America.

# APPENDIX 2

# Diagraming Sentences

The diagraming of sentences has long been a part of language study, and at times it can be one of the best aids to understanding sentence structure. In this appendix we will briefly examine two very well known ways in which diagraming is carried out. The first, *traditional sentence diagraming*, is a rather old method, while the second, *tree-structure diagraming*, was developed more recently.

## TRADITIONAL SENTENCE DIAGRAMING

One of the purposes of traditional sentence diagraming is to show sentence structure graphically. This is done by drawing a set of lines which intersect at certain points and angles so that components of a sentence can be assigned specific "places" on the lines. Naturally, a person must understand what each component is or what function it has in order to make appropriate diagrams. Five basic types of diagrams, with important "places" labeled, are shown as follows:

1    subject | verb

2    subject | verb | direct object

3    subject | linking verb \ subject complement

4    subject | verb | direct object
                    \ indirect object

| 5 | subject | verb | direct object | \ | object complement |
|---|---------|------|---------------|----|---------------------|

Notice first that these five diagrams represent five main kinds of sentences. Diagram 1 represents a sentence with an intransitive verb; diagram 2, a sentence with a transitive verb followed by a direct object; diagram 3, a sentence with a linking verb plus subject complement; diagram 4, a sentence with a transitive verb and direct and indirect objects; and diagram 5, a sentence with a transitive verb with an object and an object complement. Next, notice that in each diagram the vertical line after "subject" extends *below* the main horizontal line. This vertical line breaks each sentence into its two main components, the subject and the predicate. Everything to the left of this line is part of the subject, and everything to the right of it is part of the predicate. Further, note that direct objects and subject and object complements are set off from the verb by a line that begins *on* the main horizontal line and extends *upward*, either perpendicularly to the main line or at an angle to it. The slant of the complement line is toward the subject or object, while the direct object's line is completely vertical. An indirect object's "place" is shown as two intersecting lines *below* the verb, the first angling down and to the right, intersecting the second line, which is parallel to but still below the main line. If modifiers are present, they are always placed on lines that extend *down* at an angle from the word or construction they modify. Actual sentences would be placed on these diagrams in the following manner:

1  Crickets | chirped

2  Sandra | raises | pigeons

3  We | are \ happy

4  People | gave | gifts
       \ to
        \ Tom

5  Sam | considered | Communists \ idiots

Now that you have a general idea of what completed traditional diagrams look like, we can add some modifiers to the sentences just shown:

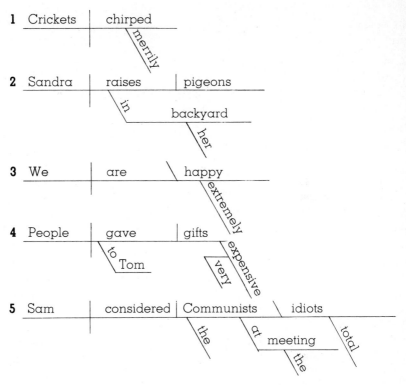

A simple declarative sentence containing many modifiers would be diagramed like this:

*Sentence:* The extremely tired astronaut very quickly signed the required lunar landing forms.

*Traditional Diagram:*

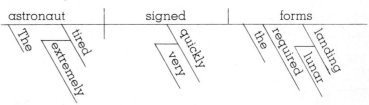

If the sentence happens to have a compound subject or a compound predicate, the diagram will assume one of the following shapes:

Dick and Jane laughed.

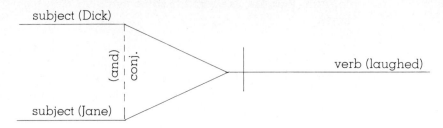

Tom hunts and fishes.

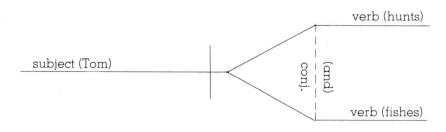

Diagrams illustrate graphically the structure of a sentence, accounting for each and every word, usually by showing that word's function and its relationship to other words in the same sentence. Vividly illustrating the complexity that sentences may attain, diagrams easily and clearly show the modifiers of the main components of a sentence, regardless of how many there might be.

# TREE-STRUCTURE DIAGRAMING

Some grammarians analyze sentences by making use of a set of rules of the following form:

1 S $\longrightarrow$ NP VP
2 VP $\longrightarrow$ V (NP)
3 NP $\longrightarrow$ (art) N

S stands for "sentence," NP for "noun phrase," and so forth. The arrow pointing to the right can be interpreted to mean "equals" or "consists of." Parentheses indicate that the element within is considered optional. The first rule says that a sentence (in English) consists of a noun phrase plus a verb phrase. The second rule says that a verb phrase consists of a verb plus, optionally, a noun phrase. The last rule claims that a noun phrase consists of an optional article and a mandatory noun. Of course, a more complete grammar would have many more rules, some of them quite complex, but these should give some idea of what this kind of rule looks like.

The rules are usually shown graphically, however, by means of a device called a *tree structure*, for the obvious reason that it resembles an upside-down tree. Here is one such tree for a simple, declarative sentence:

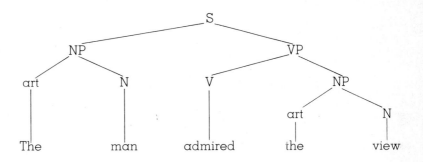

The tree begins with the symbol standing for "sentence." At each subsequent level below the top S, the symbols refer to smaller components. Therefore, the components of the S are the NP and the VP, the components of the NP are the art and the N, and so forth. Notice that the last line, or *derivation*, as it is called, consists of real words. At this level *lexical insertion* has taken place—the insertion of real words for the abstract symbols. This insertion takes place either when the symbols cannot be further broken down or when the grammarian feels that further rewriting is unnecessary. Here is another tree:

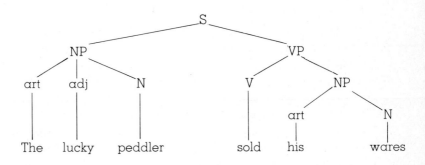

This is still a simple declarative sentence. The only difference between this tree and the preceding tree is that the left-hand NP now contains an adjective. Rule 3 could easily be rewritten to account for that:

NP ——————→ (art) (adj) N

Here is still another tree:

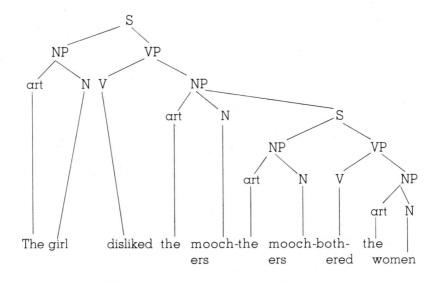

This tree analyzes a complex sentence containing an independent clause ("The girl disliked the moochers") and a dependent clause ("The moochers bothered the women") which begins at the lower S, thus clearly showing its subordination to the independent or main clause. But look at the last line:

The girl disliked the moochers the moochers bothered the women

Clearly, this is not a good English sentence. It is not supposed to be a good sentence, however, because the last line of a tree structure is meant to show "deeper" sentence relations that cannot always be seen in the written or spoken "surface" form of the sentence.

To change the derivation into the form that a sentence should have on the surface, grammarians use what are called *transformational rules*, which are really nothing more than the "grammatical operations" that have been described at various points in this book. These rules *add*, *delete*, *rearrange*, or *substitute* elements. They can do one or all of these operations on the last line of a tree structure. The transformational rules operating on the derivation of the preceding tree would perform the following operations:

**T-1**  Delete the "lower" of the two identical NPs.
**T-2**  Substitute the appropriate relative pronoun for the deleted NP.

The derivation would proceed as follows:

*Derivation:*
the girl disliked the moochers the moochers bothered the women
**T-1**  the girl disliked the moochers _____ bothered the women

**T-2**  The girl disliked the moochers _who_ bothered the women.

The derivation we obtained has now been changed into a "good" English sentence by the transformational rules. In this kind of grammar, an attempt is made not only to reveal the structure of the sentence and the relationship of its elements, but also to give some notion of the process that speakers (might) use to convert a thought into an actual utterance.

We have given you, at best, a *very* brief introduction to traditional sentence diagrams, tree-structure diagrams, and the theories that underlie them. But our intention was to introduce them to you, not to make you accomplished diagramers. Perhaps you will find diagraming a useful aid to understanding sentence structure. You might wish to explore one or more of these methods in detail and delve into the theories behind them, and to assist you we have included appropriate sources in the bibliography. But even if you just play around with diagrams, you may discover unexpected new insights now and then.

# Exercises

I  Diagram the following sentences, using traditional sentence diagraming.

*Example:* Mary avoided the oil slick easily.

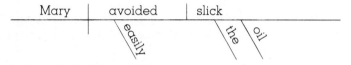

1 Greece produces excellent olives.

2 The President laughed.

**3** His new house is yellow.

**4** An unknown team won the state championship.

**5** The middle-aged man in the front office quit.

**6** Sidney never missed a performance.

**7** John and his brother argued continuously.

**8** The servants beat the rugs and aired the bedding.

**9** She threw a kiss to her departing cousin.

**10** Sally considered the remark deplorable.

**11** The man with the red suitcase was an actor.

**12** Jethro bought a bright orange truck for his oldest son.

**13** The small, dark brown hunting dog easily recovered nine ducks yesterday.

**14** Diagraming is fun.

**II** Diagram the following sentences, using tree-structure diagrams.

*Example:* The dog licked the cat.

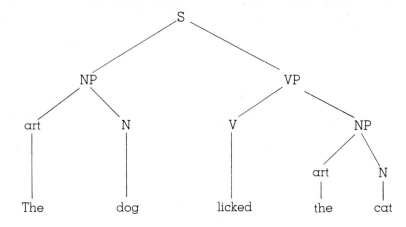

**1** The snowman melted.

**2** The child demanded an honest answer.

**3** The enormous dog defended the infant.

**4** The runner who set the record refused the prize.

# ANSWERS

# to Exercises

Chapter 2
Since the results obtained in this study will vary, the data you gather and any questions you have might be discussed in the classroom.

Chapter 3

I A. 1 Inflectional suffixes: (for nouns) worm<u>s</u>
(for verbs) find<u>s</u>        (for adjectives) bigg<u>est</u>

Derivational suffixes: frequent<u>ly</u>

Prefixes: _____

2 Inflectional suffixes: (for nouns) ship'<u>s</u>
(for verbs) radio<u>ed</u>        (for adjectives)

Derivational suffixes: youth<u>ful</u>, thoughtless<u>ly</u>

Prefixes: _____

3 Inflectional suffixes: (for nouns) Paul'<u>s</u>, stor<u>ies</u>
(for verbs) lik<u>ed</u>        (for adjectives) long<u>er</u>

Derivational suffixes: _____

Prefixes: <u>in</u>sane

4 Inflectional suffixes: (for nouns) Tom'<u>s</u>
(for verbs) tri<u>ed</u>        (for adjectives)

Derivational Suffixes: _____

Prefixes: <u>de</u>fuse

**5** Inflectional suffixes: _(for nouns) commoner**s**_
(for verbs) hat**ed**, mix**ing** (for adjectives)

Derivational suffixes: Boor**ish**, pomp**ous**, commoners

Prefixes: _____

**6** Inflectional suffixes: _(for nouns)_
(for verbs) want**s**, clos**ed** (for adjectives)

Derivational suffixes: Sens**ible**

Prefixes: _____

**7** Inflectional suffixes: _(for nouns)_
(for verbs) jump**ed** (for adjectives)

Derivational suffixes: harm**less**, side**ways**, safe**ty**

Prefixes: _____

**8** Inflectional suffixes: _(for nouns) Joan'**s**, trick**s**_
(for verbs) lik**ed**, play**ing** (for adjectives)

Derivational suffixes: fam**ous**

Prefixes: _____

**9** Inflectional suffixes: _(for nouns)_
(for verbs) claim**ed** (for adjectives) speedi**est**

Derivational suffixes: speedi**est**, rac**er**, modest**ly**

Prefixes: _____

**10** Inflectional suffixes: _(for nouns) director**s**_
(for verbs) preplann**ing**, worri**ed** (for adjectives)

Derivational suffixes: fret**ful**, direct**ors**

Prefixes: **pre**planning

---

B.  **1** Could he do it?
   **2** Jane arranged to meet Dick secretly.
   **3** The crew tried to defuse Tom's bomb.
   **4** Their objections over, he signed the new bill.
   **5** Benson always tried to come to the aid of his helpful uncle.
   **6** Only her playing the activist made him angry.
   **7** Rolf got the watch cheap.

**8** Jean's calm banker appeared friendly.

**9** The harried teacher was constantly returning papers late.

**10** My dancing instructor still finds sitting difficult.

**II**  **1** noun, verb, adjective, noun

**2** noun, verb, preposition

**3** noun, adjective, noun, verb

**4** verb, adjective, noun

**5** preposition, noun, verb, conjunction

**6** adjective, adjective, noun, preposition, noun

**7** adjective, adverb, preposition, adjective

**8** verb, noun, verb

**9** adverb, noun, adjective, verb, noun

**10** adjective, noun, adverb, verb, adjective

**III**  Phrases and Clauses.

A.  **1** Noun phrases: the family, the restaurant, a rush

Finite verb phrases: left the restaurant in a rush

Nonfinite verb phrases: Feeling very ill

Prepositional phrases: in a rush

**2** Noun phrases: The spy satellite, unknown reasons

Finite verb phrases: had been launched for unknown reasons

Nonfinite verb phrases: _____

Prepositional phrases: for unknown reasons

**3** Noun phrases: a bad sunburn, Jane, the beach

Finite verb phrases: avoided the beach

Nonfinite verb phrases: Having a bad sunburn

Prepositional phrases: _____

**4** Noun phrases: Smedley Zapp, pin-striped trousers, most occasions

Finite verb phrases: wore pin-striped trousers on most occasions

Nonfinite verb phrases: _____

Prepositional phrases: on most occasions

**5** Noun phrases: He, names, one day, the next day

Finite verb phrases: <u>can't remember names from one</u>
<u>day to the next day</u>

Nonfinite verb phrases: _____

Prepositional phrases: <u>from one day, to the next day</u>

**6** Noun phrases: <u>The startled gazelles, the fallen log</u>

Finite verb phrases: <u>leaped over the fallen log</u>

Nonfinite verb phrases: _____

Prepositional phrases: <u>over the fallen log</u>

**7** Noun phrases: <u>Solar energy, one possible solution,</u>
<u>our energy problem</u>

Finite verb phrases: <u>is one possible solution to</u>
<u>our energy problem</u>

Nonfinite verb phrases: _____

Prepositional phrases: <u>to our energy problem</u>

**8** Noun phrases: <u>The intrepid explorers, the fearsome</u>
<u>forest</u>

Finite verb phrases: <u>entered the fearsome forest</u>

Nonfinite verb phrases: _____

Prepositional phrases: _____

**9** Noun phrases: <u>The fiercest warriors, Manchuria</u>

Finite verb phrases: <u>came from Manchuria</u>

Nonfinite verb phrases: _____

Prepositional phrases: <u>from Manchuria</u>

**10** Noun phrases: <u>the young child, his mother</u>

Finite verb phrases: <u>seldom left his mother</u>

Nonfinite verb phrases: <u>Intimidated easily</u>

Prepositional phrases: _____

B.　**1** (that Lucy had just installed.)
　**2** (Although we laughed at his backhand,)
　**3** (as they stepped from the ship.)
　**4** (that Paris had surrendered)
　**5** (because they are particularly intelligent,)

**6** (after the war ended.)
**7** (which Jill wrote)
**8** (whenever he loses a tennis match.)
**9** (While Susan drove,)
**10** (Since you're involved,)
**11** (that hard work is its own reward.)
**12** (If the shoe fits,)
**13** (who lost their jobs)
**14** (when the parking lot was full.)
**15** (who are painless.)


Chapter 4
I    **1** simple past
     **2** present perfect
     **3** present progressive
     **4** past progressive
     **5** past perfect
     **6** present perfect progressive
     **7** simple past
     **8** past perfect
     **9** present progressive
     **10** future
     **11** simple past
     **12** present perfect progressive
     **13** past progressive
     **14** simple present
     **15** present perfect
     **16** present perfect
     **17** past progressive
     **18** present progressive
     **19** present perfect progressive
     **20** simple present
     **21** present perfect
     **22** present perfect
     **23** past perfect


II   **1** Tense:   past progressive
        Time:   The action was taking place in the past at the time a
                second past action occurred.
     **2** Tense:   present perfect progressive
        Time:   The action began in the past and continues into the
                present.
     **3** Tense:   simple past

Time:   The action was completed in the past.
**4** Tense:   present progressive
Time:   Emphasizes that the action is occurring right now.
**5** Tense:   past perfect
Time:   The first past action (the evidence vanishing) took place before a second past action (Mark's getting furious.)
**6** Tense:   simple present
Time:   The action is repetitive.
**7** Tense:   present perfect
Time:   The action began in the past and continues into the present.
**8** Tense:   present perfect
Time:   The action was completed at some unspecified time in the past.

Chapter 5

**I**  **1** <u>be</u>              **6** <u>is</u>
    **2** <u>is</u>              **7** <u>were</u>
    **3** <u>are</u>             **8** <u>aren't</u>, <u>being</u>
    **4** <u>was</u>             **9** <u>were</u>
    **5** <u>is</u>

**II**  **1** A, are           **6** A, was
     **2** A, is            **7** L, being
     **3** A, are           **8** L, was
     **4** L, were          **9** A, was
     **5** L, is            **10** L, been

**III**  **1** aren't         **4** isn't
      **2** were          **5** were
      **3** were          **6** were

Chapter 6

**I**  **1** The brakes were fixed by a licensed mechanic.
    **2** The school play was directed by a former actor.
    **3** The supply problem was solved by Felipe.
    **4** This church was designed by Christopher Wren.
    **5** A new home-run record was set by Henry Aaron.
    **6** Almost everyone was deceived by Jonathan.
    **7** Older homes are preferred by many people.
    **8** This course is taken by many science majors.
    **9** The tax evader was arrested by the authorities.

10 Many California missions were founded by the Franciscan missionary Junipero Serra.

11 The bank in Denver was robbed by a neatly dressed middle-aged man with a cheerful smile.

II  1 The idea was abandoned.
2 Senator Humphrey was nominated.
3 The vintage Cadillac was sold.
4 Several flaws were detected.
5 Twelve thousand pumps were manufactured.
6 The initial design was approved.
7 Your application form was lost.

III  1 The faucet got fixed.
2 Marilyn's letter got published.
3 Both Marvin and Sam got hired.
4 The San Francisco Giants got beaten.
5 The job got finished.
6 Your car got wrecked.

IV  Since answers to this exercise will vary, your instructor may choose to discuss them in the classroom.

Chapter 7
I  1 She detests the color blue.
2 He grows prize-winning beets.
3 A coward dies many deaths.
4 He loves children.
5 That student excels at mathematics.
6 The coffee plant requires a lot of moisture.
7 She always cheers for the underdog.

II  1 *Marjorie love to watch baseball on television.
2 *The teacher know the answer.
3 *Harvey swim with Randal.

Chapter 8
I  1 may, might
2 would

3 should
4 must
5 could

6 May, Can, Could, Might
7 should (*must* is also appropriate here)
8 must
9 will
10 May, Can, Could, Might

**II** **1** moved, would
   **2** ceased, would
   **3** tried, would

**III** **1** must work
    **2** can program
    **3** may think ("Benjamin thinks I may be a liar" is also possible.)
    **4** would fish
    **5** could charm
The base form (i.e., the simple form) of the verb must be used.

**IV** **1** should (probability), can (present or future ability), might (possibility), may (possibility), must (necessity), would (repetitive past action or hypothetical future event)
    **2** Can (present ability or request), Could, Might, Will, Would (requests)
    **3** will (generalization), can (present ability), must (necessity or probability), might (possibility)
    **4** can (present ability), would (repetitive past action or hypothetical future event), must (necessity or probability), may (possibility or permission granted), will (future action)
    **5** could (past ability or hypothetical future event), should (advisability or probability), must (necessity), will (future action), may (possibility), might (possibility)
    **6** used to (repetitive past action), would (repetitive past action or hypothetical future event), must (necessity or probability), had to (past necessity), should (advisability or probability)

Chapter 9
**I**   **1** Will Sylvester refuse the offer?
    **2** Were the bakers on strike?
    **3** Had the senators tried to investigate?
    **4** Could he send a substitute?
    **5** Am I too old to join the FBI?
    **6** Has a winner been chosen?
Move the auxiliary to the front of the sentence and add a question mark.
    **7** Do orchid plants require frequent watering?
    **8** Does Ann prefer Indian cuisine?
    **9** Does love conquer all?
   **10** Did the doctor save her life?
   **11** Did the judge ask for more evidence?
Add *do* to the front of the sentence and "jump" the tense from the verb to *do*.

**II**　1 When is our next holiday?
　2 How old is Billy?
　3 What will the Prince think?
　4 What does Spencer think?
　5 Where has the maid gone?
　6 Why did she insist?
　7 When can they pay?
　8 What have they gotten themselves into?
In the embedded *wh-* questions, the auxiliary (if there is one) follows the subject.

**III**　1 I can park here overnight, can't I?
　2 It is supposed to rain tomorrow, isn't it?
　3 The McGregors have checked out of their room, haven't they?
　4 The Green Bay Packers won the game, didn't they?
　5 My aunt hasn't telephoned yet, has she?
　6 Sonny isn't a real secret agent, is he?
　7 Elaine can't speak Lithuanian, can she?

Chapter 10

**I**　1 I will not go to college next year.
　2 Mrs. Bens is not eager to visit her aunt.
　3 Alice has not owned poodles before.
　4 The three soldiers would not steal from civilians.
　5 Clark is not traveling in Madagascar this summer.
　6 The young lowland gorilla had not learned its lesson.
　7 Millicent cannot throw a football 160 feet.
　8 The Emperor was not considering torture.
　9 I have not known many exciting people.
The word *not* was placed after the auxiliary.

**II**　1 Pam and Ed do not own a home in Mexico.
　2 Frank does not drive carefully.
　3 Winston did not lose his jade ring.
　4 Making new friends did not come easily for Dorothy.
　5 My father does not enjoy soap operas.
　6 Tea plants do not grow well in Wisconsin.
　7 Mr. Baynes does not envy his rich acquaintances.
　8 Thomas Jefferson did not invent the rocking chair.
They do not contain an auxiliary.
The auxiliary *do* had to be inserted before the verb.

**III**　1 Clarissa shouldn't invest so heavily in tungsten mines.
　2 The judge wasn't impressed.

**3** Those orchids haven't been watered for days.

**4** Don's car doesn't fit his personality.

**5** The California condor won't survive the century.

**6** Canadians aren't fond of lazy hockey players.

**7** This student hasn't paid his fees.

**8** I don't know where Laufenburg is.

**IV**  **1** Miss Ormsby never goes to church on Sunday.

    **2** Hector rarely made profits on his real-estate investments.

    **3** That tennis player hardly ever outsmarts the opposition.

    **4** My brother seldom does well in the sciences.

    **5** No rain is predicted for this evening.

    **6** Walter has no mechanical ability.

    **7** There is no hope.

**V**  **1** This physician's signature is illegible.

    **2** The students were very inattentive.

    **3** Most of the people were uninspired by the speech.

    **4** Farley is one of the most impolite ushers I know.

    **5** Doris is unhappy with her new contract.

    **6** The regiment's new executive officer proved to be an irresponsible administrator.

    **7** The race driver turned in an inconsistent performance in 1977.

    **8** The informer's story is untrue.

**VI**  **1** *We didn't catch nothing that day.

    **2** *Thomas didn't go nowhere(s) (or no place) yesterday.

    **3** *I don't need no help.

    **4** *The old dog didn't bother nobody.

**VII**  **1** *Can't nothing be done.

    **2** *Shouldn't nobody do that.

    **3** *Didn't nobody see it. (or *Wasn't nobody saw it.)

Chapter 11

**I**  **1** Drop the gun.

    **2** Stop lying to me.

    **3** Give me a chance.

    **4** Quit fooling around.

    **5** Kiss me.

    **6** Listen carefully.

**II**  **1** Top:   Would (or Could) you check the air in my tires, please?

      Bottom:   Check the air in my tires.

**2** Top:  Would (or Could) you sign the receipt, please?
  Bottom:  Sign the receipt.
**3** Top:  Would (or Could) you close the door, please?
  Bottom:  Close the door.
**4** Top:  Would (or Could) you do me a favor, please?
  Bottom:  Do me a favor.


Chapter 12
**I**  **1** personal
  **2** interrogative
  **3** universal
  **4** demonstrative
  **5** personal
  **6** reflexive
  **7** indefinite
  **8** interrogative
  **9** relative
  **10** interrogative
  **11** demonstrative
  **12** indefinite
  **13** reflexive
  **14** indefinite
  **15** indefinite
  **16** relative
  **17** universal
  **18** reciprocal
  **19** relative
  **20** personal
  **21** personal
  **22** personal
  **23** indefinite
  **24** demonstrative
  **25** personal

**II**  **1** Whose            **6** its
  **2** She            **7** themselves
  **3** someone, somebody      **8** me
  **4** who, that          **9** each other
  **5** all, everyone everybody    **10** They're

**III**  **1** He cut himself.
  **2** Charlotte and her mother left this morning.
  **3** If you have a question, ask those guys.
  **4** √

**5** He and I caught the biggest fish that summer.
**6** √ ("Each citizen should cherish his or her right to vote" is also correct.)
**7** I want that piece of cake.
**8** √
**9** Neither boy swims as well as he should.

Chapter 13

I  A.  **1** the, their      **6** The, the
     **2** that            **7** That
     **3** Myron's, a      **8** his
     **4** My, an        **9** Those
     **5** her, the     **10** the, their

B.

| | *Predeterminers* | *Postdeterminers* |
|---|---|---|
| **1** | Both of | |
| **2** | | |
| **3** | | five |
| **4** | | |
| **5** | half | |
| **6** | | first, second |
| **7** | | |
| **8** | | |
| **9** | | |
| **10** | All of | |

C.  Since answers to this exercise will vary, your instructor may wish to discuss them in the classroom.

II  **1** specific      **5** generic
   **2** generic      **6** specific
   **3** generic      **7** specific
   **4** specific      **8** generic

III  **1** hurricane (C), havoc (NC)
     **2** debris (NC), streets (C)
     **3** Paramedics (C), workers (C), scene (C)
     **4** milk (NC), bread (NC), meat (NC)
     **5** Bulletins (C), information (NC), public (NC)
     **6** Reconstruction (NC), area (C)
     **7** Time (NC), destruction (NC)
     **8** significance (NC), weather (NC)
     **9** Months (C), news (NC)
   **10** storm (C), vigor (NC)

11 cousin (C), homework (NC)
12 peak (C), snow (NC)
13 dust (NC), tank (C)
14 Equipment (NC), corner (C), factory (C)
15 workers (C), instruction (NC)

Chapter 14

I 1 apples
2 none
3 Tom, a weapon
4 flowers, Sandra
5 none
6 the contract
7 a roast, the elderly man
8 bombers
9 the dog, a bone
10 Mount Everest
11 the parrot
12 Gaul
13 none
14 none
15 relief, the stricken country
16 her sister, a note
17 none
18 the knife

II 1 I       7 T
2 T       8 T
3 T       9 I
4 I      10 I
5 I      11 T
6 T      12 T

III 1 Mrs. Henderson gave her daughter a new dress.
2 Ed handed his bookie a hundred dollars.
3 The coach bought the whole team dinner.
4 Mabel always sends her nieces presents.
5 not possible (object inversion cannot take place if the direct object is a personal pronoun).
6 Mr. Tracy offered me a job.
7 not possible (the direct object is a personal pronoun).

Chapter 15

1 impassable, OC
2 furious, SC
3 uneasy, OC
4 dumb, OC
5 an electrician, SC
6 NC
7 NC
8 the favorite, OC
9 upset, SC
10 a billiards player, SC
11 peculiar, SC
12 NC
13 NC
14 victorious, SC
15 incompetent, OC
16 a straight-A student, SC
17 NC
18 thin, SC
19 NC
20 easy, SC

Chapter 16
I 1 selling the bicycle, gerundive, direct object
2 Taking inventory, gerundive, subject
3 To continue, infinitive, subject
4 for screaming at employees, prepositional phrase, adjectival
at employees, prepositional phrase, adverbial
5 to declare independence, infinitive, adjectival
6 to help the young, infinitive, subject complement
7 Teaching, gerund, subject
8 Michael's singing, gerund, direct object
9 at scoring goals, prepositional phrase, adverbial
10 by making mistakes, prepositional phrase, adverbial
11 fishing in that stream, gerund, direct object
in that stream, prepositional phrase, adverbial
(A strong case can also be made for an adjectival interpretation.)
12 your getting lost, gerund, subject complement
13 to remain in India, infinitive, direct object
in India, prepositional phrase, adverbial
14 to live comfortably, infinitive, subject
15 His whining, gerund, subject
16 acting, gerund, direct object
17 to outsmart, infinitive, adverbial
18 to sue, infinitive, direct object

II 1 to try          7 trying
2 to try          8 trying
3 trying          9 to try
4 trying         10 both
5 to try         11 both
6 both
There was no rule—it depended on what the main verb was.

Chapter 17
I 1 for, purpose            11 by, instrumental
2 through, direction      12 at, place
3 of, partition           13 with, accompaniment
4 near, place             14 from, direction
5 of, attachment          15 on, time
6 after, time             16 of, attachment
7 from, source            17 as . . . as, comparison
8 like, comparison        18 of, partition
9 with, instrumental      19 for, purpose
10 with, accompaniment     20 from, source (Place and direction are also possible.)

**II** 1 Aimee put her new dress on. (optional)
  2 The bandits tied him up. (required)
  3 I will hand the assignment in. (optional)
  4 Karen made an excuse up. (optional)
  5 The young policeman turned his badge in. (optional)
  6 Roger decided to look his old roommate up. (optional)
  7 Four hikers put the fire out. (optional)
  8 Please let them in. (required)
  9 We covered it up. (required)
  10 The aides sent some refreshments in. (optional)
Particle movement was required when the direct object was a pronoun.

**III** 1 particle     6 particle
    2 particle     7 preposition
    3 preposition     8 preposition
    4 preposition     9 particle
    5 preposition     10 preposition

## Chapter 18

**I** 1 expletive     6 expletive
  2 noun     7 expletive
  3 expletive     8 adverb
  4 pronoun     9 expletive
  5 pronoun     10 expletive

**II** 1 There's a small dog inside that car.
  2 There's a ship leaving tonight.
  3 There's a stork nesting on their chimney.
  4 There's a rattlesnake directly in front of you.
  5 There's a good restaurant just around the corner.

## Chapter 19

**I** 1

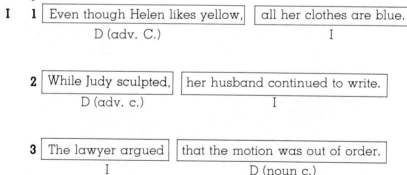

| Even though Helen likes yellow, | all her clothes are blue. |
|---|---|
| D (adv. C.) | I |

2

| While Judy sculpted, | her husband continued to write. |
|---|---|
| D (adv. c.) | I |

3

| The lawyer argued | that the motion was out of order. |
|---|---|
| I | D (noun c.) |

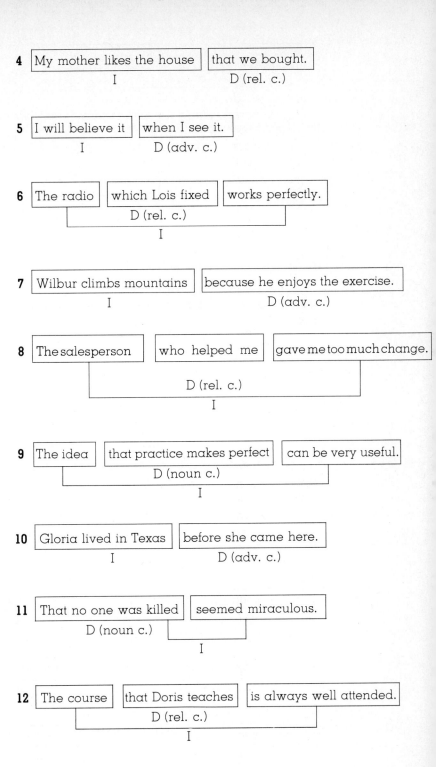

**4** | My mother likes the house | that we bought.
I — D (rel. c.)

**5** | I will believe it | when I see it.
I — D (adv. c.)

**6** | The radio | which Lois fixed | works perfectly.
D (rel. c.)
I

**7** | Wilbur climbs mountains | because he enjoys the exercise.
I — D (adv. c.)

**8** | The salesperson | who helped me | gave me too much change.
D (rel. c.)
I

**9** | The idea | that practice makes perfect | can be very useful.
D (noun c.)
I

**10** | Gloria lived in Texas | before she came here.
I — D (adv. c.)

**11** | That no one was killed | seemed miraculous.
D (noun c.)
I

**12** | The course | that Doris teaches | is always well attended.
D (rel. c.)
I

**13** The pipe | that broke | was very old.
     D (rel. c.)
       I

**14** Gary fishes for trout | whenever he visits Idaho.
    I        D (adv. c.)

**15** The agent hinted | that his client might accept the offer.
    I        D (noun c.)

**16** When Mark turned twenty,
    D (adv. c.)
he was one of the most accomplished violinists in the country.
           I

**17** The airport | that Fernando designed | has become famous.
      D (rel. c.)
        I

**18** The dog | which guards the house | is really quite affectionate.
      D (rel. c.)
        I

**19** Mary suspects | that the car will soon quit running.
    I        D (noun c.)

**20** The game will be canceled | if it rains.
     I      D (adv. c.)

**II**   **1** Let's remain here until we hear something definite.
  **2** After she graduated, Brenda toured the Middle East.
  **3** Ever since she was a child, Patty had dreamed of being a professional golfer.

**4** He could do much better if he really wanted to.

**5** The chimney leaks whenever it rains.

**6** By the time help arrived, the man was fully conscious.

**7** I'll never believe it until I see it myself.

**8** While their parents were playing cards, the children were busy raiding the refrigerator.

**III**
**1** The truck that (or which) Martin drives needs new tires.

**2** The fisherman who (or that) caught the gigantic salmon was ecstatic.

**3** A book that (or which) Peter found contains fascinating photographs.

**4** The computer that (or which) broke down cannot be repaired.

**5** The team that (or which) beat us badly will return in April.

**6** I cherish the recipes that (or which) you sent me.

**7** Karen installed the drapes that (or which) her mother made.

**8** The school that (or which) Sylvia attends encourages the study of languages.

**9** The lieutenant whom (or that) Julie likes lives in Little Rock.

**10** The artist who (or that) painted this picture understood human frailty.

**11** A movie that (or which) sounds interesting is playing downtown.

**12** The person who (or that) helped them received no thanks.

**13** Everyone respected the quarterback who (or that) refused to give up.

**14** The dog that (or which) Charlene trained became a champion.

**15** The comet that (or which) Dr. Okada discovered was truly spectacular.

**16** I favor the solution that (or which) Dorothy suggests.

**17** The wine that (or which) this island produces tastes delicious.

**18** The building that (or which) collapsed had a weak foundation.

**19** The craftsman who (or that) did the best work received the contract.

**20** Jean met the man who (or that) wrote the book.

**21** I met the woman whose husband knows the President.

**22** We visited the captain whose ship had been saved.

**IV**
**1** The problem bothering them now has no quick solution.

**2** not possible

**3** The dinner Jill prepared was sensational.

**4** The film we saw yesterday lasted five hours.

**5** The people living here seem exceptionally friendly.

**6** not possible

**7** not possible

**8** The coach, anxious about the welfare of his players, insisted that a physician travel with the team.

**9** The patient she treated recovered rapidly.

**10** An umbrella someone forgot is on the desk.

**11** Dr. Cardin, the chairman of the Thoracic Surgery Committee, believes the complaints are groundless.

**12** Anna always felt a longing for the village she had left.

**13** Karen, my next-door neighbor, knows all the important people in town.

**V** **1** The Empire State Building, which attracts thousands of tourists each year, is located in New York.

**2** Mount Everest, which was first climbed in 1953, has claimed the lives of many mountaineers.

**3** The building which my father owns does not have elevators.

**4** The mountain which we see to the south is called Old Grayback.

**5** Yesterday we went shopping for a new television set. The set which we liked best had a 25-inch screen. The price, which includes delivery and installation, is $900.

**6** I read a great book last night. The book, which is only 200 pages long, tells the story of a determined young hog farmer. The part which enthralled me the most described the complex psychology of hogs.

**VI** 

| | | | |
|---|---|---|---|
| **1** whom | | **5** who | |
| **2** who | | **6** who | |
| **3** who | | **7** whom | |
| **4** whom | | **8** whom | |

Chapter 20

| | | | |
|---|---|---|---|
| **1** S | | **9** CC | |
| **2** CX | | **10** CD | |
| **3** CX | | **11** CC | |
| **4** S | | **12** CX | |
| **5** CD | | **13** CX | |
| **6** CX | | **14** S | |
| **7** S | | **15** CD | |
| **8** CD | | **16** CC | |

Appendix 2

I  1

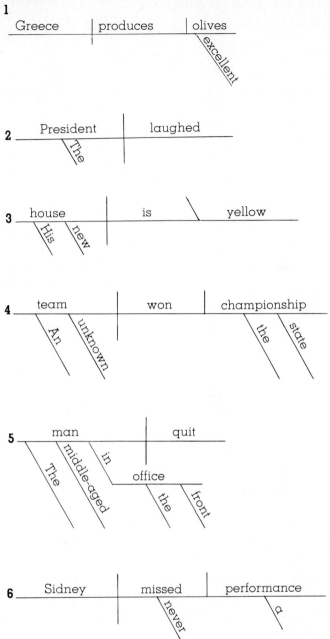

**7**
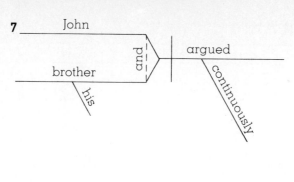

**8**
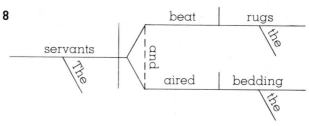

**9**
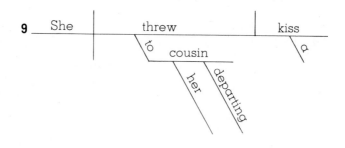

**10**

**11**
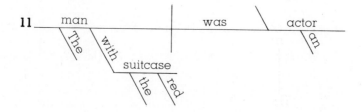

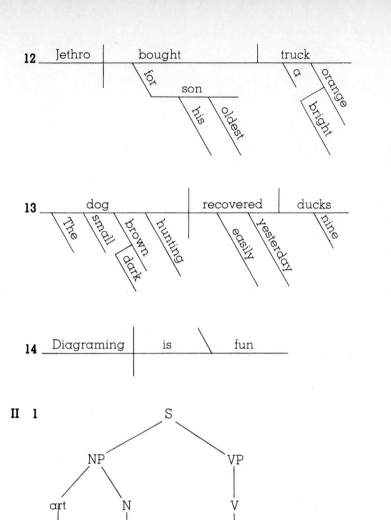

**12** Jethro | bought | truck

for / son
his / oldest

a / orange
bright

**13** dog | recovered | ducks

The / small / brown / hunting
dark

easily / yesterday
nine

**14** Diagraming | is \ fun

**II 1**

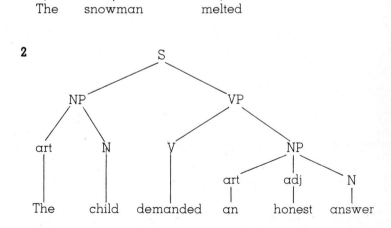

S
NP — VP
art — N — V
The — snowman — melted

**2**

S
NP — VP
art — N — V — NP
The — child — demanded — art — adj — N
an — honest — answer

**3**

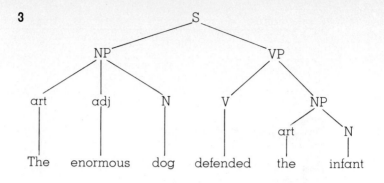

**4**

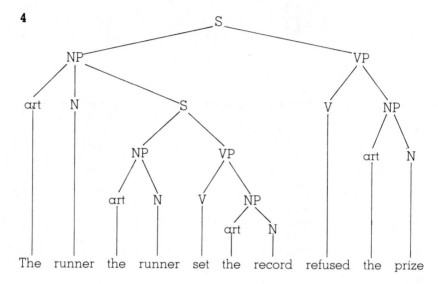

# Selective Annotated Bibliography

This brief bibliography lists some useful sources for further reading.

## SOME NOTEWORTHY GRAMMARS OF ENGLISH

Frank, Marcella. *Modern English: A Practical Reference Guide*. Englewood Cliffs, N.J.: Prentice-Hall, 1972.
Designed primarily for the advanced student of English as a second language, but a useful reference for native speakers as well.

Jespersen, Otto. *A Modern English Grammar on Historical Principles*. 7 vols. London: Allen and Unwin, 1909–1949.
Perhaps the best known of the traditional, scholarly, multivolume grammars. A great achievement that is respected and consulted even today.

Kruisinga, Etsko. *A Handbook of Present-Day English*. 4 vols. 4th ed. Utrecht, Netherlands: Kimink en Zoon, 1925.
Another of the great scholarly, traditional grammars.

Poutsma, Hendrik. *A Grammar of Late Modern English*. 5 vols. Groningen, Netherlands: P. Noordhoff, 1914–1929.
Also a traditional, scholarly grammar and one of the very best.

Quirk, Randolph, Sidney Greenbaum, Geoffrey Leech, and Jan Svartvik. *A Grammar of Contemporary English*. New York: Seminar Press, 1972.
The most recent large, comprehensive grammar. A thorough work containing a wealth of detail (the index alone comprises 28 pages).

Quirk, Randolph, and Sidney Greenbaum. *A Concise Grammar of Contemporary English*. New York: Harcourt Brace Jovanovich, 1973.
A shorter version of the work just cited.

Sledd, James. *A Short Introduction to English Grammar*. Chicago: Scott, Foresman and Company, 1959.
An example of the structuralist grammars of the 1940s and 1950s.

# TRADITIONAL SENTENCE DIAGRAMING

Emery, Donald W. *Sentence Analysis*. New York: Holt, Rinehart and Winston, 1961.
A clear and comprehensive treatment of the subject.

# INTRODUCTIONS TO TRANSFORMATIONAL GRAMMAR

Akmajian, Adrian, and Frank Heny. *An Introduction to the Principles of Transformational Syntax*. Cambridge, Mass.: MIT Press, 1975.
Introduces the theory and apparatus of the modern transformational approach to grammar. Includes tree diagrams.

Jacobs, Roderick A., and Peter S. Rosenbaum. *English Transformational Grammar*. Waltham, Mass.: Xerox Publishing Company, 1968.
A well-known introduction. Tree diagraming included.

Liles, Bruce. *An Introductory Transformational Grammar*. Englewood Cliffs, N.J.: Prentice-Hall, 1971.
Also a well-known introduction. Includes tree diagraming.

# SPECIAL DICTIONARIES

Boatner, Maxine Tull, and Edward John Gates. Update Editor: Adam Makkai. *A Dictionary of American Idioms*. Woodbury, N.Y.: Barron's Educational Series. 1975.
Defines and illustrates over 4,000 American idiomatic expressions. Many of these are not listed in other dictionaries.

Hornsby, A. S., E. V. Gatenby, and H. Wakefield. *The Advanced Learner's Dictionary of Current English*. 2d ed. London: Oxford University Press, 1963.
An unusual dictionary that includes information on whether nouns are used in the countable or noncountable sense, whether gerunds, infinitives, or other forms are required after particular verbs, and so forth. Especially helpful for advanced students of English as a second language.

MacLeish, Andrew. *A Glossary of Grammar and Linguistics*. New York: Grosset and Dunlap, 1971.
Defines and illustrates much grammatical terminology.

Partridge, Eric. *A Dictionary of Slang and Unconventional English*. 7th ed. New York: Macmillan, 1970.
A classic study of American slang.

# BOOKS ON DIALECTS

Allen, Harold B., and Gary N. Underwood, eds. *Readings in American Dialectology*. New York: Appleton-Century-Crofts, 1971.
Forty-one articles on regional and social dialects.

Brook, G. L. *English Dialects*. London: Andre Deutsch, 1963.
A good introduction to dialects of British English.

Fishman, Joshua A. *Sociolinguistics: A Brief Introduction*. Rowley, Mass.: Newbury House, 1970.
A well-balanced overview of the field of sociolinguistics.

Kurath, Hans, et al. *The Linguistic Atlas of New England*. 3 vols. in 6 parts. Providence, R.I.: Brown University, 1939–1943.
The classic study of regional dialects in the United States.

———, et al. *Handbook of the Linguistic Geography of New England*. Washington, D.C.: American Council of Learned Societies, 1939.
Designed to accompany and explain *The Linguistic Atlas of New England*.

———. *A Word Geography of the Eastern United States*. Ann Arbor, Mich.: University of Michigan Press, 1949.
Based on vocabulary information contained in the *Linguistic Atlas*.

Labov, William. *The Social Stratification of English in New York City*. Washington, D.C.: Center for Applied Linguistics, 1966.
A major, in-depth study of the speech of the Lower East Side of Manhattan in New York City and the social forces affecting the speech.

——— (with Paul Cohen, Clarence Robins, and John Lewis). *A Study of the Non-Standard English of Negro and Puerto Rican Speakers in New York City*. 2 vols. Washington, D.C.: Cooperative Research Project No. 3288, U.S. Office of Education, Department of Health, Education, and Welfare, 1968.
An extensive (over 750 pages), detailed, clear, invaluable description of the speech commonly heard in inner-city areas. Vol. I covers phonology and grammar, Vol. II the uses of this speech in social contexts. The reference librarian at your college or university library can show you how to borrow or purchase this Eric publication.

———. *The Study of Nonstandard English*. Champaign, Ill.: National Council of Teachers of English, 1970.
Surveys theoretical and educational issues that involve nonstandard English.

Malmstrom, Jean. *Language in Society*. Rev. 2d ed. Rochelle Park, N.J.: Hayden Book Company, 1973.
A look at several varieties of English. Contains exercises.

——— and Annabel Ashley. *Dialects—U.S.A*. Champaign, Ill.: National Council of Teachers of English, 1963.

A brief introduction to the study of dialects and the three main dialect areas in the United States.

Marckwardt, Albert H., and Randolph Quirk. *A Common Language: British and American English*. London: Cox and Wyman, 1966.
Twelve dialogues on the differences and similarities between British and American English.

Reed, Carroll E. *Dialects of American English*. Rev. ed. Amherst, Mass.: University of Massachusetts, 1977.
A good "first" book on dialects, including those in the Midwest and Far West.

Shuy, Roger W. *Discovering American Dialects*. Champaign, Ill.: National Council of Teachers of English, 1967.
A pedagogically oriented book on dialects.

Williamson, Juanita V., and Virginia M. Burke, eds. *A Various Language: Perspectives on American Dialects*. New York: Holt, Rinehart and Winston, 1971.
An introductory reader that surveys the history and scope of dialect studies.

# BOOKS ON USAGE

Bryant, Margaret M. *Current American Usage*. New York: Funk and Wagnalls, 1962.
Bases usage judgments on evidence from a number of authoritative sources, including the *Linguistic Atlas*.

Copperud, Roy H. *American Usage: The Consensus*. New York: Van Nostrand Reinhold, 1970.
Systematically compares the judgments of various leading usage books.

Evans, Bergen, and Cornelia Evans. *A Dictionary of Contemporary American Usage*. New York: Random House, 1957.
This book is very comprehensive, its judgments practical.

Follett, Wilson. *Modern American Usage: A Guide*. Ed. and compiled by Jacques Barzun in collaboration with Carlos Baker, Frederick W. Dupee, Dudley Fitts, James D. Hart, Phyllis McGinley, and Lionel Trilling. New York: Grosset and Dunlap, 1970.
A useful, highly regarded study—conservative and readable.

Fowler, H. W. *A Dictionary of Modern English Usage*. 2d ed. Rev. by Sir Ernest Gowers. New York: Oxford University Press, 1965.
A classic. Mainly concerned with British usage, its judgments are lively and judicious.

*Harper Dictionary of Contemporary Usage*. Ed. by William and Mary Morris with the assistance of a panel of 136 distinguished consultants on usage. New York: Harper and Row, 1975.

Based on the judgments of a usage panel of Americans including linguists, editors, authors, business people, and teachers of English and speech.

Nicholson, Margaret. *A Dictionary of American-English Usage.* Based on Fowler's *Modern English Usage.* New York: Oxford University Press, 1957.
Basically an adaptation and condensation of Fowler for Americans.

Pooley, Robert C. *Teaching English Usage.* Rev. ed. Washington, D.C.: National Council of Teachers of English, 1974.
Applies the findings of other studies in distinguishing what to teach and what not to teach in the classroom.

# HISTORIES OF ENGLISH

Baugh, Albert C. *A History of the English Language.* 2d ed. New York: Appleton-Century-Crofts, 1963.
Traces changes that have taken place over 1,500 years, with attention to related political and social events.

Gordon, James D. *The English Language: An Historical Introduction.* New York: Thomas Y. Crowell, 1972.
An account of the development of the English language for the benefit of students new to serious linguistic study.

Jespersen, Otto. *Growth and Structure of the English Language.* 9th ed. New York: Free Press, 1968.
A classic study that describes the distinctive features of the English language and explains the growth and significance of the major components of modern English.

Krapp, George Philip. *Modern English: Its Growth and Present Use.* Rev. ed. by Albert H. Marckwardt. New York: Charles Scribner's Sons, 1969.
Relates the history and development of English to its use in society.

Marckwardt, Albert H. *American English.* New York: Oxford University Press, 1958.
A short, interesting account of English in America.

Mencken, Henry L. *The American Language: The Fourth Edition and the Two Supplements, abridged.* Ed. by Raven I. McDavid. New York: Alfred A. Knopf, 1963.
A classic, individualistic study of English in America, with emphasis on its distinctive characteristics.

Myers, L. M. *The Roots of Modern English.* Boston: Little, Brown and Company, 1966.
A good "nontechnical" book for the beginning student.

Pyles, Thomas. *The Origins and Development of the English Language.* 2d ed. New York: Harcourt Brace Jovanovich, 1971.

Emphasizes the phonological and grammatical development of English.

Robertson, Stuart, and Frederic G. Cassidy. *The Development of Modern English*. 2d ed. Englewood Cliffs, N.J.: Prentice-Hall, 1954.
A useful book with interesting sections on vocabulary.

Traugott, Elizabeth Closs. *A History of English Syntax*. New York: Holt, Rinehart and Winston, 1972.
A transformational approach to the history of English sentence structure.

Williams, Joseph M. *Origins of the English Language: A Social and Linguistic History*. New York: Free Press, 1975.
A pedagogical history with a useful section on semantics.

# Index

# Index